THE POEMS OF WILLIAM CULLEN

BRYANT

THE AMERICAN POETS
EDITED BY LOUIS UNTERMEYER FOR
THE HERITAGE PRESS

WILLIAM CULLEN BRYANT

From an engraving of a painting by Samuel F. B. Morse, 1825

THE POEMS OF WILLIAM CULLEN

BRYANT

SELECTED AND EDITED, WITH A COMMENTARY,

BY *LOUIS UNTERMEYER;* ILLUSTRATED WITH

ENGRAVINGS BY *THOMAS W. NASON*

THE HERITAGE PRESS, NEW YORK

The Editor's Introduction

I

IT IS MORE than a paradox that a monolog on death has had a more enduring life than most American poems, for it was written by a seventeen-year-old boy who scarcely realized he had made a landmark of literature. It was in the autumn of 1811 that young William Cullen Bryant, still in his eighteenth year, wrote the uncannily mature and extraordinarily resounding lines beginning:

> To him who in the love of Nature holds
> Communion with her visible forms, she speaks
> A various language; for his gayer hours
> She has a voice of gladness, and a smile
> And eloquence of beauty, and she glides
> Into his darker musings, with a mild
> And healing sympathy, that steals away
> Their sharpness, ere he is aware. . . .

The conclusion was moving and majestic:

> . . . sustained and soothed
> By an unfaltering trust, approach thy grave,
> Like one that draws the drapery of his couch
> About him, and lies down to pleasant dreams.

Bryant called the poem "Thanatopsis" (literally "a contemplation upon death") and put it away in his desk. A few years later, Bryant's father found it, made a fair copy, took it to New York with another poem ("Inscription for the Entrance to a Wood") and gave the verses to the editor of *The North American Review*, who had requested contributions from the elder Bryant. Since both poems were in the father's handwriting, the staff doubted that the son was the author, and when both poems appeared in the September, 1817, issue of *The North Amercan Review* Richard Henry Dana, author of *Two Years Before the Mast*, remarked to the editor, "Phillips, you have been imposed upon. No one on this side of the Atlantic is capable of writing such verses." Subsequently it was believed that the "Inscription" might have been written by the son, but that the author of "Thanatopsis" was undoubtedly the father.

II

From the beginning, Bryant was a precocious individual. He had to be to survive. He was so frail when he was born November 3, 1794, at Cummington, Massachusetts, that his father, a country physician who was also something of a scholar and statesman, was desperate. The child's head was abnormally large, and Dr. Bryant not only reduced it to normal size but saved his son's life by plunging the boy every morning in a spring of icy water.

Descended from Mayflower stock, Puritan to the core, Bryant revealed precocity in the cradle; he learned to read at sixteen months; at ten he composed a poem which was printed in the *Hampshire Gazette.* His father's library contained some seven hundred volumes, and the boy buried himself in the books, none of which could be suspected of being frivolous. But if he was immersed in ponderous books, he was not overwhelmed by them. He enjoyed the rough life of the outdoors. In the autobiographical *The Boys of My Boyhood* we see him raising timber-frames, swinging on the ridge-pole with his head downward, helping at sugaring-off in maple syrup time, helping to bring the apple barrels to the cider-mill, profaning an occasional Sabbath by angling for trout, and doing his best to avoid the little bundle of birch rods which "was as much a part of the necessary furniture as the crane in the kitchen fireplace." In Bryant's fifteenth year his father printed the boy's first ambitious effort: an anti-Jeffersonian satire, *The Embargo,* actually written at thirteen. (See the Appendix, page 281.) He was barely out of his childhood when he was sent to study Latin with his uncle, a minister, and Greek with another clergyman. His progress was so rapid that he devoted himself to a Greek version of the New Testament and, skipping the freshman year, entered Williams College as a sophomore. He was just fifteen years old.

III

The Williams College that Bryant attended in 1810 was a small and struggling institution. Its backgrounds were those of a country school; its staff consisted of just four teachers. At the end of his first year there, the youth determined to go to Yale and prepared himself for that event. But the family fortunes—or misfortunes—turned against him. Unable to continue further schooling, the young classical student was compelled to study law in the little town of Worthington where, from seventeen to twenty, he lived unhappily. It is probable that brooding over his failure to finish his education (which, at that time, meant his life) produced the somber speculations of "Thanatopsis." Admitted to the bar at twenty-one, Bryant began, almost against his will, to practice in Plainfield, Massachusetts. At twenty-six he married Frances Fairchild, "fairest of the rural maids," and their first child was born a year later. It seemed as though he would never escape from the law, a profession he admired in theory but despised in practice. Unlike the famous New England group, all of whom except Whittier received academic degrees, Bryant was not a graduate from college; he had to make his own way without the benefit of important friends and favors.

His luck began to turn at twenty-seven. In 1821 a booklet severely entitled *Poems* appeared, and several of the pieces were widely quoted. At thirty he made his first visit to New York, entered the metropolitan literary circle, and gladly left the practice of law. He undertook to furnish a monthly contribution of at least a hundred lines of verse to the *United States Literary Gazette*, and was hailed as America's leading poet. A year later he joined the *New York Evening Post* as assistant editor. In 1829, when he was thirty-five, he became editor-in-chief, a position which he held for fifty years, until the very end of his life.

IV

Bryant was an ardent and arduous editor. His working day began at dawn and ended long after dark. The literary style of the paper not only improved but changed significantly. Bryant deleted vulgarisms with a belligerent blue pencil; he prepared an Index Expurgatorius which forbade the use of such nouns as "rough" and "rowdy."

Bryant's fame grew steadily. An English edition of his poems was sponsored and introduced by Washington Irving. Dedicating the collection to Samuel Rogers, author of the popular *Pleasures of Memory*, Irving began on a somewhat too humble note:

> "During an intimacy of some years standing, I have uniformly remarked a liberal interest on your part in the rising character and fortunes of my country, and a kind disposition to promote the success of American talent, whether engaged in literature or the arts. I am induced, therefore, as a tribute of gratitude, as well as a general testimonial of respect and friendship, to lay before you the present volume, in which, for the first time, are collected together the fugitive productions of one of our living poets, whose writings are deservedly popular throughout the United States.
>
> "Many of these poems have appeared at various times in periodical publications; and some of them, I am aware, have met your eye, and received the stamp of your approbation. They could scarcely fail to do so, characterised as they are by a purity of moral, an elevation and refinement of thought, and a terseness and elegance of diction, congenial to the bent of your own genius and to your cultivated taste."

But Irving did not truckle. He went on to persuade Rogers that Bryant's poems were not only "essentially American" but belonged to "the best school of English poetry and entitled to rank among the highest of their class. . . . They transport us," continued Irving:

"into the depths of the solemn primeval forest—to the shores of the lonely lake—the banks of the wild nameless stream, or the brow of the rocky upland rising like a promontory from amidst a wide ocean of foliage; while they shed around us the glories of a climate fierce in its extremes, but splendid in all its vicissitudes. His close observation of the phenomena of nature, and the graphic felicity of his details, prevent his descriptions from ever becoming general and commonplace; while he has the gift of shedding over them a pensive grace that blends them all into harmony, and of clothing them with moral associations that make them speak to the heart. Neither, I am convinced, will it be the least of his merits in your eyes, that his writings are imbued with the independent spirit and the buoyant aspirations incident to a youthful, a free, and a rising country."

V

The youthful and rising country rewarded Bryant. Before he was forty he had successfully published five editions of his poetry; four more volumes appeared by the time he was fifty. He traveled extensively at home and abroad, was sought out by the artists and literati of his day; when Dickens visited America his first question on landing was "Where is Bryant?" When, in his mid-sixties, he presided at a lecture given by Abraham Lincoln, Lincoln said, "It was worth the journey to see such a man." Admirers claimed he was "the first citizen of the Republic."

Nearing seventy, Bryant was still young in heart. He wrote eloquently and worked fervently in the cause of the Union. "Not Yet" and "Our Country's Call" were as vigorous as battle cries. At seventy-seven he finished his excellent translation of the first volume of the twelve-book *Odyssey* and completed the huge work a year later.

He began his eightieth year with an address on Benjamin Franklin. Still vigorous—he started each day with calisthenic exercises and walked hours at a time—he composed hymns, projected new poems, and helped edit a revised edition of the mammoth *Library of Poetry and Song*. In his eighties he continued to be a frequent speaker at various receptions. In late May of his eighty-fourth year he made an address in Central Park at the unveiling of a statue to the Italian patriot Mazzini. Standing with head uncovered, he suffered the full force of the intense sun. After the ceremonies, as he was ascending the steps of General Wilson's house, he became dizzy and fell. Concussion of the brain followed and, after remaining in a coma several weeks, he died June 12, 1878.

VI

Someone has remarked that in his youth Bryant wrote for elderly people and in his old age for children. It is apparent that his verse, never noted for its sensuousness or passion, grew freer if not more flexible as Bryant grew older. Often referred to as "the American Wordsworth" because of his preoccupation with the soil, Bryant earned the appellation. But, unlike Wordsworth, Bryant was more interested in nature than in human nature. The poet commonly called "the father of American poetry" was serene to the point of aloofness; the self-discipline achieved a calmness which almost denies emotion as dignity freezes into austerity. James Russell Lowell teased the elderly bard in *A Fable for Critics*, yet his rhymed puns and critical persiflage are not unjustified:

> There is Bryant, as quiet, as cool, and as dignified,
> As a smooth, silent iceberg that never is ignified,
> Save when by reflection 'tis kindled o' nights
> With a semblance of flame by the chill Northern Lights.
> He may rank (Griswold says so) first bard of your nation
> (There's no doubt that he stands in supreme ice-olation);
> Your topmost Parnassus he may set his heel on,
> But no warm applauses come, peal following peal on,—
> He's too smooth and too polished to hang any zeal on.
> Unqualified merits, I'll grant, if you choose, he has 'em,
> But he lacks the one merit of kindling enthusiasm.

Such an estimate is only a half-true summary. Bryant loved the world with earnest forthrightness. His affection went out to bobolinks and waterfowl, early yellow violets, a dissolving cloud and the frozen earth of November. He celebrated the rank leafage of wet woods as well as the delicacy of the fringed gentian, that blossom as blue:

> as if that sky let fall
> A flower from its cerulean wall.

"In character no man stands more loftily than Bryant," wrote Edgar Allan Poe, putting aside his usually biting manner. "The peculiarly melancholy expression of his countenance has caused him to be accused of harshness, or coldness of heart. Never was there a greater mistake. His soul is charity itself, in all respects generous and noble." The generosity and nobility are always there, obvious at the most casual reading. Bryant sounded the Puritan note at its purest. He maintained that Beauty was both more and less than its own excuse for being; to serve its (and Bryant's) aim it had to be linked to purpose, upheld by justice. The moralizing, the sense of divinity, was implicit, not a mere sanctimonious appendage. For the first time in America, the true voices of poet and prophet were united.

It cannot be said that Bryant was startlingly original. He was influenced at the very beginning by Pope and Cowper and also by Southey, Kirk White, and "The Graveyard Poets." The later indebtedness to Wordsworth was not only acknowledged but emphasized by Bryant himself. Originality was not Bryant's forte; his was a genuine pastoral note rather than a brilliantly inventive one.

The world in which Bryant was at home is neither the dizzy mountainous terrain of Emerson nor the haunted midnight landscape of Poe. But, though it may never be a dazzling or romantic domain, after turbulent days we are glad for its quiet assurance. It may not be enchanted ground, but it has the comfort of good earth: it is sure haven.

The Table of Contents

II

THE DEATH OF THE FLOWERS AND OTHER POEMS

III

LATER POEMS

IV

HYMNS WRITTEN AT VARIOUS TIMES

V

APPENDIX: EARLY AND UNCOLLECTED POEMS

A List of the Engravings

THE BRYANT HOMESTEAD AT CUMMINGTON

The Poems of William Cullen Bryant

I

THANATOPSIS AND OTHER POEMS

The Editor's Commentary

AMERICAN POETRY may be said to have emerged from its colonial or incubating period in 1817 with the simultaneous publication of Bryant's "Thanatopsis" and his "Inscription for the Entrance to a Wood." When his first collection of poems appeared, it contained half a dozen pieces written in the author's youth: "The Yellow Violet," written three years after the composition of "Thanatopsis," when Bryant was seventeen, "Green River," "A Hymn to Death," "The West Wind," the unforgettable "To a Waterfowl," and the ambitious "The Ages," in which the author endeavored "from a survey of the past ages of the world, and of the successive advances of mankind in knowledge, virtue, and happiness, to justify and confirm the hopes of the philanthropist for the future destinies of the human race."

Edgar Allan Poe was particularly enthusiastic about two of Bryant's early lyrics. He insisted that "Oh Fairest of the Rural Maids" would strike every poet as "the truest poem ever written by Bryant. It is richly ideal." Poe was even more expansive about "June," which he found "sweet and well modulated in rhythm, and inexpressibly pathetic. It serves well to illustrate my remarks about passion in its connection with poetry. In 'June' there is, very properly, nothing of the intense *passion* of grief; but the subdued sorrow which comes up, as if perforce, to the surface of the poet's gay sayings about his grave, we find thrilling to the soul while there is yet a spiritual *elevation* in the thrill."

The youthful philosophizer did not lose himself in meditation. As Poe discovered, Bryant turned gladly to song, and from song to story. Not enough has been written about Bryant's narrative range: his preoccupation with aboriginal backgrounds in "The Indian Girl's Lament," "An Indian Story," and the Great Barrington legend embodied in "Monument Mountain"; his concern with the Greek struggle for independence in "The Massacre at Scio"; his response to Hebraic tradition in "Rizpah" and "The Song of the Stars"; his use of purely native material in "The Murdered Traveler," which originated in a mysterious murder near Stockbridge.

Such poems emphasize that Bryant did not harp on the single note of elegaic musing. His mind was alive to a variety of riches; he combined classic dignity with contemporary distinction.

A Winter Piece

The time has been that these wild solitudes,
Yet beautiful as wild, were trod by me
Oftener than now; and when the ills of life
Had chafed my spirit—when the unsteady pulse
Beat with strange flutterings—I would wander forth
And seek the woods. The sunshine on my path
Was to me as a friend. The swelling hills,
The quiet dells retiring far between,
With gentle invitation to explore
Their windings, were a calm society
That talked with me and soothed me. Then the chant
Of birds, and chime of brooks, and soft caress
Of the fresh sylvan air, made me forget
The thoughts that broke my peace, and I began
To gather simples by the fountain's brink,
And lose myself in day-dreams. While I stood
In Nature's loneliness, I was with one
With whom I early grew familiar, one
Who never had a frown for me, whose voice
Never rebuked me for the hours I stole
From cares I loved not, but of which the world
Deems highest, to converse with her. When shrieked
The bleak November winds, and smote the woods,
And the brown fields were herbless, and the shades,
That met above the merry rivulet,
Were spoiled, I sought, I loved them still; they seemed
Like old companions in adversity.
Still there was beauty in my walks; the brook,
Bordered with sparkling frost-work, was as gay
As with its fringe of summer flowers. Afar,
The village with its spires, the path of streams
And dim receding valleys, hid before
By interposing trees, lay visible
Through the bare grove, and my familiar haunts
Seemed new to me. Nor was I slow to come
Among them, when the clouds, from their still skirts,
Had shaken down on earth the feathery snow,
And all was white. The pure keen air abroad,
Albeit it breathed no scent of herb, nor heard
Love-call of bird nor merry hum of bee,
Was not the air of death. Bright mosses crept
Over the spotted trunks, and the close buds,
That lay along the boughs, instinct with life,
Patient, and waiting the soft breath of Spring,

Feared not the piercing spirit of the North.
The snow-bird twittered on the beechen bough,
And 'neath the hemlock, whose thick branches bent
Beneath its bright cold burden, and kept dry
A circle, on the earth, of withered leaves,
The partridge found a shelter. Through the snow
The rabbit sprang away. The lighter track
Of fox, and the raccoon's broad path, were there,
Crossing each other. From his hollow tree
The squirrel was abroad, gathering the nuts
Just fallen, that asked the winter cold and sway
Of winter blast, to shake them from their hold.

But Winter has yet brighter scenes—he boasts
Splendors beyond what gorgeous Summer knows;
Or Autumn with his many fruits, and woods
All flushed with many hues. Come when the rains
Have glazed the snow and clothed the trees with ice,
While the slant sun of February pours
Into the bowers a flood of light. Approach!
The incrusted surface shall upbear thy steps,
And the broad arching portals of the grove
Welcome thy entering. Look! the massy trunks
Are cased in the pure crystal; each light spray,
Nodding and tinkling in the breath of heaven,
Is studded with its trembling water-drops,
That glimmer with an amethystine light.
But round the parent-stem the long low boughs
Bend, in a glittering ring, and arbors hide
The glassy floor. Oh! you might deem the spot
The spacious cavern of some virgin mine,
Deep in the womb of earth—where the gems grow,
And diamonds put forth radiant rods and bud
With amethyst and topaz—and the place
Lit up, most royally, with the pure beam
That dwells in them. Or haply the vast hall
Of fairy palace, that outlasts the night,
And fades not in the glory of the sun;—
Where crystal columns send forth slender shafts
And crossing arches; and fantastic aisles
Wind from the sight in brightness, and are lost
Among the crowded pillars. Raise thine eye;
Thou seest no cavern roof, no palace vault;
There the blue sky and the white drifting cloud

Look in. Again the wildered fancy dreams
Of spouting fountains, frozen as they rose.
And fixed, with all their branching jets, in air,
And all their sluices sealed. All, all is light;
Light without shade. But all shall pass away
With the next sun. From numberless vast trunks
Loosened, the crashing ice shall make a sound
Like the far roar of rivers, and the eve
Shall close o'er the brown woods as it was wont.

And it is pleasant, when the noisy streams
Are just set free, and milder suns melt off
The plashy snow, save only the firm drift
In the deep glen or the close shade of pines—
'Tis pleasant to behold the wreaths of smoke
Roll up among the maples of the hill,
Where the shrill sound of youthful voices wakes
The shriller echo, as the clear pure lymph,
That from the wounded trees, in twinkling drops,
Falls, mid the golden brightness of the morn,
Is gathered in with brimming pails, and oft,
Wielded by sturdy hands, the stroke of axe
Makes the woods ring. Along the quiet air,
Come and float calmly off the soft light clouds,
Such as you see in summer, and the winds
Scarce stir the branches. Lodged in sunny cleft,
Where the cold breezes come not, blooms alone
The little wind-flower, whose just opened eye
Is blue as the spring heaven it gazes at—
Startling the loiterer in the naked groves
With unexpected beauty, for the time
Of blossoms and green leaves is yet afar.
And ere it comes, the encountering winds shall oft
Muster their wrath again, and rapid clouds
Shade heaven, and bounding on the frozen earth
Shall fall their volleyed stores, rounded like hail
And white like snow, and the loud North again
Shall buffet the vexed forest in his rage.

Rizpah

And he delivered them into the hands of the Gibeonites, and they hanged them in the hill before the Lord; and they fell all seven together, and were put to death in the days of the harvest, in the first days, in the beginning of barley-harvest.

And Rizpah, the daughter of Aiah, took sackcloth, and spread it for her upon the rock, from the beginning of harvest until the water dropped upon them out of heaven, and suffered neither the birds of the air to rest upon them by day, nor the beasts of the field by night. 2 Samuel, xxi. 10.

Hear what the desolate Rizpah said,
As on Gibeah's rocks she watched the dead.
The sons of Michal before her lay,
And her own fair children, dearer than they:
By a death of shame they all had died,
And were stretched on the bare rock, side by side.
And Rizpah, once the loveliest of all
That bloomed and smiled in the court of Saul,
All wasted with watching and famine now,
And scorched by the sun her haggard brow,
Sat mournfully guarding their corpses there,
And murmured a strange and solemn air;
The low, heart-broken, and wailing strain
Of a mother that mourns her children slain:

"I have made the crags my home, and spread
On their desert backs my sackcloth bed;
I have eaten the bitter herb of the rocks,
And drunk the midnight dew in my locks;
I have wept till I could not weep, and the pain
Of the burning eyeballs went to my brain.
Seven blackened corpses before me lie,
In the blaze of the sun and the winds of the sky.
I have watched them through the burning day,
And driven the vulture and raven away;
And the cormorant wheeled in circles round,
Yet feared to alight on the guarded ground.
And when the shadows of twilight came,
I have seen the hyena's eyes of flame,
And heard at my side his stealthy tread,
But aye at my shout the savage fled:
And I threw the lighted brand to fright
The jackal and wolf that yelled in the night.

"Ye were foully murdered, my hapless sons,
By the hands of wicked and cruel ones;
Ye fell, in your fresh and blooming prime,
All innocent, for your father's crime.

He sinned—but he paid the price of his guilt
When his blood by a nameless hand was spilt;
When he strove with the heathen host in vain,
And fell with the flower of his people slain,
And the sceptre his children's hands should sway
From his injured lineage passed away.

"But I hoped that the cottage-roof would be
A safe retreat for my sons and me;
And that while they ripened to manhood fast,
They should wean my thoughts from the woes of the past;
And my bosom swelled with a mother's pride,
As they stood in their beauty and strength by my side,
Tall like their sire, with the princely grace
Of his stately form, and the bloom of his face.

"Oh, what an hour for a mother's heart,
When the pitiless ruffians tore us apart!
When I clasped their knees and wept and prayed,
And struggled and shrieked to Heaven for aid,
And clung to my sons with desperate strength,
Till the murderers loosed my hold at length,
And bore me breathless and faint aside,
In their iron arms, while my children died.
They died—and the mother that gave them birth
Is forbid to cover their bones with earth.

"The barley-harvest was nodding white,
When my children died on the rocky height,
And the reapers were singing on hill and plain,
When I came to my task of sorrow and pain.
But now the season of rain is nigh,
The sun is dim in the thickening sky,
And the clouds in sullen darkness rest
Where he hides his light at the doors of the west.
I hear the howl of the wind that brings
The long drear storm on its heavy wings;
But the howling wind and the driving rain
Will beat on my houseless head in vain:
I shall stay, from my murdered sons to scare
The beasts of the desert, and fowls of air."

Thanatopsis

To him who in the love of Nature holds
Communion with her visible forms, she speaks
A various language; for his gayer hours
She has a voice of gladness, and a smile
And eloquence of beauty, and she glides
Into his darker musings, with a mild
And healing sympathy, that steals away
Their sharpness, ere he is aware. When thoughts
Of the last bitter hour come like a blight
Over thy spirit, and sad images
Of the stern agony, and shroud, and pall,
And breathless darkness, and the narrow house,
Make thee to shudder, and grow sick at heart;—
Go forth, under the open sky, and list
To Nature's teachings, while from all around—
Earth and her waters, and the depths of air—
Comes a still voice—Yet a few days, and thee
The all-beholding sun shall see no more
In all his course; nor yet in the cold ground,
Where thy pale form was laid, with many tears,
Nor in the embrace of ocean, shall exist
Thy image. Earth, that nourished thee, shall claim
Thy growth, to be resolved to earth again,
And, lost each human trace, surrendering up
Thine individual being, shalt thou go
To mix forever with the elements,
To be a brother to the insensible rock
And to the sluggish clod, which the rude swain
Turns with his share, and treads upon. The oak
Shall send his roots abroad, and pierce thy mould.
Yet not to thine eternal resting-place
Shalt thou retire alone—nor couldst thou wish
Couch more magnificent. Thou shalt lie down
With patriarchs of the infant world—with kings,
The powerful of the earth—the wise, the good,
Fair forms, and hoary seers of ages past,
All in one mighty sepulchre.—The hills
Rock-ribbed and ancient as the sun,—the vales
Stretching in pensive quietness between;
The venerable woods—rivers that move
In majesty, and the complaining brooks
That make the meadows green; and, poured round all,
Old ocean's gray and melancholy waste,—
Are but the solemn decorations all

Of the great tomb of man. The golden sun,
The planets, all the infinite host of heaven,
Are shining on the sad abodes of death,
Through the still lapse of ages. All that tread
The globe are but a handful to the tribes
That slumber in its bosom.—Take the wings
Of morning—and the Barcan desert pierce,
Or lose thyself in the continuous woods
Where rolls the Oregon, and hears no sound,
Save his own dashings—yet—the dead are there;
And millions in those solitudes, since first
The flight of years began, have laid them down
In their last sleep—the dead reign there alone.
So shalt thou rest—and what if thou withdraw
Unheeded by the living—and no friend
Take note of thy departure? All that breathe
Will share thy destiny. The gay will laugh
When thou art gone, the solemn brood of care
Plod on, and each one as before will chase
His favorite phantom; yet all these shall leave
Their mirth and their employments, and shall come
And make their bed with thee. As the long train
Of ages glide away, the sons of men,
The youth in life's green spring, and he who goes

In the full strength of years, matron and maid,
The speechless babe, and the gray-headed man—
Shall one by one be gathered to thy side,
By those, who in their turn shall follow them.

So live, that when thy summons comes to join
The innumerable caravan, which moves
To that mysterious realm, where each shall take
His chamber in the silent halls of death,
Thou go not, like the quarry-slave at night,
Scourged to his dungeon, but, sustained and soothed
By an unfaltering trust, approach thy grave,
Like one who wraps the drapery of his couch
About him, and lies down to pleasant dreams.

Consumption

Ay, thou art for the grave; thy glances shine
Too brightly to shine long; another Spring
Shall deck her for men's eyes—but not for thine—
Sealed in a sleep which knows no wakening.
The fields for thee have no medicinal leaf,
And the vexed ore no mineral of power;
And they who love thee wait in anxious grief
Till the slow plague shall bring the fatal hour.
Glide softly to thy rest then; Death should come
Gently, to one of gentle mould like thee,
As light winds wandering through groves of bloom
Detach the delicate blossom from the tree.
Close thy sweet eyes, calmly, and without pain;
And we will trust in God to see thee yet again.

The West Wind

Beneath the forest's skirt I rest,
　Whose branching pines rise dark and high,
And hear the breezes of the West
　Among the thread-like foliage sigh.

Sweet Zephyr! why that sound of woe?
　Is not thy home among the flowers?
Do not the bright June roses blow,
　To meet thy kiss at morning hours?

And lo! thy glorious realm outspread—
　Yon stretching valleys, green and gay,
And yon free hill-tops, o'er whose head
　The loose white clouds are borne away.

And there the full broad river runs,
　And many a fount wells fresh and sweet,
To cool thee when the mid-day suns
　Have made thee faint beneath their heat.

Thou wind of joy, and youth, and love;
　Spirit of the new-wakened year!
The sun in his blue realm above
　Smooths a bright path when thou art here.

In lawns the murmuring bee is heard,
　The wooing ring-dove in the shade;
On thy soft breath, the new-fledged bird
　Takes wing, half happy, half afraid.

Ah! thou art like our wayward race;—
　When not a shade of pain or ill
Dims the bright smile of Nature's face,
　Thou lov'st to sigh and murmur still.

The Yellow Violet

When beechen buds begin to swell,
   And woods the blue-bird's warble know,
The yellow violet's modest bell
   Peeps from the last year's leaves below.

Ere russet fields their green resume,
   Sweet flower, I love, in forest bare,
To meet thee, when thy faint perfume
   Alone is in the virgin air.

Of all her train, the hands of Spring
   First plant thee in the watery mould,
And I have seen thee blossoming
   Beside the snow-bank's edges cold.

Thy parent sun, who bade thee view
   Pale skies, and chilling moisture sip,
Has bathed thee in his own bright hue,
   And streaked with jet thy glowing lip.

Yet slight thy form, and low thy seat,
   And earthward bent thy gentle eye,
Unapt the passing view to meet,
   When loftier flowers are flaunting nigh.

Oft, in the sunless April day,
  Thy early smile has stayed my walk;
But midst the gorgeous blooms of May,
  I passed thee on thy humble stalk.

So they, who climb to wealth, forget
  The friends in darker fortunes tried.
I copied them—but I regret
  That I should ape the ways of pride.

And when again the genial hour
  Awakes the painted tribes of light,
I'll not o'erlook the modest flower
  That made the woods of April bright.

Ode for an Agricultural Celebration

Far back in the ages,
  The plough with wreaths was crowned;
The hands of kings and sages
  Entwined the chaplet round;
Till men of spoil disdained the toil
  By which the world was nourished,
And dews of blood enriched the soil
  Where green their laurels flourished.
—Now the world her fault repairs—
  The guilt that stains her story;
And weeps her crimes amid the cares
  That formed her earliest glory.

The proud throne shall crumble,
  The diadem shall wane,
The tribes of earth shall humble
  The pride of those who reign;
And War shall lay his pomp away;—
  The fame that heroes cherish,
The glory earned in deadly fray
  Shall fade, decay, and perish.
Honor waits, o'er all the earth,
  Through endless generations,
The art that calls her harvest forth,
  And feeds th' expectant nations.

Green River

When breezes are soft and skies are fair,
I steal an hour from study and care,
And hie me away to the woodland scene,
Where wanders the stream with waters of green,
As if the bright fringe of herbs on its brink
Had given their stain to the waves they drink;
And they, whose meadows it murmurs through,
Have named the stream from its own fair hue.

Yet pure its waters—its shallows are bright
With colored pebbles and sparkles of light,
And clear the depths where its eddies play,
And dimples deepen and whirl away,
And the plane-tree's speckled arms o'ershoot
The swifter current that mines its root,
Through whose shifting leaves, as you walk the hill,
The quivering glimmer of sun and rill
With a sudden flash on the eye is thrown,
Like the ray that streams from the diamond-stone.
Oh, loveliest there the spring days come,
With blossoms, and birds, and wild-bees' hum;
The flowers of summer are fairest there,
And freshest the breath of the summer air;
And sweetest the golden autumn day
In silence and sunshine glides away.

Yet, fair as thou art, thou shunnest to glide,
Beautiful stream! by the village side;
But windest away from haunts of men,
To quiet valley and shaded glen;
And forest, and meadow, and slope of hill,
Around thee, are lonely, lovely, and still,
Lonely—save when, by thy rippling tides,
From thicket to thicket the angler glides;
Or the simpler comes, with basket and book,
For herbs of power on thy banks to look;
Or haply, some idle dreamer, like me,
To wander, and muse, and gaze on thee,
Still—save the chirp of birds that feed
On the river cherry and seedy reed,
And thy own wild music gushing out
With mellow murmur of fairy shout,
From dawn to the blush of another day,
Like traveller singing along his way.

That fairy music I never hear,
Nor gaze on those waters so green and clear,
And mark them winding away from sight,
Darkened with shade or flashing with light,
While o'er them the vine to its thicket clings,
And the zephyr stoops to freshen his wings,
But I wish that fate had left me free
To wander these quiet haunts with thee,
Till the eating cares of earth should depart,
And the peace of the scene pass into my heart;
And I envy thy stream, as it glides along
Through its beautiful banks in a trance of song.

Though forced to drudge for the dregs of men,
And scrawl strange words with the barbarous pen,
And mingle among the jostling crowd,
Where the sons of strife are subtle and loud—
I often come to this quiet place,
To breathe the airs that ruffle thy face,
And gaze upon thee in silent dream,
For in thy lonely and lovely stream
An image of that calm life appears
That won my heart in my greener years.

The Burial-Place

A FRAGMENT

Erewhile, on England's pleasant shores, our sires
Left not their churchyards unadorned with shades
Or blossoms, but indulgent to the strong
And natural dread of man's last home, the grave,
Its frost and silence—they disposed around,
To soothe the melancholy spirit that dwelt
Too sadly on life's close, the forms and hues
Of vegetable beauty. There the yew,
Green ever amid the snows of winter, told
Of immortality, and gracefully
The willow, a perpetual mourner, drooped;
And there the gadding woodbine crept about,
And there the ancient ivy. From the spot
Where the sweet maiden, in her blossoming years
Cut off, was laid with streaming eyes, and hands
That trembled as they placed her there, the rose
Sprung modest, on bowed stalk, and better spoke
Her graces, than the proudest monument.
There children set about their playmate's grave
The pansy. On the infant's little bed,
Wet at its planting with maternal tears,
Emblem of early sweetness, early death,
Nestled the lowly primrose. Childless dames,
And maids that would not raise the reddened eye—
Orphans, from whose young lids the light of joy
Fled early—silent lovers, who had given
All that they lived for to the arms of earth,
Came often, o'er the recent graves to strew
Their offerings, rue, and rosemary, and flowers.

The pilgrim bands who passed the sea to keep
Their Sabbaths in the eye of God alone,
In his wide temple of the wilderness,
Brought not these simple customs of the heart
With them. It might be, while they laid their dead
By the vast solemn skirts of the old groves,
And the fresh virgin soil poured forth strange flowers
About their graves; and the familiar shades
Of their own native isle, and wonted blooms,
And herbs were wanting, which the pious hand
Might plant or scatter there, these gentle rites
Passed out of use. Now they are scarcely known,
And rarely in our borders may you meet

The tall larch, sighing in the burial-place,
Or willow, training low its boughs to hide
The gleaming marble. Naked rows of graves
And melancholy ranks of monuments
Are seen instead, where the coarse grass, between,
Shoots up its dull green spikes, and in the wind
Hisses, and the neglected bramble nigh,
Offers its berries to the schoolboy's hand,
In vain—they grow too near the dead. Yet here,
Nature, rebuking the neglect of man,
Plants often, by the ancient mossy stone,
The brier-rose, and upon the broken turf
That clothes the fresher grave, the strawberry plant
Sprinkles its swell with blossoms, and lays forth
Her ruddy, pouting fruit. . . .

November

Yet one smile more, departing, distant sun!
  One mellow smile through the soft vapory air,
Ere, o'er the frozen earth, the loud winds run,
  Or snows are sifted o'er the meadows bare.
One smile on the brown hills and naked trees,
  And the dark rocks whose summer wreaths are cast,
And the blue gentian-flower, that, in the breeze,
  Nods lonely, of her beauteous race the last.
Yet a few sunny days, in which the bee
  Shall murmur by the hedge that skirts the way,
The cricket chirp upon the russet lea,
  And man delight to linger in thy ray.
Yet one rich smile, and we will try to bear
The piercing winter frost, and winds, and darkened air.

The Indian Girl's Lament

An Indian girl was sitting where
  Her lover, slain in battle, slept;
Her maiden veil, her own black hair,
  Came down o'er eyes that wept;
And wildly, in her woodland tongue,
This sad and simple lay she sung:

"I've pulled away the shrubs that grew
  Too close above thy sleeping head,
And broke the forest-boughs that threw
  Their shadows o'er thy bed,
That, shining from the sweet southwest,
The sunbeams might rejoice thy rest.

"It was a weary, weary road
  That led thee to the pleasant coast,
Where thou, in his serene abode,
  Hast met thy father's ghost;
Where everlasting autumn lies
On yellow woods and sunny skies.

" 'Twas I the broidered mocsen made,
  That shod thee for that distant land;
'Twas I thy bow and arrows laid
  Beside thy still cold hand;
Thy bow in many a battle bent,
Thy arrows never vainly sent.

"With wampum-belts I crossed thy breast,
  And wrapped thee in the bison's hide,
And laid the food that pleased thee best,
  In plenty, by thy side,
And decked thee bravely, as became
A warrior of illustrious name.

"Thou'rt happy now, for thou hast passed
  The long dark journey of the grave,
And in the land of light, at last,
  Hast joined the good and brave;
Amid the flushed and balmy air,
The bravest and the loveliest there.

"Yet, oft to thine own Indian maid
  Even there thy thoughts will earthward stray—

To her who sits where thou wert laid,
And weeps the hours away,
Yet almost can her grief forget,
To think that thou dost love her yet.

"And thou, by one of those still lakes
That in a shining cluster lie,
On which the south wind scarcely breaks
The image of the sky,
A bower for thee and me hast made
Beneath the many-colored shade.

"And thou dost wait and watch to meet
My spirit sent to join the blessed,
And, wondering what detains my feet
From that bright land of rest,
Dost seem, in every sound, to hear
The rustling of my footsteps near."

Song

Soon as the glazed and gleaming snow
Reflects the day-dawn cold and clear,
The hunter of the West must go
In depth of woods to seek the deer.

His rifle on his shoulder placed,
His stores of death arranged with skill,
His moccasins and snow-shoes laced—
Why lingers he beside the hill?

Far, in the dim and doubtful light,
Where woody slopes a valley leave,
He sees what none but lover might,
The dwelling of his Genevieve.

And oft he turns his truant eye,
And pauses oft, and lingers near;
But when he marks the reddening sky,
He bounds away to hunt the deer.

The Rivulet

This little rill, that from the springs
Of yonder grove its current brings,
Plays on the slope awhile, and then
Goes prattling into groves again,
Oft to its warbling waters drew
My little feet, when life was new.
When woods in early green were dressed,
And from the chambers of the west
The warm breezes, travelling out,
Breathed the new scent of flowers about,
My truant steps from home would stray,
Upon its grassy side to play,
List the brown thrasher's vernal hymn,
And crop the violet on its brim,
With blooming cheek and open brow,
As young and gay, sweet rill, as thou.

And when the days of boyhood came,
And I had grown in love with fame,
Duly I sought thy banks, and tried
My first rude numbers by thy side.
Words cannot tell how bright and gay
The scenes of life before me lay.
Then glorious hopes, that now to speak
Would bring the blood into my cheek,
Passed o'er me; and I wrote, on high,
A name I deemed should never die.

Years change thee not. Upon yon hill
The tall old maples, verdant still,
Yet tell, in grandeur of decay,
How swift the years have passed away,
Since first, a child, and half afraid,
I wandered in the forest shade.
Thou, ever-joyous rivulet,
Dost dimple, leap, and prattle yet;
And sporting with the sands that pave
The windings of thy silver wave,
And dancing to thy own wild chime,
Thou laughest at the lapse of time.
The same sweet sounds are in my ear
My early childhood loved to hear;
As pure thy limpid waters run;
As bright they sparkle to the sun;

As fresh and thick the bending ranks
Of herbs that line thy oozy banks;
The violet there, in soft May dew,
Comes up, as modest and as blue;
As green amid thy current's stress,
Floats the scarce-rooted watercress;
And the brown ground-bird, in thy glen,
Still chirps as merrily as then.

Thou changest not—but I am changed
Since first thy pleasant banks I ranged;
And the grave stranger, come to see
The play-place of his infancy,
Has scarce a single trace of him
Who sported once upon thy brim.
The visions of my youth are past—
Too bright, too beautiful to last.
I've tried the world—it wears no more
The coloring of romance it wore.
Yet well has Nature kept the truth
She promised in my earliest youth.
The radiant beauty shed abroad
On all the glorious works of God,
Shows freshly, to my sobered eye,
Each charm it wore in days gone by.

Yet a few years shall pass away,
And I, all trembling, weak, and gray,
Bowed to the earth, which waits to fold

My ashes in the embracing mould,
(If haply the dark will of Fate
Indulge my life so long a date),
May come for the last time to look
Upon my childhood's favorite brook.
Then dimly on my eye shall gleam
The sparkle of thy dancing stream;
And faintly on my ear shall fall
Thy prattling current's merry call;
Yet shalt thou flow as glad and bright
As when thou met'st my infant sight.

And I shall sleep—and on thy side,
As ages after ages glide,
Children their early sports shall try,
And pass to hoary age and die.
But thou, unchanged from year to year,
Gayly shalt play and glitter here;
Amid young flowers and tender grass
Thy endless infancy shall pass;
And, singing down thy narrow glen,
Shalt mock the fading race of men.

To a Cloud

Beautiful cloud! with folds so soft and fair,
   Swimming in the pure quiet air!
Thy fleeces bathed in sunlight, while below
   Thy shadow o'er the vale moves slow;
Where, midst their labor, pause the reaper train,
   As cool it comes along the grain.
Beautiful cloud! I would I were with thee
   In thy calm way o'er land and sea;
To rest on thy unrolling skirts, and look
   On Earth as on an open book;
On streams that tie her realms with silver bands,
   And the long ways that seam her lands;
And hear her humming cities, and the sound
   Of the great ocean breaking round.
Ay—I would sail, upon thy air-borne car,
   To blooming regions distant far,
To where the sun of Andalusia shines
   On his own olive-groves and vines,
Or the soft lights of Italy's clear sky
   In smiles upon her ruins lie.
But I would woo the winds to let us rest
   O'er Greece, long fettered and oppressed,
Whose sons at length have heard the call that comes
   From the old battle-fields and tombs,
And risen, and drawn the sword, and on the foe
   Have dealt the swift and desperate blow,
And the Othman power is cloven, and the stroke
   Has touched its chains, and they are broke.
Ay, we would linger, till the sunset there
   Should come, to purple all the air,
And thou reflect upon the sacred ground
   The ruddy radiance streaming round.
Bright meteor! for the summer noontide made!
   Thy peerless beauty yet shall fade.
The sun, that fills with light each glistening fold,
   Shall set, and leave thee dark and cold:
The blast shall rend thy skirts, or thou mayst frown
   In the dark heaven when storms come down;
And weep in rain, till man's inquiring eye
   Miss thee, forever, from the sky.

To a Waterfowl

Whither, midst falling dew,
While glow the heavens with the last steps of day,
Far, through their rosy depths, dost thou pursue
Thy solitary way?

Vainly the fowler's eye
Might mark thy distant flight to do thee wrong,
As, darkly seen against the crimson sky,
Thy figure floats along.

Seek'st thou the plashy brink
Of weedy lake, or marge of river wide,
Or where the rocking billows rise and sink
On the chafed ocean-side?

There is a Power whose care
Teaches thy way along that pathless coast—
The desert and illimitable air—
Lone wandering, but not lost.

All day thy wings have fanned,
At that far height, the cold, thin atmosphere,
Yet stoop not, weary, to the welcome land,
Though the dark night is near.

And soon that toil shall end;
Soon shalt thou find a summer home, and rest,
And scream among thy fellows; reeds shall bend,
Soon, o'er thy sheltered nest.

Thou'rt gone, the abyss of heaven
Hath swallowed up thy form; yet, on my heart
Deeply has sunk the lesson thou hast given,
And shall not soon depart.

He who, from zone to zone,
Guides through the boundless sky thy certain flight,
In the long way that I must tread alone,
Will lead my steps aright.

"I Broke the Spell That Held Me Long"

I broke the spell that held me long,
The dear, dear witchery of song.
I said, the poet's idle lore
Shall waste my prime of years no more,
For Poetry, though heavenly born,
Consorts with poverty and scorn.

I broke the spell—nor deemed its power
Could fetter me another hour.
Ah, thoughtless! how could I forget
Its causes were around me yet?
For wheresoe'er I looked, the while,
Was Nature's everlasting smile.

Still came and lingered on my sight
Of flowers and streams the bloom and light,
And glory of the stars and sun;—
And these and poetry are one.
They, ere the world had held me long,
Recalled me to the love of song.

Hymn to Death

Oh! could I hope the wise and pure in heart
Might hear my song without a frown, nor deem
My voice unworthy of the theme it tries,—
I would take up the hymn to Death, and say
To the grim power, The world hath slandered thee
And mocked thee. On thy dim and shadowy brow
They place an iron crown, and call thee king
Of terrors, and the spoiler of the world,
Deadly assassin, that strik'st down the fair,
The loved, the good—that breathest on the lights
Of virtue set along the vale of life,
And they go out in darkness. I am come,
Not with reproaches, not with cries and prayers,
Such as have stormed thy stern, insensible ear
From the beginning; I am come to speak
Thy praises. True it is, that I have wept
Thy conquests, and may weep them yet again,
And thou from some I love wilt take a life
Dear to me as my own. Yet while the spell
Is on my spirit, and I talk with thee
In sight of all thy trophies, face to face,
Meet it is that my voice should utter forth
Thy nobler triumphs; I will teach the world
To thank thee. Who are thine accusers?—Who?
The living!—they who never felt thy power,
And know thee not. The curses of the wretch
Whose crimes are ripe, his sufferings when thy hand
Is on him, and the hour he dreads is come,
Are writ among thy praises. But the good—
Does he whom thy kind hand dismissed to peace,
Upbraid the gentle violence that took off
His fetters, and unbarred his prison-cell?

Raise then the hymn to Death. Deliverer!
God hath anointed thee to free the oppressed
And crush the oppressor. When the armed chief,
The conqueror of nations, walks the world,
And it is changed beneath his feet, and all
Its kingdoms melt into one mighty realm—
Thou, while his head is loftiest and his heart
Blasphemes, imagining his own right hand
Almighty, thou dost set thy sudden grasp
Upon him, and the links of that strong chain
Which bound mankind are crumbled; thou dost break

Sceptre and crown, and beat his throne to dust.
Then the earth shouts with gladness, and her tribes
Gather within their ancient bounds again.
Else had the mighty of the olden time,
Nimrod, Sesostris, or the youth who feigned
His birth from Libyan Ammon, smitten yet
The nations with a rod of iron, and driven
Their chariot o'er our necks. Thou dost avenge,
In thy good time, the wrongs of those who know
No other friend. Nor dost thou interpose
Only to lay the sufferer asleep,
Where he who made him wretched troubles not
His rest—thou dost strike down his tyrant too.
Oh, there is joy when hands that held the scourge
Drop lifeless, and the pitiless heart is cold.
Thou too dost purge from earth its horrible
And old idolatries;—from the proud fanes
Each to his grave their priests go out, till none
Is left to teach their worship; then the fires
Of sacrifice are chilled, and the green moss
O'ercreeps their altars; the fallen images
Cumber the weedy courts, and for loud hymns,
Chanted by kneeling multitudes, the wind
Shrieks in the solitary aisles. When he
Who gives his life to guilt, and laughs at all
The laws that God or man has made, and round
Hedges his seat with power, and shines in wealth,—
Lifts up his atheist front to scoff at Heaven,
And celebrates his shame in open day,
Thou, in the pride of all his crimes, cutt'st off
The horrible example. Touched by thine,
The extortioner's hard hand foregoes the gold
Wrung from the o'er-worn poor. The perjurer,
Whose tongue was lithe, e'en now, and voluble
Against his neighbor's life, and he who laughed
And leaped for joy to see a spotless fame
Blasted before his own foul calumnies,
Are smit with deadly silence. He, who sold
His conscience to preserve a worthless life,
Even while he hugs himself on his escape,
Trembles, as, doubly terrible, at length,
Thy steps o'ertake him, and there is no time
For parley, nor will bribes unclench thy grasp.
Oft, too, dost thou reform thy victim, long

Ere his last hour. And when the reveller,
Mad in the chase of pleasure, stretches on,
And strains each nerve, and clears the path of life
Like wind, thou point'st him to the dreadful goal,
And shak'st thy hour-glass in his reeling eye,
And check'st him in mid course. Thy skeleton hand
Shows to the faint of spirit the right path,
And he is warned, and fears to step aside.
Thou sett'st between the ruffian and his crime
Thy ghastly countenance, and his slack hand
Drops the drawn knife. But, oh, most fearfully
Dost thou show forth Heaven's justice, when thy shafts
Drink up the ebbing spirit—then the hard
Of heart and violent of hand restores
The treasure to the friendless wretch he wronged.
Then from the writhing bosom thou dost pluck
The guilty secret; lips, for ages sealed,
Are faithless to their dreadful trust at length,
And give it up; the felon's latest breath
Absolves the innocent man who bears his crime;
The slanderer, horror-smitten, and in tears,
Recalls the deadly obloquy he forged
To work his brother's ruin. Thou dost make
Thy penitent victim utter to the air
The dark conspiracy that strikes at life,
And aims to whelm the laws; ere yet the hour
Is come, and the dread sign of murder given.

Thus, from the first of time, hast thou been found
On virtue's side; the wicked, but for thee,
Had been too strong for the good; the great of earth
Had crushed the weak for ever. Schooled in guile
For ages, while each passing year had brought
Its baneful lesson, they had filled the world
With their abominations; while its tribes,
Trodden to earth, imbruted, and despoiled,
Had knelt to them in worship; sacrifice
Had smoked on many an altar, temple-roofs
Had echoed with the blasphemous prayer and hymn:
But thou, the great reformer of the world,
Tak'st off the sons of violence and fraud
In their green pupilage, their lore half learned—
Ere guilt had quite o'errun the simple heart
God gave them at their birth, and blotted out

His image. Thou dost mark them flushed with hope,
As on the threshold of their vast designs
Doubtful and loose they stand, and strik'st them down.

. . . .

Alas! I little thought that the stern power,
Whose fearful praise I sang, would try me thus
Before the strain was ended. It must cease—
For he is in his grave who taught my youth
The art of verse, and in the bud of life
Offered me to the Muses. Oh, cut off
Untimely! when thy reason in its strength,
Ripened by years of toil and studious search,
And watch of Nature's silent lessons, taught
Thy hand to practise best the lenient art
To which thou gavest thy laborious days,
And, last, thy life. And, therefore, when the earth
Received thee, tears were in unyielding eyes
And on hard cheeks, and they who deemed thy skill
Delayed their death-hour, shuddered and turned pale
When thou wert gone. This faltering verse, which thou
Shalt not, as wont, o'erlook, is all I have
To offer at thy grave—this—and the hope
To copy thy example, and to leave
A name of which the wretched shall not think
As of an enemy's, whom they forgive
As all forgive the dead. Rest, therefore, thou
Whose early guidance trained my infant steps—
Rest, in the bosom of God, till the brief sleep
Of death is over, and a happier life
Shall dawn to waken thine insensible dust.

Now thou art not—and yet the men whose guilt
Has wearied Heaven for vengeance—he who bears
False witness—he who takes the orphan's bread,
And robs the widow—he who spreads abroad
Polluted hands in mockery of prayer,
Are left to cumber earth. Shuddering I look
On what is written, yet I blot not out
The desultory numbers; let them stand,
The record of an idle revery.

An Indian Story

"I know where the timid fawn abides
In the depths of the shaded dell,
Where the leaves are broad and the thicket hides,
With its many stems and its tangled sides,
From the eye of the hunter well.

"I know where the young May violet grows,
In its lone and lowly nook,
On the mossy bank, where the larch-tree throws
Its broad dark bough, in solemn repose,
Far over the silent brook.

"And that timid fawn starts not with fear
When I steal to her secret bower;
And that young May violet to me is dear,
And I visit the silent streamlet near,
To look on the lovely flower."

Thus Maquon sings as he lightly walks
To the hunting-ground on the hills;
'Tis a song of his maid of the woods and rocks,
With her bright black eyes and long black locks,
And voice like the music of rills.

He goes to the chase—but evil eyes
Are at watch in the thicker shades;
For she was lovely that smiled on his sighs,
And he bore, from a hundred lovers, his prize,
The flower of the forest maids.

The boughs in the morning wind are stirred,
And the woods their song renew,
With the early carol of many a bird,
And the quickened tune of the streamlet heard
Where the hazels trickle with dew.

And Maquon has promised his dark-haired maid,
Ere eve shall redden the sky,
A good red deer from the forest shade,
That bounds with the herd through grove and glade,
At her cabin-door shall lie.

[AN INDIAN STORY]

The hollow woods, in the setting sun,
  Ring shrill with the fire-bird's lay;
And Maquon's sylvan labors are done,
And his shafts are spent, but the spoil they won
  He bears on his homeward way.

He stops near his bower—his eye perceives
  Strange traces along the ground—
At once to the earth his burden he heaves;
He breaks through the veil of boughs and leaves;
  And gains its door with a bound.

But the vines are torn on its walls that leant,
  And all from the young shrubs there
By struggling hands have the leaves been rent,
And there hangs on the sassafras, broken and bent,
  One tress of the well-known hair.

But where is she who, at this calm hour,
  Ever watched his coming to see?
She is not at the door, nor yet in the bower;
He calls—but he only hears on the flower
  The hum of the laden bee.

It is not a time for idle grief,
  Nor a time for tears to flow;
The horror that freezes his limbs is brief—
He grasps his war-axe and bow, and a sheaf
  Of darts made sharp for the foe.

And he looks for the print of the ruffian's feet
  Where he bore the maiden away;
And he darts on the fatal path more fleet
Than the blast hurries the vapor and sleet
  O'er the wild November day.

'Twas early summer when Maquon's bride
  Was stolen away from his door;
But at length the maples in crimson are dyed,
And the grape is black on the cabin-side—
  And she smiles at his hearth once more.

But far in the pine-grove, dark and cold,
  Where the yellow leaf falls not,

Nor the autumn shines in scarlet and gold,
There lies a hillock of fresh dark mould,
In the deepest gloom of the spot.

And the Indian girls, that pass that way,
Point out the ravisher's grave;
"And how soon to the bower she loved," they say,
"Returned the maid that was borne away
From Maquon, the fond and the brave."

"Blessed Are They That Mourn"

Oh, deem not they are blest alone
Whose lives a peaceful tenor keep;
The Power who pities man, hath shown
A blessing for the eyes that weep.

The light of smiles shall fill again
The lids that overflow with tears;
And weary hours of woe and pain
Are promises of happier years.

There is a day of sunny rest
For every dark and troubled night:
And grief may bide an evening guest,
Buy joy shall come with early light.

And thou, who, o'er thy friend's low bier,
Dost shed the bitter drops like rain,
Hope that a brighter, happier sphere
Will give him to thy arms again.

Nor let the good man's trust depart,
Though life its common gifts deny,—
Though with a pierced and bleeding heart
And spurned of men, he goes to die.

For God hath marked each sorrowing day
And numbered every secret tear,
And heaven's long age of bliss shall pay
For all his children suffer here.

Summer Wind

It is a sultry day; the sun has drunk
The dew that lay upon the morning grass;
There is no rustling in the lofty elm
That canopies my dwelling, and its shade
Scarce cools me. All is silent, save the faint
And interrupted murmur of the bee,
Settling on the sick flowers, and then again
Instantly on the wing. The plants around
Feel the too potent fervors: the tall maize
Rolls up its long green leaves; the clover droops
Its tender foliage, and declines its blooms.
But far in the fierce sunshine tower the hills,
With all their growth of woods, silent and stern,
As if the scorching heat and dazzling light
Were but an element they loved. Bright clouds,
Motionless pillars of the brazen heaven—
Their bases on the mountains—their white tops
Shining in the far ether—fire the air
With a reflected radiance, and make turn
The gazer's eye away. For me, I lie
Languidly in the shade, where the thick turf,
Yet virgin from the kisses of the sun,
Retains some freshness, and I woo the wind
That still delays his coming. Why so slow,
Gentle and voluble spirit of the air?
Oh, come and breathe upon the fainting earth
Coolness and life. Is it that in his caves
He hears me? See, on yonder woody ridge,
The pine is bending his proud top, and now
Among the nearer groves, chestnut and oak
Are tossing their green boughs about. He comes;
Lo, where the grassy meadow runs in waves!
The deep distressful silence of the scene
Breaks up with mingling of unnumbered sounds
And universal motion. He is come,
Shaking a shower of blossoms from the shrubs,
And bearing on their fragrance; and he brings
Music of birds, and rustling of young boughs,
And sound of swaying branches, and the voice
Of distant waterfalls. All the green herbs
Are stirring in his breath; a thousand flowers,
By the road-side and the borders of the brook,
Nod gayly to each other; glossy leaves

Are twinkling in the sun, as if the dew
Were on them yet, and silver waters break
Into small waves and sparkle as he comes.

March

The stormy March is come at last,
With wind, and cloud, and changing skies;
I hear the rushing of the blast,
That through the snowy valley flies.

Ah, passing few are they who speak,
Wild, stormy month! in praise of thee;
Yet though thy winds are loud and bleak,
Thou art a welcome month to me.

For thou, to northern lands, again
The glad and glorious sun dost bring,
And thou hast joined the gentle train
And wear'st the gentle name of Spring.

And, in thy reign of blast and storm,
Smiles many a long, bright, sunny day,
When the changed winds are soft and warm,
And heaven puts on the blue of May.

Then sing aloud the gushing rills
In joy that they again are free,
And, brightly leaping down the hills,
Renew their journey to the sea.

The year's departing beauty hides
Of wintry storms the sullen threat;
But in thy sternest frown abides
A look of kindly promise yet.

Thou bring'st the hope of those calm skies,
And that soft time of sunny showers,
When the wide bloom, on earth that lies,
Seems of a brighter world than ours.

The Old Man's Funeral

I saw an aged man upon his bier,
His hair was thin and white, and on his brow
A record of the cares of many a year;—
Cares that were ended and forgotten now.
And there was sadness round, and faces bowed,
And woman's tears fell fast, and children wailed aloud.

Then rose another hoary man and said,
In faltering accents, to that weeping train.
"Why mourn ye that our aged friend is dead?
Ye are not sad to see the gathered grain,
Nor when their mellow fruit the orchards cast,
Nor when the yellow woods let fall the ripened mast.

"Ye sigh not when the sun, his course fulfilled,
His glorious course, rejoicing earth and sky,
In the soft evening, when the winds are stilled,
Sinks where his islands of refreshment lie,
And leaves the smile of his departure, spread
O'er the warm-colored heaven and ruddy mountain head.

"Why weep ye then for him, who, having won
The bound of man's appointed years, at last,
Life's blessings all enjoyed, life's labors done,
Serenely to his final rest has passed;
While the soft memory of his virtues, yet,
Lingers like twilight hues, when the bright sun is set?

"His youth was innocent; his riper age
Marked with some act of goodness every day;
And watched by eyes that loved him, calm and sage,
Faded his late declining years away.
Meekly he gave his being up, and went
To share the holy rest that waits a life well spent.

"That life was happy; every day he gave
Thanks for the fair existence that was his;
For a sick fancy made him not her slave,
To mock him with her phantom miseries.
No chronic tortures racked his aged limb,
For luxury and sloth had nourished none for him.

"And I am glad that he has lived thus long,
And glad that he has gone to his reward;

Nor can I deem that Nature did him wrong,
  Softly to disengage the vital cord.
For when his hand grew palsied, and his eye
Dark with the mists of age, it was his time to die."

Mutation

They talk of short-lived pleasure—be it so—
  Pain dies as quickly: stern, hard-featured pain
Expires, and lets her weary prisoner go.
  The fiercest agonies have shortest reign;
  And after dreams of horror, comes again
The welcome morning with its rays of peace.
  Oblivion, softly wiping out the stain,
Makes the strong secret pangs of shame to cease:
Remorse is virtue's root; its fair increase
  Are fruits of innocence and blessedness:
Thus joy, o'erborne and bound, doth still release
  His young limbs from the chains that round him press.
Weep not that the world changes—did it keep
A stable, changeless state, 'twere cause indeed to weep.

Song

Dost thou idly ask to hear
At what gentle seasons
Nymphs relent, when lovers near
Press the tenderest reasons?
Ah, they give their faith too oft
To the careless wooer;
Maidens' hearts are always soft:
Would that men's were truer!

Woo the fair one when around
Early birds are singing;
When, o'er all the fragrant ground,
Early herbs are springing:
When the brookside, bank, and grove,
All with blossoms laden,
Shine with beauty, breathe of love,—
Woo the timid maiden.

Woo her when, with rosy blush,
Summer eve is sinking;
When, on rills that softly gush,
Stars are softly winking;
When through boughs that knit the bower
Moonlight gleams are stealing;
Woo her, till the gentle hour
Wake a gentler feeling.

Woo her when autumnal dyes
Tinge the woody mountain;
When the dropping foliage lies
In the weedy fountain;
Let the scene, that tells how fast
Youth is passing over,
Warn her, ere her bloom is past,
To secure her lover.

Woo her when the north winds call
At the lattice nightly;
When, within the cheerful hall,
Blaze the fagots brightly;
While the wintry tempest round
Sweeps the landscape hoary,
Sweeter in her ear shall sound
Love's delightful story.

The Ages

I When to the common rest that crowns our days,
Called in the noon of life, the good man goes,
Or full of years, and ripe in wisdom, lays
His silver temples in their last repose;
When, o'er the buds of youth, the death-wind blows
And blights the fairest; when our bitter tears
Stream, as the eyes of those that love us close,
We think on what they were, with many fears
Lest goodness die with them, and leave the coming years.

II And therefore, to our hearts, the days gone by,
When lived the honored sage whose death we wept,
And the soft virtues beamed from many an eye,
And beat in many a heart that long has slept—
Like spots of earth where angel-feet have stepped,
Are holy; and high-dreaming bards have told
Of times when worth was crowned, and faith was kept
Ere friendship grew a snare, or love waxed cold—
Those pure and happy times—the golden days of old.

III Peace to the just man's memory; let it grow
Greener with years, and blossom through the flight
Of ages; let the mimic canvas show
His calm benevolent features; let the light
Stream on his deeds of love, that shunned the sight
Of all but heaven, and in the book of fame
The glorious record of his virtues write
And hold it up to men, and bid them claim
A palm like his, and catch from him the hallowed flame.

IV But oh, despair not of their fate who rise
To dwell upon the earth when we withdraw!
Lo! the same shaft by which the righteous dies,
Strikes through the wretch that scoffed at mercy's law
And trode his brethren down, and felt no awe
Of Him who will avenge them. Stainless worth,
Such as the sternest age of virtue saw,
Ripens, meanwhile, till time shall call it forth
From the low modest shade, to light and bless the earth.

V Has Nature, in her calm, majestic march,
Faltered with age at last? does the bright sun
Grow dim in heaven? or, in their far blue arch,

Sparkle the crowd of stars, when day is done,
Less brightly? when the dew-lipped Spring comes on,
Breathes she with airs less soft, or scents the sky
With flowers less fair than when her reign begun?
Does prodigal Autumn, to our age, deny
The plenty that once swelled beneath his sober eye?

VI Look on this beautiful world, and read the truth
In her fair page; see, every season brings
New change, to her, of everlasting youth;
Still the green soil, with joyous living things,
Swarms, the wide air is full of joyous wings,
And myriads, still, are happy in the sleep
Of ocean's azure gulfs, and where he flings
The restless surge. Eternal Love doth keep,
In his complacent arms, the earth, the air, the deep.

VII Will then the merciful One, who stamped our race
With his own image, and who gave them sway
O'er earth, and the glad dwellers on her face,
Now that our swarming nations far away
Are spread, where'er the moist earth drinks the day,
Forget the ancient care that taught and nursed
His latest offspring? will he quench the ray
Infused by his own forming smile at first,
And leave a work so fair all blighted and accursed?

VIII Oh, no! a thousand cheerful omens give
Hope of yet happier days, whose dawn is nigh.
He who has tamed the elements, shall not live
The slave of his own passions; he whose eye
Unwinds the eternal dances of the sky,
And in the abyss of brightness dares to span
The sun's broad circle, rising yet more high,
In God's magnificent works his will shall scan—
And love and peace shall make their paradise with man.

IX Sit at the feet of History—through the night
Of years the steps of virtue she shall trace,
And show the earlier ages, where her sight
Can pierce the eternal shadows o'er their face;—
When, from the genial cradle of our race,
Went forth the tribes of men, their pleasant lot
To choose, where palm-groves cooled their dwelling-place,

Or freshening rivers ran; and there forgot
The truth of heaven, and kneeled to gods that heard them not.

X Then waited not the murderer for the night,
But smote his brother down in the bright day,
And he who felt the wrong, and had the might,
His own avenger, girt himself to slay;
Beside the path the unburied carcass lay;
The shepherd, by the fountains of the glen,
Fled, while the robber swept his flock away,
And slew his babes. The sick, untended then,
Languished in the damp shade, and died afar from men.

XI But misery brought in love; in passion's strife
Man gave his heart to mercy, pleading long,
And sought out gentle deeds to gladden life;
The weak, against the sons of spoil and wrong,
Banded, and watched their hamlets, and grew strong;
States rose, and, in the shadow of their might,
The timid rested. To the reverent throng,
Grave and time-wrinkled men, with locks all white,
Gave laws, and judged their strifes, and taught the way of right;

XII Till bolder spirits seized the rule, and nailed
On men the yoke that man should never bear,
And drave them forth to battle. Lo! unveiled
The scene of those stern ages! What is there?
A boundless sea of blood, and the wild air
Moans with the crimsoned surges that entomb
Cities and bannered armies; forms that wear
The kingly circlet rise, amid the gloom,
O'er the dark wave, and straight are swallowed in its womb.

XIII Those ages have no memory, but they left
A record in the desert—columns strown
On the waste sands, and statues fallen and cleft,
Heaped like a host in battle overthrown;
Vast ruins, where the mountain's ribs of stone
Were hewn into a city; streets that spread
In the dark earth, where never breath has blown
Of heaven's sweet air, nor foot of man dares tread
The long and perilous ways—the Cities of the Dead!

XIV And tombs of monarchs to the clouds up-piled—
They perished, but the eternal tombs remain—
And the black precipice, abrupt and wild,
Pierced by long toil and hollowed to a fane;—
Huge piers and frowning forms of gods sustain
The everlasting arches, dark and wide,
Like the night-heaven, when clouds are black with rain.
But idly skill was tasked, and strength was plied,
All was the work of slaves to swell a despot's pride.

XV And Virtue cannot dwell with slaves, nor reign
O'er those who cower to take a tyrant's yoke;
She left the down-trod nations in disdain,
And flew to Greece, when Liberty awoke,
New-born, amid those glorious vales, and broke
Sceptre and chain with her fair youthful hands:
As rocks are shivered in the thunder-stroke.
And lo! in full-grown strength, an empire stands
Of leagued and rival states, the wonder of the lands.

XVI Oh, Greece! thy flourishing cities were a spoil
Unto each other; thy hard hand oppressed
And crushed the helpless; thou didst make thy soil
Drunk with the blood of those that loved thee best;
And thou didst drive, from thy unnatural breast,
Thy just and brave to die in distant climes;
Earth shuddered at thy deeds, and sighed for rest
From thine abominations; after-times,
That yet shall read thy tale, will tremble at thy crimes!

XVII Yet there was that within thee which has saved
Thy glory, and redeemed thy blotted name;
The story of thy better deeds, engraved
On fame's unmouldering pillar, puts to shame
Our chiller virtue; the high art to tame
The whirlwind of the passions was thy own;
And the pure ray, that from thy bosom came,
Far over many a land and age has shone,
And mingles with the light that beams from God's own throne.

XVIII And Rome—thy sterner, younger sister, she
Who awed the world with her imperial frown—

Rome drew the spirit of her race from thee,
The rival of thy shame and thy renown.
Yet her degenerate children sold the crown
Of earth's wide kingdoms to a line of slaves;
Guilt reigned, and woe with guilt, and plagues came down,
Till the North broke its floodgates, and the waves
Whelmed the degraded race, and weltered o'er their graves.

XIX Vainly that ray of brightness from above,
That shone around the Galilean lake,
The light of hope, the leading star of love,
Struggled, the darkness of that day to break;
Even its own faithless guardians strove to slake,
In fogs of earth, the pure ethereal flame;
And priestly hands, for Jesus' blessed sake,
Were red with blood, and charity became,
In that stern war of forms, a mockery and a name.

XX They triumphed, and less bloody rites were kept
Within the quiet of the convent-cell;
The well-fed inmates pattered prayer, and slept,
And sinned, and liked their easy penance well,
Where pleasant was the spot for men to dwell,
Amid its fair broad lands the abbey lay,
Sheltering dark orgies that were shame to tell,
And cowled and barefoot beggars swarmed the way,
All in their convent weeds, of black, and white, and grey.

XXI Oh, sweetly the returning muses' strain
Swelled over that famed stream, whose gentle tide
In their bright lap the Etrurian vales detain,
Sweet, as when winter storms have ceased to chide,
And all the new-leaved woods, resounding wide,
Send out wild hymns upon the scented air.
Lo! to the smiling Arno's classic side
The emulous nations of the West repair,
And kindle their quenched urns, and drink fresh spirit there.

XXII Still, Heaven deferred the hour ordained to rend
From saintly rottenness the sacred stole;
And cowl and worshipped shrine could still defend
The wretch with felon stains upon his soul;
And crimes were set to sale, and hard his dole

Who could not bribe a passage to the skies;
And vice, beneath the mitre's kind control,
Sinned gayly on, and grew to giant size,
Shielded by priestly power, and watched by priestly eyes.

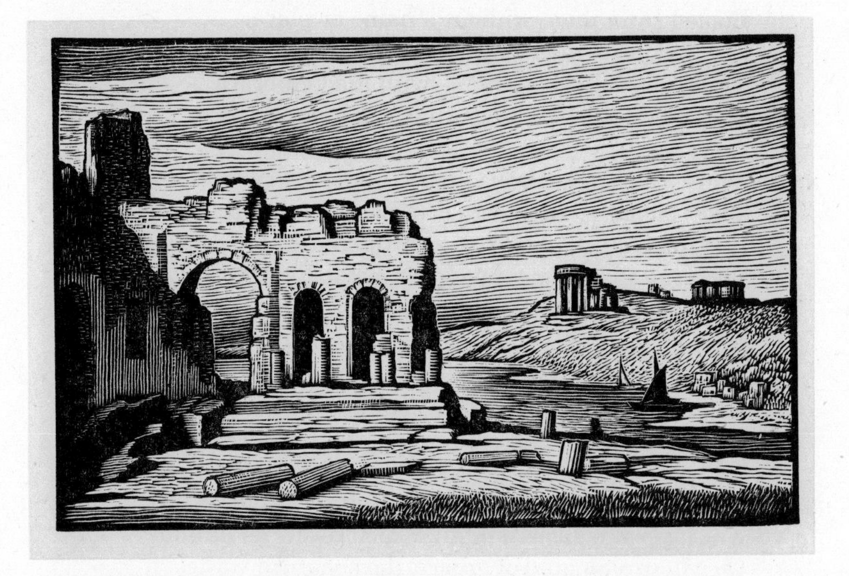

XXIII At last the earthquake came—the shock, that hurled
To dust, in many fragments dashed and strown,
The throne, whose roots were in another world,
And whose far-stretching shadow awed our own.
From many a proud monastic pile, o'erthrown,
Fear-struck, the hooded inmates rushed and fled;
The web, that for a thousand years had grown
O'er prostrate Europe, in that day of dread
Crumbled and fell, as fire dissolves the flaxen thread.

XXIV The spirit of that day is still awake,
And spreads himself, and shall not sleep again;
But through the idle mesh of power shall break
Like billows o'er the Asian monarch's chain;
Till men are filled with him, and feel how vain,
Instead of the pure heart and innocent hands,
Are all the proud and pompous modes to gain
The smile of Heaven;—till a new age expands
Its white and holy wings above the peaceful lands.

XXV For look again on the past years;—behold,
How like the nightmare's dreams have flown away
Horrible forms of worship, that, of old,
Held, o'er the shuddering realms, unquestioned sway:
See crimes, that feared not once the eye of day,
Rooted from men, without a name or place:
See nations blotted out from earth, to pay
The forfeit of deep guilt;—with glad embrace
The fair disburdened lands welcome a nobler race.

XXVI Thus error's monstrous shapes from earth are driven;
They fade, they fly—but Truth survives their flight;
Earth has no shades to quench that beam of heaven;
Each ray that shone, in early time, to light
The faltering footstep in the path of right,
Each gleam of clearer brightness shed to aid
In man's maturer day his bolder sight,
All blended, like the rainbow's radiant braid,
Pour yet, and still shall pour, the blaze that cannot fade.

XXVII Late, from this Western shore, that morning chased
The deep and ancient night, which threw its shroud
O'er the green land of groves, the beautiful waste,
Nurse of full streams, and lifter-up of proud
Sky-mingling mountains that o'erlook the cloud.
Erewhile, where yon gay spires their brightness rear,
Trees waved, and the brown hunter's shouts were loud
Amid the forest; and the bounding deer
Fled at the glancing plume, and the gaunt wolf yelled near.

XXVIII And where his willing waves yon bright blue bay
Sends up, to kiss his decorated brim,
And cradles, in his soft embrace, the gay
Young group of grassy islands born of him,
And crowding nigh, or in the distance dim,
Lifts the white throng of sails, that bear or bring
The commerce of the world;—with tawny limb,
And belt and beads in sunlight glistening,
The savage urged his skiff like wild bird on the wing.

XXIX Then all this youthful paradise around,
And all the broad and boundless mainland, lay
Cooled by the interminable wood, that frowned
O'er mount and vale, where never summer ray

Glanced, till the strong tornado broke his way
Through the gray giants of the sylvan wild;
Yet many a sheltered glade, with blossoms gay
Beneath the showery sky and sunshine mild,
Within the shaggy arms of that dark forest smiled.

XXX There stood the Indian hamlet, there the lake
Spread its blue sheet that flashed with many an oar,
Where the brown otter plunged him from the brake,
And the deer drank: as the light gale flew o'er,
The twinkling maize-field rustled on the shore;
And while that spot, so wild, and lone, and fair,
A look of glad and guiltless beauty wore,
And peace was on the earth and in the air,
The warrior lit the pile, and bound his captive there.

XXXI Not unavenged—the foeman, from the wood,
Beheld the deed, and, when the midnight shade
Was stillest, gorged his battle-axe with blood;
All died—the wailing babe—the shrinking maid—
And in the flood of fire that scathed the glade,
The roofs went down; but deep the silence grew,
When on the dewy woods the day-beam played;
No more the cabin-smokes rose wreathed and blue,
And ever, by their lake, lay moored the bark canoe.

XXXII Look now abroad—another race has filled
These populous borders—wide the wood recedes,
And towns shoot up, and fertile realms are tilled;
The land is full of harvests and green meads;
Streams numberless, that many a fountain feeds,
Shine, disembowered, and give to sun and breeze
Their virgin waters; the full region leads
New colonies forth, that toward the western seas
Spread, like a rapid flame among the autumnal trees.

XXXIII Here the free spirit of mankind, at length,
Throws its last fetters off; and who shall place
A limit to the giant's unchained strength,
Or curb his swiftness in the forward race?
On, like the comet's way through infinite space,
Stretches the long untravelled path of light,
Into the depths of ages; we may trace,

Afar, the brightening glory of its flight,
Till the receding rays are lost to human sight.

XXXIV Europe is given a prey to sterner fates,
And writhes in shackles; strong the arms that chain
To earth her struggling multitude of states;
She too is strong, and might not chafe in vain
Against them, but might cast to earth the train
That trample her, and break their iron net.
Yes, she shall look on brighter days and gain
The meed of worthier deeds; the moment set
To rescue and raise up, draws near—but is not yet.

XXXV But thou, my country, thou shalt never fall,
Save with thy children—thy maternal care,
Thy lavish love, thy blessings showered on all—
These are thy fetters—seas and stormy air
Are the wide barrier of thy borders, where,
Among thy gallant sons who guard thee well,
Thou laugh'st at enemies: who shall then declare
The date of thy deep-founded strength, or tell
How happy, in thy lap, the sons of men shall dwell?

The Massacre at Scio

Weep not for Scio's children slain;
Their blood, by Turkish falchions shed,
Sends not its cry to Heaven in vain
For vengeance on the murderer's head.

Though high the warm red torrent ran
Between the flames that lit the sky,
Yet, for each drop, an armèd man
Shall rise, to free the land, or die.

And for each corpse, that in the sea
Was thrown, to feast the scaly herds,
A hundred of the foe shall be
A banquet for the mountain-birds.

Stern rites and sad shall Greece ordain
To keep that day along her shore,
Till the last link of slavery's chain
Is shattered, to be worn no more.

Inscription for the Entrance to a Wood

Stranger, if thou hast learned a truth which needs
No school of long experience, that the world
Is full of guilt and misery, and hast seen
Enough of all its sorrows, crimes, and cares,
To tire thee of it, enter this wild wood
And view the haunts of Nature. The calm shade
Shall bring a kindred calm, and the sweet breeze
That makes the green leaves dance, shall waft a balm
To thy sick heart. Thou wilt find nothing here
Of all that pained thee in the haunts of men,
And made thee loathe thy life. The primal curse
Fell, it is true, upon the unsinning earth,
But not in vengeance. God hath yoked to guilt
Her pale tormentor, misery. Hence, these shades
Are still the abodes of gladness; the thick roof
Of green and stirring branches is alive
And musical with birds, that sing and sport
In wantonness of spirit; while below
The squirrel, with raised paws and form erect,
Chirps merrily. Throngs of insects in the shade
Try their thin wings and dance in the warm beam
That waked them into life. Even the green trees
Partake the deep contentment; as they bend
To the soft winds, the sun from the blue sky
Looks in and sheds a blessing on the scene.
Scarce less the cleft-born wild-flower seems to enjoy
Existence, than the wingèd plunderer
That sucks its sweets. The mossy rocks themselves
And the old and ponderous trunks of postrate trees
That lead from knoll to knoll a causey rude
Or bridge the sunken brook, and their dark roots,
With all their earth upon them, twisting high,
Breathe fixed tranquillity. The rivulet
Sends forth glad sounds, and tripping o'er its bed
Of pebbly sands, or leaping down the rocks,
Seems, with continuous laughter, to rejoice
In its own being. Softly tread the marge,
Lest from her midway perch thou scare the wren
That dips her bill in water. The cool wind,
That stirs the stream in play, shall come to thee,
Like one that loves thee nor will let thee pass
Ungreeted, and shall give its light embrace.

After a Tempest

The day had been a day of wind and storm,
The wind was laid, the storm was overpast,
And stooping from the zenith, bright and warm,
Shone the great sun on the wide earth at last.
I stood upon the upland slope, and cast
Mine eye upon a broad and beauteous scene,
Where the vast plain lay girt by mountains vast,
And hills o'er hills lifted their heads of green,
With pleasant vales scooped out and villages between.

The rain-drops glistened on the trees around,
Whose shadows on the tall grass were not stirred,
Save when a shower of diamonds, to the ground,
Was shaken by the flight of startled bird;
For birds were warbling round, and bees were heard
About the flowers; the cheerful rivulet sung
And gossiped, as he hastened oceanward;
To the gray oak the squirrel, chiding, clung,
And chirping from the ground the grasshopper upsprung.

And from beneath the leaves that kept them dry
Flew many a glittering insect here and there,
And darted up and down the butterfly,
That seemed a living blossom of the air,
The flocks came scattering from the thicket, where
The violent rain had pent them; in the way
Strolled groups of damsels frolicsome and fair;
The farmer swung the scythe or turned the hay,
And 'twixt the heavy swaths his children were at play.

It was a scene of peace—and, like a spell,
Did that serene and golden sunlight fall
Upon the motionless wood that clothed the fell,
And precipice upspringing like a wall,
And glassy river and white waterfall,
And happy living things that trod the bright
And beauteous scene; while far beyond them all,
On many a lovely valley, out of sight,
Was poured from the blue heavens the same soft golden light.

I looked, and thought the quiet of the scene
An emblem of the peace that yet shall be,
When o'er earth's continents, and isles between,
The noise of war shall cease from sea to sea,

And married nations dwell in harmony;
When millions, crouching in the dust to one,
No more shall beg their lives on bended knee,
Nor the black stake be dressed, nor in the sun
The o'erlabored captive toil, and wish his life were done.

Too long, at clash of arms amid her bowers
And pools of blood, the earth has stood aghast,
The fair earth, that should only blush with flowers
And ruddy fruits; but not for aye can last
The storm, and sweet the sunshine when 'tis past.
Lo, the clouds roll away—they break—they fly,
And, like the glorious light of summer, cast
O'er the wide landscape from the embracing sky,
On all the peaceful world the smile of heaven shall lie.

Hymn of the Waldenses

Hear, Father, hear thy faint afflicted flock
Cry to thee, from the desert and the rock;
While those, who seek to slay thy children, hold
Blasphemous worship under roofs of gold;
And the broad goodly lands, with pleasant airs
That nurse the grape and wave the grain, are theirs.
Yet better were this mountain wilderness,
And this wild life of danger and distress—
Watchings by night and perilous flight by day,
And meetings in the depths of earth to pray—
Better, far better, than to kneel with them,
And pay the impious rite thy laws condemn.

Thou, Lord, dost hold the thunder; the firm land
Tosses in billows when it feels thy hand;
Thou dashest nation against nation, then
Stillest the angry world to peace again.
Oh, touch their stony hearts who hunt thy sons—
The murderers of our wives and little ones.
Yet, mighty God, yet shall thy frown look forth
Unveiled, and terribly shall shake the earth.
Then the foul power of priestly sin and all
Its long-upheld idolatries shall fall.
Thou shalt raise up the trampled and oppressed,
And thy delivered saints shall dwell in rest.

A Walk at Sunset

When insect wings are glistening in the beam
Of the low sun, and mountain-tops are bright,
Oh, let me, by the crystal valley-stream,
Wander amid the mild and mellow light;
And while the wood-thrush pipes his evening lay,
Give me one lonely hour to hymn the setting day.

Oh, sun! that o'er the western mountains now
Go'st down in glory! ever beautiful
And blessed is thy radiance, whether thou
Colorest the eastern heaven and night-mist cool,
Till the bright day-star vanish, or on high
Climbest and streamest thy white splendors from mid-sky.

Yet, loveliest are thy setting smiles, and fair,
Fairest of all that earth beholds, the hues,
That live among the clouds, and flush the air,
Lingering and deepening at the hour of dews.
Then softest gales are breathed, and softest heard
The plaining voice of streams, and pensive note of bird.

They who here roamed, of yore, the forest wide,
Felt, by such charm, their simple bosoms won;
They deemed their quivered warrior, when he died,
Went to bright isles beneath the setting sun;
Where winds are aye at peace, and skies are fair,
And purple-skirted clouds curtain the crimson air.

So, with the glories of the dying day,
Its thousand trembling lights and changing hues,
The memory of the brave who passed away
Tenderly mingled;—fitting hour to muse
On such grave theme, and sweet the dream that shed
Brightness and beauty round the destiny of the dead.

For ages, on the silent forests here,
Thy beams did fall before the red man came
To dwell beneath them; in their shade the deer
Fed, and feared not the arrow's deadly aim.
Nor tree was felled, in all that world of woods,
Save by the beaver's tooth, or winds, or rush of floods.

Then came the hunter tribes, and thou didst look,
For ages, on their deeds in the hard chase,

And well-fought wars; green sod and silver brook
Took the first stain of blood; before thy face
The warrior generations came and passed,
And glory was laid up for many an age to last.

Now they are gone, gone as thy setting blaze
Goes down the west, while night is pressing on,
And with them the old tale of better days,
And trophies of remembered power, are gone.
Yon field that gives the harvest, where the plough
Strikes the white bone, is all that tells their story now.

I stand upon their ashes in thy beam,
The offspring of another race, I stand,
Beside a stream they loved, this valley-stream;
And where the night-fire of the quivered band
Showed the gray oak by fits, and war-song rung,
I teach the quiet shades the strains of this new tongue.

Farewell! but thou shalt come again—thy light
Must shine on other changes, and behold
The place of the thronged city still as night—
States fallen—new empires built upon the old—
But never shalt thou see these realms again
Darkened by boundless groves, and roamed by savage men.

Monument Mountain

Thou who wouldst see the lovely and the wild
Mingled in harmony on Nature's face,
Ascend our rocky mountains. Let thy foot
Fail not with weariness, for on their tops
The beauty and the majesty of earth,
Spread wide beneath, shall make thee to forget
The steep and toilsome way. There, as thou stand'st,
The haunts of men below thee, and around
The mountain-summits, thy expanding heart
Shall feel a kindred with that loftier world
To which thou art translated, and partake
The enlargement of thy vision. Thou shalt look
Upon the green and rolling forest-tops,
And down into the secrets of the glens,
And streams that with their bordering thickets strive
To hide their windings. Thou shalt gaze, at once,
Here on white villages, and tilth, and herds,
And swarming roads, and there on solitudes
That only hear the torrent, and the wind,
And eagle's shriek. There is a precipice
That seems a fragment of some mighty wall,
Built by the hand that fashioned the old world,
To separate its nations, and thrown down
When the flood drowned them. To the north, a path
Conducts you up the narrow battlement.
Steep is the western side, shaggy and wild
With mossy trees, and pinnacles of flint,
And many a hanging crag. But, to the east,
Sheer to the vale go down the bare old cliffs—
Huge pillars, that in middle heaven upbear
Their weather-beaten capitals, here dark
With moss, the growth of centuries, and there
Of chalky whiteness where the thunderbolt
Has splintered them. It is a fearful thing
To stand upon the beetling verge, and see
Where storm and lightning, from that huge gray wall,
Have tumbled down vast blocks, and at the base
Dashed them in fragments, and to lay thine ear
Over the dizzy depth, and hear the sound
Of winds, that struggle with the woods below,
Come up like ocean murmurs. But the scene
Is lovely round; a beautiful river there
Wanders amid the fresh and fertile meads,
The paradise he made unto himself,

Mining the soil for ages. On each side
The fields swell upward to the hills; beyond,
Above the hills, in the blue distance, rise
The mountain-columns with which earth props heaven.

There is a tale about these reverend rocks,
A sad tradition of unhappy love,
And sorrows borne and ended, long ago,
When over these fair vales the savage sought
His game in the thick woods. There was a maid,
The fairest of the Indian maids, bright-eyed,
With wealth of raven tresses, a light form,
And a gay heart. About her cabin-door
The wide old woods resounded with her song
And fairy laughter all the summer day.
She loved her cousin; such a love was deemed,
By the morality of those stern tribes,
Incestuous, and she struggled hard and long
Against her love, and reasoned with her heart,
As simple Indian maiden might. In vain.
Then her eye lost its lustre, and her step
Its lightness, and the gray-haired men that passed
Her dwelling, wondered that they heard no more
The accustomed song and laugh of her, whose looks
Were like the cheerful smile of Spring, they said,
Upon the Winter of their age. She went
To weep where no eye saw, and was not found
Where all the merry girls were met to dance,
And all the hunters of the tribe were out;
Nor when they gathered from the rustling husk
The shining ear; nor when, by the river's side,
They pulled the grape and startled the wild shades
With sounds of mirth. The keen-eyed Indian dames
Would whisper to each other, as they saw
Her wasting form, and say, *The girl will die.*

One day into the bosom of a friend,
A playmate of her young and innocent years,
She poured her griefs. "Thou know'st, and thou alone,"
She said, "for I have told thee, all my love,
And guilt, and sorrow. I am sick of life.
All night I weep in darkness, and the morn
Glares on me, as upon a thing accursed,
That has no business on the earth. I hate

The pastimes and the pleasant toils that once
I loved; the cheerful voices of my friends
Sound in my ear like mockings, and, at night,
In dreams, my mother, from the land of souls,
Calls me and chides me. All that look on me
Do seem to know my shame; I cannot bear
Their eyes; I cannot from my heart root out
The love that wrings it so, and I must die."

It was a summer morning, and they went
To this old precipice. About the cliffs
Lay garlands, ears of maize, and shaggy skins
Of wolf and bear, the offerings of the tribe

Here made to the Great Spirit, for they deemed,
Like worshippers of the elder time, that God
Doth walk on the high places and affect
The earth-o'erlooking mountains. She had on
The ornaments with which her father loved
To deck the beauty of his bright-eyed girl,
And bade her wear when stranger warriors came
To be his guests. Here the friends sat them down,
And sang, all day, old songs of love and death,
And decked the poor wan victim's hair with flowers,
And prayed that safe and swift might be her way
To the calm world of sunshine, where no grief
Makes the heart heavy and the eyelids red.
Beautiful lay the region of her tribe
Below her—waters resting in the embrace
Of the wide forest, and maize-planted glades
Opening amid the leafy wilderness.
She gazed upon it long, and at the sight
Of her own village peeping through the trees,
And her own dwelling, and the cabin roof
Of him she loved with an unlawful love,
And came to die for, a warm gush of tears
Ran from her eyes. But when the sun grew low
And the hill shadows long, she threw herself
From the steep rock and perished. There was scooped,
Upon the mountain's southern slope, a grave;
And there they laid her, in the very garb
With which the maiden decked herself for death,
With the same withering wild-flowers in her hair.
And o'er the mould that covered her, the tribe
Built up a simple monument, a cone
Of small loose stones. Thenceforward all who passed,
Hunter, and dame, and virgin, laid a stone
In silence on the pile. It stands there yet.
And Indians from the distant West, who come
To visit where their fathers' bones are laid,
Yet tell the sorrowful tale, and to this day
The mountain where the hapless maiden died
Is called the Mountain of the Monument.

Autumn Woods

Ere, in the northern gale,
The summer tresses of the trees are gone,
The woods of Autumn, all around our vale,
Have put their glory on.

The mountains that infold,
In their wide sweep, the colored landscape round,
Seem groups of giant kings, in purple and gold,
That guard the enchanted ground.

I roam the woods that crown
The uplands, where the mingled splendors glow,
Where the gay company of trees look down
On the green fields below.

My steps are not alone
In these bright walks; the sweet southwest, at play,
Flies, rustling, where the painted leaves are strown
Along the winding way.

And far in heaven, the while,
The sun, that sends that gale to wander here,
Pours out on the fair earth his quiet smile—
The sweetest of the year.

Where now the solemn shade,
Verdure and gloom where many branches meet;
So grateful, when the noon of summer made
The valleys sick with heat?

Let in through all the trees
Come the strange rays; the forest depths are bright;
Their sunny colored foliage, in the breeze,
Twinkles, like beams of light.

The rivulet, late unseen,
Where bickering through the shrubs its waters run,
Shines with the image of its golden screen,
And glimmerings of the sun.

But 'neath yon crimson tree,
Lover to listening maid might breathe his flame,
Nor mark, within its roseate canopy,
Her blush of maiden shame.

Oh, Autumn! why so soon
Depart the hues that make thy forests glad,
Thy gentle wind and thy fair sunny noon,
And leave thee wild and sad!

Ah! 'twere a lot too blest
Forever in thy colored shades to stray;
Amid the kisses of the soft southwest
To roam and dream for aye;

And leave the vain low strife
That makes men mad—the tug for wealth and power—
The passions and the cares that wither life,
And waste its little hour.

"Oh Fairest of the Rural Maids"

Oh fairest of the rural maids!
Thy birth was in the forest shades;
Green boughs, and glimpses of the sky,
Were all that met thine infant eye.

Thy sports, thy wanderings, when a child,
Were ever in the sylvan wild;
And all the beauty of the place
Is in thy heart and on thy face.

The twilight of the trees and rocks
Is in the light shade of thy locks;
Thy step is as the wind, that weaves
Its playful way among the leaves.

Thine eyes are springs, in whose serene
And silent waters heaven is seen;
Their lashes are the herbs that look
On their young figures in the brook.

The forest depths, by foot unpressed,
Are not more sinless than thy breast;
The holy peace, that fills the air
Of those calm solitudes, is there.

Hymn to the North Star

The sad and solemn night
Hath yet her multitude of cheerful fires;
The glorious host of light
Walk the dark hemisphere till she retires;
All through her silent watches, gliding slow,
Her constellations come, and climb the heavens, and go.

Day, too, hath many a star
To grace his gorgeous reign, as bright as they:
Through the blue fields afar,
Unseen, they follow in his flaming way:
Many a bright lingerer, as the eve grows dim,
Tells what a radiant troop arose and set with him.

And thou dost see them rise,
Star of the Pole! and thou dost see them set.
Alone, in thy cold skies,
Thou keep'st thy old unmoving station yet,
Nor join'st the dances of that glittering train,
Nor dipp'st thy virgin orb in the blue western main.

There, at morn's rosy birth,
Thou lookest meekly through the kindling air,
And eve, that round the earth
Chases the day, beholds thee watching there;
There noontide finds thee, and the hour that calls
The shapes of polar flame to scale heaven's azure walls.

Alike, beneath thine eye,
The deeds of darkness and of light are done;
High toward the starlit sky
Towns blaze, the smoke of battle blots the sun,
The night storm on a thousand hills is loud,
And the strong wind of day doth mingle sea and cloud.

On thy unaltering blaze
The half-wrecked mariner, his compass lost,
Fixes his steady gaze,
And steers, undoubting, to the friendly coast;
And they who stray in perilous wastes, by night,
Are glad when thou dost shine to guide their footsteps right.

And, therefore, bards of old,
Sages and hermits of the solemn wood,

Did in thy beams behold
A beauteous type of that unchanging good,
That bright eternal beacon, by whose ray
The voyager of time should shape his heedful way.

Song of the Greek Amazon

I buckle to my slender side
The pistol and the scimitar,
And in my maiden flower and pride
Am come to share the task of war.
And yonder stands the fiery steed,
That paws the ground and neighs to go,
My charger of the Arab breed—
I took him from the routed foe.

My mirror is the mountain-spring,
At which I dress my ruffled hair;
My dimmed and dusty arms I bring,
And wash away the blood-stain there.
Why should I guard from wind and sun
This cheek, whose virgin rose is fled?
It was for one—oh, only one—
I kept its bloom, and he is dead.

But they who slew him—unaware
Of coward murderers lurking nigh—
And left him to the fowls of air,
Are yet alive—and they must die!
They slew him—and my virgin years
Are vowed to Greece and vengeance now,
And many an Othman dame, in tears,
Shall rue the Grecian maiden's vow.

I touched the lute in better days,
I led in dance the joyous band;
Ah! they may move to mirthful lays
Whose hands can touch a lover's hand.
The march of hosts that haste to meet
Seems gayer than the dance to me;
The lute's sweet tones are not so sweet
As the fierce shout of victory.

June

I gazed upon the glorious sky
And the green mountains round,
And thought that when I came to lie
At rest within the ground,
'Twere pleasant, that in flowery June,
When brooks send up a cheerful tune,
And groves a joyous sound,
The sexton's hand, my grave to make,
The rich, green mountain-turf should break.

A cell within the frozen mould,
A coffin borne through sleet,
And icy clods above it rolled,
While fierce the tempests beat—
Away!—I will not think of these—
Blue be the sky and soft the breeze,
Earth green beneath the feet,
And be the damp mould gently pressed
Into my narrow place of rest.

There through the long, long summer hours,
The golden light should lie,
And thick young herbs and groups of flowers
Stand in their beauty by.
The oriole should build and tell
His love-tale close beside my cell;
The idle butterfly
Should rest him there, and there be heard
The housewife bee and humming-bird.

And what if cheerful shouts at noon
Come, from the village sent,
Or songs of maids, beneath the moon
With fairy laughter blent?
And what if, in the evening light,
Betrothèd lovers walk in sight
Of my low monument?
I would the lovely scene around
Might know no sadder sight nor sound.

I know that I no more should see
The season's glorious show,
Nor would its brightness shine for me,
Nor its wild music flow;

But if, around my place of sleep,
The friends I love should come to weep,
They might not haste to go.
Soft airs, and song, and light, and bloom
Should keep them lingering by my tomb.

These to their softened hearts should bear
The thought of what has been,
And speak of one who cannot share
The gladness of the scene;
Whose part, in all the pomp that fills
The circuit of the summer hills,
Is that his grave is green;
And deeply would their hearts rejoice
To hear again his living voice.

"No Man Knoweth His Sepulchre"

When he, who, from the scourge of wrong,
Aroused the Hebrew tribes to fly,
Saw the fair region, promised long,
And bowed him on the hills to die;

God made his grave, to men unknown,
Where Moab's rocks a vale infold,
And laid the aged seer alone
To slumber while the world grows old.

Thus still, whene'er the good and just
Close the dim eye on life and pain,
Heaven watches o'er their sleeping dust
Till the pure spirit comes again.

Though nameless, trampled, and forgot,
Her servant's humble ashes lie,
Yet God has marked and sealed the spot,
To call its inmate to the sky.

The Song of the Stars

When the radiant morn of creation broke,
And the world in the smile of God awoke,
And the empty realms of darkness and death
Were moved through their depths by his mighty breath,
And orbs of beauty and spheres of flame
From the void abyss by myriads came—
In the joy of youth as they darted away,
Through the widening wastes of space to play,
Their silver voices in chorus rang,
And this was the song the bright ones sang:

"Away, away, through the wide, wide sky,
The fair blue fields that before us lie—
Each sun with the worlds that round him roll,
Each planet, poised on her turning pole;
With her isles of green, and her clouds of white,
And her waters that lie like fluid light.

"For the source of glory uncovers his face,
And the brightness o'erflows unbounded space,
And we drink as we go to the luminous tides
In our ruddy air and our blooming sides:
Lo, yonder the living splendors play;
Away, on our joyous path, away!

"Look, look, through our glittering ranks afar,
In the infinite azure, star after star,
How they brighten and bloom as they swiftly pass!
How the verdure runs o'er each rolling mass!
And the path of the gentle winds is seen,
Where the small waves dance, and the young woods lean.

"And see, where the brighter day-beams pour,
How the rainbows hang in the sunny shower;
And the morn and eve, with their pomp of hues,
Shift o'er the bright planets and shed their dews;
And 'twixt them both, o'er the teeming ground,
With her shadowy cone the night goes round!

"Away, away! in our blossoming bowers,
In the soft airs wrapping these spheres of ours,
In the seas and fountains that shine with morn,
See, Love is brooding, and Life is born,

And breathing myriads are breaking from night,
To rejoice, like us, in motion and light.

"Glide on in your beauty, ye youthful spheres,
To weave the dance that measures the years;
Glide on, in the glory and gladness sent
To the furthest wall of the firmament—
The boundless visible smile of Him
To the veil of whose brow your lamps are dim."

An Indian at the Burial-Place of His Fathers

It is the spot I came to seek—
   My father's ancient burial-place,
Ere from these vales, ashamed and weak,
   Withdrew our wasted race.
It is the spot—I know it well—
Of which our old traditions tell.

For here the upland bank sends out
   A ridge toward the river-side;
I know the shaggy hills about,
   The meadows smooth and wide,
The plains, that, toward the southern sky,
Fenced east and west by mountains lie.

A white man, gazing on the scene,
   Would say a lovely spot was here,
And praise the lawns, so fresh and green,
   Between the hills so sheer.
I like it not— I would the plain
Lay in its tall old groves again.

The sheep are on the slopes around,
   The cattle in the meadows feed,

And laborers turn the crumbling ground,
  Or drop the yellow seed,
And prancing steeds, in trappings gay,
Whirl the bright chariot o'er the way.

Methinks it were a nobler sight
  To see these vales in woods arrayed,
Their summits in the golden light,
  Their trunks in grateful shade,
And herds of deer that bounding go
O'er hills and prostrate trees below.

And then to mark the lord of all,
  The forest hero, trained to wars,
Quivered and plumed, and lithe and tall,
  And seamed with glorious scars,
Walk forth, amid his reign, to dare
The wolf, and grapple with the bear.

This bank, in which the dead were laid,
  Was sacred when its soil was ours;
Hither the silent Indian maid
  Brought wreaths of beads and flowers,
And the gray chief and gifted seer
Worshipped the god of thunders here.

But now the wheat is green and high
  On clods that hid the warrior's breast,
And scattered in the furrows lie
  The weapons of his rest;
And there, in the loose sand, is thrown
Of his large arm the mouldering bone.

Ah, little thought the strong and brave
  Who bore their lifeless chieftain forth—
Or the young wife that weeping gave
  Her first-born to the earth—
That the pale race, who waste us now,
Among their bones should guide the plough.

They waste us—ay—like April snow
  In the warm noon, we shrink away;
And fast they follow, as we go
  Toward the setting day—

Till they shall fill the land, and we
Are driven into the Western sea.

But I behold a fearful sign,
To which the white men's eyes are blind;
Their race may vanish hence, like mine,
And leave no trace behind,
Save ruins o'er the region spread,
And the white stones above the dead.

Before these fields were shorn and tilled,
Full to the brim our rivers flowed;
The melody of waters filled
The fresh and boundless wood;
And torrents dashed and rivulets played,
And fountains spouted in the shade.

Those grateful sounds are heard no more,
The springs are silent in the sun;
The rivers, by the blackened shore,
With lessening current run;
The realm our tribes are crushed to get
May be a barren desert yet.

The Firmament

Ay! gloriously thou standest there,
Beautiful, boundless firmament!
That, swelling wide o'er earth and air,
And round the horizon bent,
With thy bright vault, and sapphire wall,
Dost overhang and circle all.

Far, far below thee, tall gray trees
Arise, and piles built up of old,
And hills, whose ancient summits freeze
In the fierce light and cold.
The eagle soars his utmost height,
Yet far thou stretchest o'er his flight.

Thou hast thy frowns—with thee on high
The storm has made his airy seat,

Beyond that soft blue curtain lie
His stores of hail and sleet.
Thence the consuming lightnings break,
There the strong hurricanes awake.

Yet art thou prodigal of smiles—
Smiles, sweeter than thy frowns are stern,
Earth sends, from all her thousand isles,
A shout at their return.
The glory that comes down from thee,
Bathes, in deep joy, the land and sea.

The sun, the gorgeous sun is thine,
The pomp that brings and shuts the day,
The clouds that round him change and shine,
The airs that fan his way.
Thence look the thoughtful stars, and there
The meek moon walks the silent air.

The sunny Italy may boast
The beauteous tints that flush her skies,
And lovely, round the Grecian coast,
May thy blue pillars rise.
I only know how fair they stand
Around my own beloved land.

And they are fair—a charm is theirs,
That earth, the proud green earth, has not,
With all the forms, and hues, and airs,
That haunt her sweetest spot.
We gaze upon thy calm pure sphere,
And read of Heaven's eternal year.

Oh, when, amid the throng of men,
The heart grows sick of hollow mirth,
How willingly we turn us then
Away from this cold earth,
And look into thy azure breast,
For seats of innocence and rest!

A Song of Pitcairn's Island

Come, take our boy, and we will go
  Before our cabin-door;
The winds shall bring us, as they blow,
  The murmurs of the shore;
And we will kiss his young blue eyes,
And I will sing him, as he lies,
  Songs that were made of yore:
I'll sing, in his delighted ear,
The island lays thou lov'st to hear.

And thou, while stammering I repeat,
  Thy country's tongue shalt teach;
'Tis not so soft, but far more sweet
  Than my own native speech:
For thou no other tongue didst know,
When, scarcely twenty moons ago,
  Upon Tahete's beach,
Thou cam'st to woo me to be thine,
With many a speaking look and sign.

I knew thy meaning—thou didst praise
  My eyes, my locks of jet;
Ah! well for me they won thy gaze,
  But thine were fairer yet!
I'm glad to see my infant wear
Thy soft blue eyes and sunny hair,
  And when my sight is met
By his white brow and blooming cheek,
I feel a joy I cannot speak.

Come, talk of Europe's maids with me,
  Whose necks and cheeks, they tell,
Outshine the beauty of the sea,
  White foam and crimson shell.
I'll shape like theirs my simple dress,
And bind like them each jetty tress,
  A sight to please thee well;
And for my dusky brow will braid
A bonnet like an English maid.

Come, for the soft low sunlight calls,
  We lose the pleasant hours;
'Tis lovelier than these cottage walls,—
  That seat among the flowers.

And I will learn of thee a prayer,
To Him who gave a home so fair,
A lot so blest as ours—
The God who made, for thee and me,
This sweet lone isle amid the sea.

"I Cannot Forget with What Fervid Devotion"

I cannot forget with what fervid devotion
I worshipped the visions of verse and of fame;
Each gaze at the glories of earth, sky, and ocean,
To my kindled emotions, was wind over flame.

And deep were my musings in life's early blossom,
Mid the twilight of mountain-groves wandering long;
How thrilled my young veins, and how throbbed my full bosom,
When o'er me descended the spirit of song!

'Mong the deep-cloven fells that for ages had listened
To the rush of the pebble-paved river between,
Where the kingfisher screamed and gray precipice glistened,
All breathless with awe have I gazed on the scene;

Till I felt the dark power o'er my reveries stealing,
From the gloom of the thicket that over me hung,
And the thoughts that awoke, in that rapture of feeling,
Were formed into verse as they rose to my tongue.

Bright visions! I mixed with the world, and ye faded,
No longer your pure rural worshipper now;
In the haunts your continual presence pervaded,
Ye shrink from the signet of care on my brow.

In the old mossy groves on the breast of the mountain,
In deep lonely glens where the waters complain,
By the shade of the rock, by the gush of the fountain,
I seek your loved footsteps, but seek them in vain.

Oh, leave not, forlorn and forever forsaken,
Your pupil and victim, to life and its tears!
But sometimes return, and in mercy awaken
The glories ye showed to his earlier years.

A Forest Hymn

The groves were God's first temples. Ere man learned
To hew the shaft, and lay the architrave,
And spread the roof above them—ere he framed
The lofty vault, to gather and roll back
The sound of anthems; in the darkling wood,
Amid the cool and silence, he knelt down,
And offered to the Mightiest solemn thanks
And supplication. For his simple heart
Might not resist the sacred influences
Which, from the stilly twilight of the place,
And from the gray old trunks that high in heaven
Mingled their mossy boughs, and from the sound
Of the invisible breath that swayed at once
All their green tops, stole over him, and bowed
His spirit with the thought of boundless power
And inaccessible majesty. Ah, why
Should we, in the world's riper years, neglect
God's ancient sanctuaries, and adore
Only among the crowd, and under roofs
That our frail hands have raised? Let me, at least,
Here, in the shadow of this aged wood,
Offer one hymn—thrice happy, if it find
Acceptance in His ear.

Father, thy hand
Hath reared these venerable columns, thou
Didst weave this verdant roof. Thou didst look down
Upon the naked earth, and, forthwith, rose
All these fair ranks of trees. They, in thy sun,
Budded, and shook their green leaves in thy breeze,
And shot toward heaven. The century-living crow
Whose birth was in their tops, grew old and died
Among their branches, till, at last, they stood,
As now they stand, massy, and tall, and dark,
Fit shrine for humble worshipper to hold
Communion with his Maker. These dim vaults,
These winding aisles, of human pomp or pride
Report not. No fantastic carvings show
The boast of our vain race to change the form
Of thy fair works. But thou art here—thou fill'st
The solitude. Thou art in the soft winds
That run along the summit of these trees
In music; thou art in the cooler breath
That from the inmost darkness of the place

Comes, scarcely felt; the barky trunks, the ground,
The fresh moist ground, are all instinct with thee.
Here is continual worship;—Nature, here,
In the tranquillity that thou dost love,
Enjoys thy presence. Noiselessly, around,
From perch to perch, the solitary bird
Passes; and yon clear spring, that, midst its herbs,
Wells softly forth and wandering steeps the roots
Of half the mighty forest, tells no tale
Of all the good it does. Thou hast not left
Thyself without a witness, in the shades,
Of thy perfections. Grandeur, strength, and grace
Are here to speak of thee. This mighty oak—
By whose immovable stem I stand and seem
Almost annihilated—not a prince,
In all that proud old world beyond the deep,
E'er wore his crown as loftily as he
Wears the green coronal of leaves with which
Thy hand has graced him. Nestled at his root
Is beauty, such as blooms not in the glare
Of the broad sun. That delicate forest flower,
With scented breath and look so like a smile,
Seems, as it issues from the shapeless mould,
An emanation of the indwelling Life,
A visible token of the upholding Love,
That are the soul of this great universe.

My heart is awed within me when I think
Of the great miracle that still goes on,
In silence, round me—the perpetual work
Of thy creation, finished, yet renewed
Forever. Written on thy works I read
The lesson of thy own eternity.
Lo! all grow old and die—but see again,
How on the faltering footsteps of decay
Youth presses—ever gay and beautiful youth
In all its beautiful forms. These lofty trees
Wave not less proudly that their ancestors
Moulder beneath them. Oh, there is not lost
One of earth's charms: upon her bosom yet,
After the flight of untold centuries,
The freshness of her far beginning lies
And yet shall lie. Life mocks the idle hate
Of his arch-enemy Death—yea, seats himself

Upon the tyrant's throne—the sepulchre,
And of the triumphs of his ghastly foe
Makes his own nourishment. For he came forth
From thine own bosom, and shall have no end.

There have been holy men who hid themselves
Deep in the woody wilderness, and gave
Their lives to thought and prayer, till they outlived
The generation born with them, nor seemed
Less aged than the hoary trees and rocks
Around them;—and there have been holy men
Who deemed it were not well to pass life thus.
But let me often to these solitudes
Retire, and in thy presence reassure
My feeble virtue. Here its enemies,
The passions, at thy plainer footsteps shrink
And tremble and are still. O God! when thou
Dost scare the world with tempests, set on fire
The heavens with falling thunderbolts, or fill,
With all the waters of the firmament,
The swift dark whirlwind that uproots the woods
And drowns the villages; when, at thy call,
Uprises the great deep and throws himself
Upon the continent, and overwhelms
Its cities—who forgets not, at the sight
Of these tremendous tokens of thy power,
His pride, and lays his strifes and follies by?
Oh, from these sterner aspects of thy face
Spare me and mine, nor let us need the wrath
Of the mad unchained elements to teach
Who rules them. Be it ours to meditate,
In these calm shades, thy milder majesty,
And to the beautiful order of thy works
Learn to conform the order of our lives.

The Murdered Traveller

When Spring, to woods and wastes around,
  Brought bloom and joy again,
The murdered traveller's bones were found,
  Far down a narrow glen.

The fragrant birch, above him, hung
  Her tassels in the sky;
And many a vernal blossom sprung,
  And nodded careless by.

The red-bird warbled, as he wrought
  His hanging nest o'erhead,
And fearless, near the fatal spot,
  Her young the partridge led.

But there was weeping far away,
  And gentle eyes, for him,
With watching many an anxious day,
  Were sorrowful and dim.

They little knew, who loved him so,
  The fearful death he met,
When shouting o'er the desert snow,
  Unarmed, and hard beset;—

Nor how, when round the frosty pole
  The northern dawn was red,
The mountain-wolf and wild-cat stole
  To banquet on the dead;—

Nor how, when strangers found his bones,
  They dressed the hasty bier,
And marked his grave with nameless stones,
  Unmoistened by a tear.

But long they looked, and feared, and wept,
  Within his distant home;
And dreamed, and started as they slept,
  For joy that he was come.

Long, long they looked—but never spied
  His welcome step again,
Nor knew the fearful death he died
  Far down that narrow glen.

The Poems of William Cullen Bryant

II

THE DEATH OF THE FLOWERS
AND OTHER POEMS

The Editor's Commentary

THOSE WHO ARE skeptical of Bryant's range and variety should read the first three poems in this section. Noble serenity breathes through the famous "The Death of the Flowers," which commemorates the passing of Bryant's sister; pure burlesque plays through the mock pomposity of "To a Mosquito"; a fierce emotion intensifies "The African Chief."

Perhaps the most high-spirited of Bryant's moods was the one which found expression in the resonant "Song of Marion's Men." Bryant's ironic note is, in itself, a significant commentary: "The exploits of General Francis Marion, the famous warrior of South Carolina, form an interesting chapter in the annals of the American Revolution. The British troops were so harassed by the irregular and successful warfare which he kept up at the head of a few daring followers, that they sent an officer to remonstrate with him for not coming into the open field and fighting 'like a gentleman and a Christian.' "

"The Prairies" is another poem which extends Bryant's gamut. The blend of American landscape and classic imagery results in a succession of delicate yet effective pictures which almost justify Richard Henry Stoddard's enthusiastic outburst: "It was worth going to the ends of the world to be able to write 'The Prairies.' "

To point Bryant's variety with one more contrast, this section ends with one of the tenderest lyrics in American literature. "To the Fringed Gentian" glows with its own cerulean light. It is a nature poem which is also a didactic poem; but its "moral" is not only integrated but implicit. It quickens the mind with beauty and strengthens the heart with hope.

The Death of the Flowers

The melancholy days are come, the saddest of the year,
Of wailing winds, and naked woods, and meadows brown and sere.
Heaped in the hollows of the grove, the autumn leaves lie dead;
They rustle to the eddying gust, and to the rabbit's tread;
The robin and the wren are flown, and from the shrubs the jay,
And from the wood-top calls the crow through all the gloomy day.

Where are the flowers, the fair young flowers, that lately sprang and
stood
In brighter light and softer airs, a beauteous sisterhood?
Alas! they all are in their graves, the gentle race of flowers
Are lying in their lowly beds, with the fair and good of ours.
The rain is falling where they lie, but the cold November rain
Calls not from out the gloomy earth the lovely ones again.

The wind-flower and the violet, they perished long ago,
And the brier-rose and the orchis died amid the summer glow;
But on the hills the golden-rod, and the aster in the wood,
And the yellow sun-flower by the brook in autumn beauty stood,
Till fell the frost from the clear cold heaven, as falls the plague on men,
And the brightness of their smile was gone, from upland, glade, and
glen.

And now, when comes the calm mild day, as still such days will come,
To call the squirrel and the bee from out their winter home,
When the sound of dropping nuts is heard, though all the trees are still,
And twinkle in the smoky light the waters of the rill,
The south wind searches for the flowers whose fragrance late he bore,
And sighs to find them in the wood and by the stream no more.

And then I think of one who in her youthful beauty died,
The fair meek blossom that grew up and faded by my side.
In the cold moist earth we laid her, when the forests cast the leaf,
And we wept that one so lovely should have a life so brief:
Yet not unmeet it was that one, like that young friend of ours,
So gentle and so beautiful, should perish with the flowers.

The Gladness of Nature

Is this a time to be cloudy and sad,
  When our mother Nature laughs around;
When even the deep blue heavens look glad,
  And gladness breathes from the blossoming ground?

There are notes of joy from the hang-bird and wren,
  And the gossip of swallows through all the sky;
The ground-squirrel gayly chirps by his den,
  And the wilding bee hums merrily by.

The clouds are at play in the azure space
  And their shadows at play on the bright-green vale,
And here they stretch to the frolic chase,
  And there they roll on the easy gale.

There's a dance of leaves in that aspen bower,
  There's a titter of winds in that beechen tree,
There's a smile on the fruit, and a smile on the flower,
  And a laugh from the brook that runs to the sea.

And look at the broad-faced sun, how he smiles
  On the dewy earth that smiles in his ray,
On the leaping waters and gay young isles;
  Ay, look, and he'll smile thy gloom away.

To a Mosquito

Fair insect! that, with threadlike legs spread out,
  And blood-extracting bill and filmy wing,
Dost murmur, as thou slowly sail'st about,
  In pitiless ears full many a plaintive thing,
And tell how little our large veins should bleed,
Would we but yield them to thy bitter need.

Unwillingly, I own, and, what is worse,
  Full angrily, men hearken to thy plaint,
Thou gettest many a brush, and many a curse,
  For saying thou art gaunt, and starved, and faint:
Even the old beggar, while he asks for food,
Would kill thee, hapless stranger, if he could.

I call thee stranger, for the town, I ween,
  Has not the honor of so proud a birth,
Thou com'st from Jersey meadows, fresh and green,
  The offspring of the gods, though born on earth;
For Titan was thy sire, and fair was she,
The ocean nymph, that nursed thy infancy.

Beneath the rushes was thy cradle swung,
  And when, at length, thy gauzy wings grew strong,
Abroad to gentle airs their folds were flung,
  Rose in the sky and bore thee soft along:
The south wind breathed to waft thee on thy way,
And danced and shone beneath the billowy bay.

Calm rose afar the city spires, and thence
  Came the deep murmur of its throng of men,
And as its grateful odors met thy sense,
  They seemed the perfumes of thy native fen.
Fair lay its crowded streets, and at the sight
Thy tiny song grew shriller with delight.

At length thy pinions fluttered in Broadway—
  Ah, there were fairy steps, and white necks kissed
By wanton airs, and eyes whose killing ray
  Shone through the snowy veils like stars through mist;
And fresh as morn, on many a cheek and chin,
Bloomed the bright blood through the transparent skin.

Sure these were sights to touch an anchorite!
  What! do I hear thy slender voice complain?

Thou wailest when I talk of beauty's light,
  As if it brought the memory of pain:
Thou art a wayward being—well—come near,
And pour thy tale of sorrow in my ear.

What sayest thou—slanderer!—rouge makes thee sick?
  And China bloom at best is sorry food?
And Rowland's Kalydor, if laid on thick,
  Poisons the thirsty wretch that bores for blood?
Go! 'twas a just reward that met thy crime—
But shun the sacrilege another time.

That bloom was made to look at, not to touch;
  To worship, not approach, that radiant white;
And well might sudden vengeance light on such
  As dared, like thee, most impiously to bite.
Thou shouldst have gazed at distance and admired,
Murmured thy adoration, and retired.

Thou'rt welcome to the town; but why come here
  To bleed a brother poet, gaunt like thee?
Alas! the little blood I have is dear,
  And thin will be the banquet drawn from me.
Look round—the pale-eyed sisters in my cell,
Thy old acquaintance, Song and Famine, dwell.

Try some plump alderman, and suck the blood
  Enriched by generous wine and costly meat;
On well-filled skins, sleek as thy native mud,
  Fix thy light pump and press thy freckled feet.
Go to the men for whom, in ocean's halls,
The oyster breeds, and the green turtle sprawls.

There corks are drawn, and the red vintage flows
  To fill the swelling veins for thee, and now
The ruddy cheek and now the ruddier nose
  Shall tempt thee, as thou flittest round the brow;
And when the hour of sleep its quiet brings,
No angry hands shall rise to brush thy wings.

The African Chief

The story of the African Chief, related in this ballad, may be found in the *African Repository* for April, 1825. The subject of it was a warrior of majestic stature, the brother of Yarradee, king of the Solima nation. He had been taken in battle, and was brought in chains for sale to the Rio Pongas, where he was exhibited in the market-place, his ankles still adorned with the massy rings of gold which he wore when captured. The refusal of his captor to listen to his offers of ransom drove him mad, and he died a maniac.

Chained in the market-place he stood,
  A man of giant frame,
Amid the gathering multitude
  That shrunk to hear his name—
All stern of look and strong of limb,
  His dark eye on the ground:—
And silently they gazed on him,
  As on a lion bound.

Vainly, but well, that chief had fought,
  He was a captive now,
Yet pride, that fortune humbles not,
  Was written on his brow.
The scars his dark broad bosom wore
  Showed warrior true and brave;
A prince among his tribe before,
  He could not be a slave.

Then to his conqueror he spake—
  "My brother is a king;
Undo this necklace from my neck,
  And take this bracelet ring,
And send me where my brother reigns
  And I will fill thy hands
With store of ivory from the plains,
  And gold-dust from the sands."

"Not for thy ivory nor thy gold
  Will I unbind thy chain;
That bloody hand shall never hold
  The battle-spear again.
A price thy nation never gave,
  Shall yet be paid for thee;
For thou shalt be the Christian's slave,
  In lands beyond the sea."

Then wept the warrior chief, and bade
   To shred his locks away;
And, one by one, each heavy braid
   Before the victor lay.
Thick were the platted locks, and long,
   And deftly hidden there
Shone many a wedge of gold among
   The dark and crispèd hair.

"Look, feast thy greedy eye with gold
   Long kept for sorest need;
Take it—thou askest sums untold,
   And say that I am freed.
Take it—my wife, the long, long day,
   Weeps by the cocoa-tree,
And my young children leave their play,
   And ask in vain for me."

"I take thy gold—but I have made
   Thy fetters fast and strong,
And ween that by the cocoa shade
   Thy wife will wait thee long."
Strong was the agony that shook
   The captive's frame to hear,
And the proud meaning of his look
   Was changed to mortal fear.

His heart was broken—crazed his brain:
   At once his eye grew wild;
He struggled fiercely with his chain,
   Whispered, and wept, and smiled;
Yet wore not long those fatal bands,
   And once, at shut of day,
They drew him forth upon the sands,
   The foul hyena's prey.

Romero

When freedom, from the land of Spain,
  By Spain's degenerate sons was driven,
Who gave their willing limbs again
  To wear the chain so lately riven;
Romero broke the sword he wore—
  "Go, faithful brand," the warrior said,
"Go undishonored, never more
  The blood of man shall make thee red;
  I grieve for that already shed;
And I am sick at heart to know,
That faithful friend and noble foe
Have only bled to make more strong
The yoke that Spain has worn so long.
Wear it who will, in abject fear—
  I wear it not who have been free;
The perjured Ferdinand shall hear
  No oath of loyalty from me."
Then, hunted by the hounds of power,
  Romero chose a safe retreat,
Where bleak Nevada's summits tower
  Above the beauty at their feet.

There once, when on his cabin lay
The crimson light of setting day,
When even on the mountain's breast
The chainless winds were all at rest,
And he could hear the river's flow
From the calm paradise below;
Warmed with his former fires again,
He framed this rude but solemn strain.

I

"Here will I make my home—for here at least I see,
Upon this wild Sierra's side, the steps of Liberty;
Where the locust chirps unscared beneath the unpruned lime,
And the merry bee doth hide from man the spoil of the mountain
  thyme;
Where the pure winds come and go, and the wild vine strays at will,
An outcast from the haunts of men, she dwells with Nature still.

II

"I see the valleys, Spain! where thy mighty rivers run,
And the hills that lift thy harvests and vineyards to the sun,
And the flocks that drink thy brooks and sprinkle all the green,

Where lie thy plains, with sheep-walks seamed, and olive shades between:
I see thy fig-trees bask, with the fair pomegranate near,
And the fragrance of thy lemon-groves can almost reach me here.

III

"Fair—fair—but fallen Spain! 'tis with a swelling heart,
That I think on all thou might'st have been, and look at what thou art;
But the strife is over now—and all the good and brave,
That would have raised thee up, are gone, to exile or the grave.
Thy fleeces are for monks, thy grapes for the convent feast,
And the wealth of all thy harvest-fields for the pampered lord and priest.

IV

"But I shall see the day—it will come before I die—
I shall see it in my silver hairs, and with an age-dimmed eye;—
When the spirit of the land to liberty shall bound,
As yonder fountain leaps away from the darkness of the ground;
And, to my mountain cell, the voices of the free
Shall rise, as from the beaten shore the thunders of the sea."

William Tell

Chains may subdue the feeble spirit, but thee,
Tell, of the iron heart! they could not tame!
For thou wert of the mountains; they proclaim
The everlasting creed of liberty.
That creed is written on the untrampled snow,
Thundered by torrents which no power can hold,
Save that of God, when He sends forth His cold,
And breathed by winds that through the free heaven blow.
Thou, while thy prison-walls were dark around,
Didst meditate the lesson Nature taught,
And to thy brief captivity was brought
A vision of thy Switzerland unbound.
The bitter cup they mingled, strengthened thee
For the great work to set thy country free.

Spring in Town

The country ever has a lagging Spring,
Waiting for May to call its violets forth,
And June its roses; showers and sunshine bring,
Slowly, the deepening verdure o'er the earth;
To put their foliage out, the woods are slack,
And one by one the singing-birds come back.

Within the city's bounds the time of flowers
Comes earlier. Let a mild and sunny day,
Such as full often, for a few bright hours,
Breathes through the sky of March the airs of May
Shine on our roofs and chase the wintry gloom—
And lo! our borders glow with sudden bloom.

For the wide sidewalks of Broadway are then
Gorgeous as are a rivulet's banks in June,
That overhung with blossoms, through its glen,
Slides soft away beneath the sunny noon,
And they who search the untrodden wood for flowers
Meet in its depths no lovelier ones than ours.

For here are eyes that shame the violet,
Or the dark drop that on the pansy lies,
And foreheads, white, as when in clusters set,
The anemones by forest-mountains rise;
And the spring-beauty boasts no tenderer streak
Than the soft red on many a youthful cheek.

And thick about those lovely temples lie
Locks that the lucky Vignardonne has curled,
Thrice happy man! whose trade it is to buy,
And bake, and braid those love-knots of the world;
Who curls of every glossy color keepest,
And sellest, it is said, the blackest cheapest.

And well thou mayst—for Italy's brown maids
Send the dark locks with which their brows are dressed,
And Gascon lasses, from their jetty braids,
Crop half, to buy a ribbon for the rest;
But the fresh Norman girls their tresses spare,
And the Dutch damsel keeps her flaxen hair.

Then, henceforth, let no maid nor matron grieve,
To see her locks of an unlovely hue,

Frouzy or thin, for liberal art shall give
  Such piles of curls as Nature never knew.
Eve, with her veil of tresses, at the sight
Had blushed, outdone, and owned herself a fright.

Soft voices and light laughter wake the street,
  Like notes of woodbirds, and where'er the eye
Threads the long way, plumes wave, and twinkling feet
  Fall light, as hastes that crowd of beauty by.
The ostrich, hurrying o'er the desert space,
Scarce bore those tossing plumes with fleeter pace.

No swimming Juno gait, of languor born,
  Is theirs, but a light step of freest grace,—
Light as Camilla's o'er the unbent corn,—
  A step that speaks the spirit of the place,
Since Quiet, meek old dame, was driven away
To Sing Sing and the shores of Tappan Bay.

Ye that dash by in chariots! who will care
  For steeds or footmen now? ye cannot show
Fair face, and dazzling dress, and graceful air,
  And last edition of the shape! Ah, no,
These sights are for the earth and open sky,
And your loud wheels unheeded rattle by.

Midsummer

A power is on the earth and in the air
  From which the vital spirit shrinks afraid,
  And shelters him, in nooks of deepest shade,
From the hot steam and from the fiery glare.
Look forth upon the earth—her thousand plants
  Are smitten; even the dark sun-loving maize
  Faints in the field beneath the torrid blaze;
The herd beside the shaded fountain pants;
For life is driven from all the landscape brown;
  The bird has sought his tree, the snake his den,
  The trout floats dead in the hot stream, and men
Drop by the sun-stroke in the populous town;
  As if the Day of Fire had dawned, and sent
  Its deadly breath into the firmament.

The New Moon

When, as the garish day is done,
Heaven burns with the descended sun,
    'Tis passing sweet to mark,
Amid that flush of crimson light,
The new moon's modest bow grow bright,
    As earth and sky grow dark.

Few are the hearts too cold to feel
A thrill of gladness o'er them steal,
    When first the wandering eye
Sees faintly, in the evening blaze,
That glimmering curve of tender rays
    Just planted in the sky.

The sight of that young crescent brings
Thoughts of all fair and youthful things—
    The hopes of early years;
And childhood's purity and grace,
And joys that like a rainbow chase
    The passing shower of tears.

The captive yields him to the dream
Of freedom, when that virgin beam
    Comes out upon the air;
And painfully the sick man tries
To fix his dim and burning eyes
    On the sweet promise there.

Most welcome to the lover's sight
Glitters that pure, emerging light;

For prattling poets say,
That sweetest is the lovers' walk,
And tenderest is their murmured talk,
Beneath its gentle ray.

And there do graver men behold
A type of errors, loved of old,
Forsaken and forgiven;
And thoughts and wishes not of earth
Just opening in their early birth,
Like that new light in heaven.

The Journey of Life

Beneath the waning moon I walk at night,
And muse on human life—for all around
Are dim uncertain shapes that cheat the sight,
And pitfalls lurk in shade along the ground,
And broken gleams of brightness, here and there,
Glance through, and leave unwarmed the death-like air.

The trampled earth returns a sound of fear—
A hollow sound, as if I walked on tombs;
And lights, that tell of cheerful homes, appear
Far off, and die like hope amid the glooms.
A mournful wind across the landscape flies,
And the wide atmosphere is full of sighs.

And I, with faltering footsteps, journey on,
Watching the stars that roll the hours away,
Till the faint light that guides me now is gone,
And, like another life, the glorious day
Shall open o'er me from the empyreal height,
With warmth, and certainty, and boundless light.

The Two Graves

'Tis a bleak wild hill, but green and bright
In the summer warmth and the mid-day light;
There's the hum of the bee and the chirp of the wren
And the dash of the brook from the alder-glen.
There's the sound of a bell from the scattered flock,
And the shade of the beech lies cool on the rock,
And fresh from the west is the free wind's breath;—
There is nothing here that speaks of death.

Far yonder, where orchards and gardens lie,
And dwellings cluster, 'tis there men die,
They are born, they die, and are buried near,
Where the populous graveyard lightens the bier.
For strict and close are the ties that bind
In death the children of human-kind;
Yea, stricter and closer than those of life,—
'Tis a neighborhood that knows no strife.
They are noiselessly gathered—friend and foe—
To the still and dark assemblies below.
Without a frown or a smile they meet,
Each pale and calm in his winding-sheet;
In that sullen home of peace and gloom,
Crowded, like guests in a banquet-room.

Yet there are graves in this lonely spot
Two humble graves,—but I meet them not.
I have seen them,—eighteen years are past
Since I found their place in the brambles last,—
The place where, fifty winters ago
An aged man in his locks of snow,
And an aged matron, withered with years,
Were solemnly laid!—but not with tears.
For none, who sat by the light of their hearth,
Beheld their coffins covered with earth;
Their kindred were far, and their children dead,
When the funeral-prayer was coldly said.

Two low green hillocks, two small gray stones,
Rose over the place that held their bones;
But the grassy hillocks are levelled again,
And the keenest eye might search in vain,
'Mong briers, and ferns, and paths of sheep,
For the spot where the aged couple sleep.

Yet well might they lay, beneath the soil
Of this lonely spot, that man of toil,
And trench the strong hard mould with the spade,
Where never before a grave was made;
For he hewed the dark old woods away,
And gave the virgin fields to the day;
And the gourd and the bean, beside his door,
Bloomed where their flowers ne'er opened before;
And the maize stood up, and the bearded rye
Bent low in the breath of an unknown sky.

'Tis said that when life is ended here,
The spirit is borne to a distant sphere;
That it visits its earthly home no more,
Nor looks on the haunts it loved before.
But why should the bodiless soul be sent
Far off, to a long, long banishment?
Talk not of the light and the living green!
It will pine for the dear familiar scene;
It will yearn, in that strange bright world, to behold
The rock and the stream it knew of old.

'Tis a cruel creed, believe it not!
Death to the good is a milder lot.
They are here,—they are here,—that harmless pair,
In the yellow sunshine and flowing air,
In the light cloud-shadows that slowly pass,

In the sounds that rise from the murmuring grass.
They sit where their humble cottage stood,
They walk by the waving edge of the wood,
And list to the long-accustomed flow
Of the brook that wets the rocks below,
Patient, and peaceful, and passionless,
As seasons on seasons swiftly press,
They watch, and wait, and linger around,
Till the day when their bodies shall leave the ground.

"Innocent Child and Snow-White Flower"

Innocent child and snow-white flower!
Well are ye paired in your opening hour.
Thus should the pure and the lovely meet,
Stainless with stainless, and sweet with sweet.

White as those leaves, just blown apart,
Are the folds of thy own young heart;
Guilty passion and cankering care
Never have left their traces there.

Artless one! though thou gazest now
O'er the white blossom with earnest brow,
Soon will it tire thy childish eye;
Fair as it is, thou wilt throw it by.

Throw it aside in thy weary hour,
Throw to the ground the fair white flower;
Yet, as thy tender years depart,
Keep that white and innocent heart.

A Meditation on Rhode Island Coal

Decolor, obscurus, vilis, non ille repexam
Cesariem regum, non candida virginis ornat
Colla, nec insigni splendet per cingula morsu
Sed nova si nigri videas miracula saxi,
Tune superat pulchros cultus et quicquid Eois
Indus litoribus rubra scrutatur in alga. CLAUDIAN

I sat beside the glowing grate, fresh heaped
With Newport coal, and as the flame grew bright
—The many-colored flame—and played and leaped,
I thought of rainbows, and the northern light,
Moore's Lalla Rookh, the Treasury Report,
And other brilliant matters of the sort.

And last I thought of that fair isle which sent
The mineral fuel; on a summer day
I saw it once, with heat and travel spent,
And scratched by dwarf-oaks in the hollow way.
Now dragged through sand, now jolted over stone—
A rugged road through rugged Tiverton.

And hotter grew the air, and hollower grew
The deep-worn path, and horror-struck, I thought,
Where will this dreary passage lead me to?
This long dull road, so narrow, deep, and hot?
I looked to see it dive in earth outright;
I looked—but saw a far more welcome sight.

Like a soft mist upon the evening shore,
At once a lovely isle before me lay,
Smooth, and with tender verdure covered o'er,
As if just risen from its calm inland bay;
Sloped each way gently to the grassy edge,
And the small waves that dallied with the sedge.

The barley was just reaped; the heavy sheaves
Lay on the stubble-field; the tall maize stood
Dark in its summer growth, and shook its leaves,
And bright the sunlight played on the young wood—
For fifty years ago, the old men say,
The Briton hewed their ancient groves away.

I saw where fountains freshened the green land,
And where the pleasant road, from door to door,
With rows of cherry-trees on either hand,
Went wandering all that fertile region o'er—

Rogue's Island once—but when the rogues were dead,
Rhode Island was the name it took instead.

Beautiful island! then it only seemed
A lovely stranger; it has grown a friend.
I gazed on its smooth slopes, but never dreamed
How soon that green and quiet isle would send
The treasures of its womb across the sea,
To warm a poet's room and boil his tea.

Dark anthracite! that reddenest on my hearth,
Thou in those island mines didst slumber long;
But now thou art come forth to move the earth,
And put to shame the men that mean thee wrong:
Thou shalt be coals of fire to those that hate thee,
And warm the shins of all that underrate thee.

Yea, they did wrong thee foully—they who mocked
Thy honest face, and said thou wouldst not burn;
Of hewing thee to chimney-pieces talked,
And grew profane, and swore, in bitter scorn,
That men might to thy inner caves retire,
And there, unsinged, abide the day of fire.

Yet is thy greatness nigh. I pause to state,
That I too have seen greatness—even I—
Shook hands with Adams, stared at La Fayette,
When, barehead, in the hot noon of July,
He would not let the umbrella be held o'er him,
For which three cheers burst from the mob before him.

And I have seen—not many months ago—
An eastern Governor in chapeau bras
And military coat, a glorious show!
Ride forth to visit the reviews, and ah!
How oft he smiled and bowed to Jonathan!
How many hands were shook and votes were won!

'Twas a great Governor; thou too shalt be
Great in thy turn, and wide shall spread thy fame
And swiftly; furthest Maine shall hear of thee,
And cold New Brunswick gladden at thy name;
And, faintly through its sleets, the weeping isle
That sends the Boston folks their cod shall smile.

For thou shalt forge vast railways, and shalt heat
The hissing rivers into steam, and drive
Huge masses from thy mines, on iron feet,
Walking their steady way, as if alive,
Northward, till everlasting ice besets thee,
And South as far as the grim Spaniard lets thee.

Thou shalt make mighty engines swim the sea,
Like its own monsters—boats that for a guinea
Will take a man to Havre—and shalt be
The moving soul of many a spinning-jenny,
And ply thy shuttles, till a bard can wear
As good a suit of broadcloth as the mayor.

Then we will laugh at winter when we hear
The grim old churl about our dwellings rave:
Thou, from that "ruler of the inverted year,"
Shalt pluck the knotty sceptre Cowper gave,
And pull him from his sledge, and drag him in,
And melt the icicles from off his chin.

October

Ay, thou art welcome, heaven's delicious breath!
When woods begin to wear the crimson leaf,
And suns grow meek, and the meek suns grow brief,
And the year smiles as it draws near its death.
Wind of the sunny south! oh, still delay
In the gay woods and in the golden air,
Like to a good old age released from care,
Journeying, in long serenity, away.
In such a bright, late quiet, would that I
Might wear out life like thee, mid bowers and brooks,
And, dearer yet, the sunshine of kind looks,
And music of kind voices ever nigh;
And when my last sand twinkled in the glass,
Pass silently from men, as thou dost pass.

The Disinterred Warrior

Gather him to his grave again,
  And solemnly and softly lay,
Beneath the verdure of the plain,
  The warrior's scattered bones away.
Pay the deep reverence, taught of old,
  The homage of man's heart to death;
Nor dare to trifle with the mould
  Once hallowed by the Almighty's breath.

The soul hath quickened every part—
  That remnant of a martial brow,
Those ribs that held the mighty heart,
  That strong arm—strong no longer now.
Spare them, each mouldering relic spare,
  Of God's own image; let them rest,
Till not a trace shall speak of where
  The awful likeness was impressed.

For he was fresher from the hand
  That formed of earth the human face,
And to the elements did stand
  In nearer kindred than our race.
In many a flood to madness tossed,
  In many a storm has been his path;
He hid him not from heat or frost,
  But met them, and defied their wrath.

Then they were kind—the forests here,
  Rivers, and stiller waters, paid
A tribute to the net and spear
  Of the red ruler of the shade.
Fruits on the woodland branches lay,
  Roots in the shaded soil below;
The stars looked forth to teach his way;
  The still earth warned him of the foe.

A noble race! but they are gone,
  With their old forests wide and deep,
And we have built our homes upon
  Fields where their generations sleep.
Their fountains slake our thirst at noon,
  Upon their fields our harvest waves,
Our lovers woo beneath their moon—
  Then let us spare, at least, their graves.

The Damsel of Peru

Where olive-leaves were twinkling in every wind that blew,
There sat beneath the pleasant shade a damsel of Peru.
Betwixt the slender boughs, as they opened to the air,
Came glimpses of her ivory neck and of her glossy hair;
And sweetly rang her silver voice, within that shady nook,
As from the shrubby glen is heard the sound of hidden brook.
'Tis a song of love and valor, in the noble Spanish tongue,
That once upon the sunny plains of old Castile was sung;
When, from their mountain-holds, on the Moorish rout below,
Had rushed the Christians like a flood, and swept away the foe.
Awhile that melody is still, and then breaks forth anew
A wilder rhyme, a livelier note, of freedom and Peru.
For she has bound the sword to a youthful lover's side,
And sent him to the war the day she should have been his bride,
And bade him bear a faithful heart to battle for the right,
And held the fountains of her eyes till he was out of sight.
Since the parting kiss was given, six weary months are fled,
And yet the foe is in the land, and blood must yet be shed.
A white hand parts the branches, a lovely face looks forth,
And bright dark eyes gaze steadfastly and sadly toward the north.
Thou look'st in vain, sweet maiden, the sharpest sigh would fail
To spy a sign of human life abroad in all the vale;
For the noon is coming on, and the sunbeams fiercely beat,
And the silent hills and forest-tops seem reeling in the heat.
That white hand is withdrawn, that fair sad face is gone,
But the music of that silver voice is flowing sweetly on,
Not as of late, in cheerful tones, but mournfully and low,—
A ballad of a tender maid heart-broken long ago,
Of him who died in battle, the youthful and the brave,
And her who died of sorrow, upon his early grave.
And see, along that mountain-slope, a fiery horseman ride;
Mark his torn plume, his tarnished belt, the sabre at his side.
His spurs are buried rowel-deep, he rides with loosened rein,
There's blood upon his charger's flank and foam upon the mane.
He speeds him toward the olive-grove, along that shaded hill!
God shield the helpless maiden there, if he should mean her ill!
And suddenly that song has ceased, and suddenly I hear
A shriek sent up amid the shade, a shriek—but not of fear.
For tender accents follow, and tender pauses speak
The overflow of gladness, when words are all too weak;
"I lay my good sword at thy feet, for now Peru is free,
And I am come to dwell beside the olive-grove with thee."

The Greek Partisan

Our free flag is dancing
  In the free mountain air,
And burnished arms are glancing,
  And warriors gathering there;
And fearless is the little train
  Whose gallant bosoms shield it;
The blood that warms their hearts shall stain
  That banner, ere they yield it.
—Each dark eye is fixed on earth,
  And brief each solemn greeting;
There is no look nor sound of mirth,
  Where those stern men are meeting.

They go to the slaughter
  To strike the sudden blow,
And pour on earth, like water,
  The best blood of the foe;
To rush on them from rock and height,
  And clear the narrow valley,
Or fire their camp at dead of night,
  And fly before they rally.
—Chains are round our country pressed,
  And cowards have betrayed her,
And we must make her bleeding breast
  The grave of the invader.

Not till from her fetters
  We raise up Greece again,
And write, in bloody letters,
  That tyranny is slain,—
Oh, not till then the smile shall steal
  Across those darkened faces,
Nor one of all those warriors feel
  His children's dear embraces.
—Reap we not the ripened wheat,
  Till yonder hosts are flying,
And all their bravest, at our feet,
  Like autumn sheaves are lying.

The Prairies

These are the gardens of the Desert, these
The unshorn fields, boundless and beautiful,
For which the speech of England has no name—
The Prairies. I behold them for the first,
And my heart swells, while the dilated sight
Takes in the encircling vastness. Lo! they stretch,
In airy undulations, far away,
As if the ocean, in his gentlest swell,
Stood still, with all his rounded billows fixed,
And motionless forever.—Motionless?—
No—they are all unchained again. The clouds
Sweep over with their shadows, and, beneath,
The surface rolls and fluctuates to the eye;
Dark hollows seem to glide along and chase
The sunny ridges. Breezes of the South!
Who toss the golden and the flame-like flowers,
And pass the prairie-hawk that, poised on high,
Flaps his broad wings, yet moves not—ye have played
Among the palms of Mexico and vines
Of Texas, and have crisped the limpid brooks
That from the fountains of Sonora glide
Into the calm Pacific—have ye fanned
A nobler or a lovelier scene than this?
Man hath no power in all this glorious work:
The hand that built the firmament hath heaved
And smoothed these verdant swells, and sown their slopes
With herbage, planted them with island groves,
And hedged them round with forests. Fitting floor
For this magnificent temple of the sky—
With flowers whose glory and whose multitude
Rival the constellations! The great heavens
Seem to stoop down upon the scene in love,—
A nearer vault, and of a tenderer blue,
Than that which bends above our eastern hills.

As o'er the verdant waste I guide my steed,
Among the high rank grass that sweeps his sides
The hollow beating of his footstep seems
A sacrilegious sound. I think of those
Upon whose rest he tramples. Are they here—
The dead of other days?—and did the dust
Of these fair solitudes once stir with life
And burn with passion? Let the mighty mounds

That overlook the rivers, or that rise
In the dim forest crowded with old oaks,
Answer. A race, that long has passed away,
Built them;—a disciplined and populous race
Heaped, with long toil, the earth, while yet the Greek
Was hewing the Pentelicus to forms
Of symmetry, and rearing on its rock
The glittering Parthenon. These ample fields
Nourished their harvests, here their herds were fed,
When haply by their stalls the bison lowed,
And bowed his manèd shoulder to the yoke.
All day this desert murmured with their toils,
Till twilight blushed, and lovers walked, and wooed
In a forgotten language, and old tunes,
From instruments of unremembered form,
Gave the soft winds a voice. The red man came—
The roaming hunter tribes, warlike and fierce,
And the mound-builders vanished from the earth.
The solitude of centuries untold
Has settled where they dwelt. The prairie-wolf
Hunts in their meadows, and his fresh-dug den
Yawns by my path. The gopher mines the ground
Where stood their swarming cities. All is gone;
All—save the piles of earth that hold their bones,
The platforms where they worshipped unknown gods,
The barriers which they builded from the soil
To keep the foe at bay—till o'er the walls
The wild beleaguerers broke, and, one by one,
The strongholds of the plain were forced, and heaped
With corpses. The brown vultures of the wood
Flocked to those vast uncovered sepulchres,
And sat unscared and silent at their feast.
Haply some solitary fugitive,
Lurking in marsh and forest, till the sense
Of desolation and of fear became
Bitterer than death, yielded himself to die.
Man's better nature triumphed then. Kind words
Welcomed and soothed him; the rude conquerors
Seated the captive with their chiefs; he chose
A bride among their maidens, and at length
Seemed to forget—yet ne'er forgot—the wife
Of his first love, and her sweet little ones,
Butchered, amid their shrieks, with all his race.

Thus change the forms of being. Thus arise
Races of living things, glorious in strength,
And perish, as the quickening breath of God
Fills them, or is withdrawn. The red man, too,
Has left the blooming wilds he ranged so long,
And, nearer to the Rocky Mountains, sought
A wilder hunting-ground. The beaver builds
No longer by these streams, but far away,
On waters whose blue surface ne'er gave back
The white man's face—among Missouri's springs,
And pools whose issues swell the Oregon—
He rears his little Venice. In these plains
The bison feeds no more. Twice twenty leagues
Beyond remotest smoke of hunter's camp,
Roams the majestic brute, in herds that shake
The earth with thundering steps—yet here I meet
His ancient footprints stamped beside the pool.

Still this great solitude is quick with life.
Myriads of insects, gaudy as the flowers
They flutter over, gentle quadrupeds,
And birds, that scarce have learned the fear of man,

Are here, and sliding reptiles of the ground,
Startlingly beautiful. The graceful deer
Bounds to the wood at my approach. The bee,
A more adventurous colonist than man,
With whom he came across the eastern deep,
Fills the savannas with his murmurings,
And hides his sweets, as in the golden age,
Within the hollow oak. I listen long
To his domestic hum, and think I hear
The sound of that advancing multitude
Which soon shall fill these deserts. From the ground
Comes up the laugh of children, the soft voice
Of maidens, and the sweet and solemn hymn
Of Sabbath worshippers. The low of herds
Blends with the rustling of the heavy grain
Over the dark brown furrows. All at once
A fresher wind sweeps by, and breaks my dream,
And I am in the wilderness alone.

"Upon the Mountain's Distant Head"

Upon the mountain's distant head,
With trackless snows forever white,
Where all is still, and cold, and dead,
Late shines the day's departing light.

But far below those icy rocks,
The vales, in summer bloom arrayed,
Woods full of birds, and fields of flocks,
Are dim with mist and dark with shade.

'Tis thus, from warm and kindly hearts,
And eyes where generous meanings burn,
Earliest the light of life departs,
But lingers with the cold and stern.

The Conjunction of Jupiter and Venus

I would not always reason. The straight path
Wearies us with the never-varying lines,
And we grow melancholy. I would make
Reason my guide, but she should sometimes sit
Patiently by the way-side, while I traced
The mazes of the pleasant wilderness
Around me. She should be my counsellor,
But not my tyrant. For the spirit needs
Impulses from a deeper source than hers,
And there are motions, in the mind of man,
That she must look upon with awe. I bow
Reverently to her dictates, but not less
Hold to the fair illusions of old time—
Illusions that shed brightness over life,
And glory over Nature. Look, even now,
Where two bright planets in the twilight meet,
Upon the saffron heaven,—the imperial star
Of Jove, and she that from her radiant urn
Pours forth the light of love. Let me believe,
Awhile, that they are met for ends of good,
Amid the evening glory, to confer
Of men and their affairs, and to shed down
Kind influence. Lo! they brighten as we gaze,
And shake out softer fires! The great earth feels
The gladness and the quiet of the time.
Meekly the mighty river, that infolds
This mighty city, smooths his front, and far
Glitters and burns even the rocky base
Of the dark heights that bound him to the west;
And a deep murmur, from the many streets,
Rises like a thanksgiving. Put we hence
Dark and sad thoughts awhile—there's time for them
Hereafter—on the morrow we will meet,
With melancholy looks, to tell our griefs,
And make each other wretched; this calm hour,
This balmy, blessed evening, we will give
To cheerful hopes and dreams of happy days,
Born of the meeting of those glorious stars.

Enough of drought has parched the year, and scared
The land with dread of famine. Autumn, yet,
Shall make men glad with unexpected fruits.
The dog-star shall shine harmless: genial days
Shall softly glide away into the keen

And wholesome cold of winter; he that fears
The pestilence, shall gaze on those pure beams,
And breathe, with confidence, the quiet air.

Emblems of power and beauty! well may they
Shine brightest on our borders, and withdraw
Toward the great Pacific, marking out
The path of empire. Thus in our own land,
Ere long, the better Genius of our race,
Having encompassed earth, and tamed its tribes,
Shall sit him down beneath the farthest west,
By the shore of that calm ocean, and look back
On realms made happy.

Light the nuptial torch,
And say the glad, yet solemn rite, that knits
The youth and maiden. Happy days to them
That wed this evening!—a long life of love,
And blooming sons and daughters! Happy they
Born at this hour, for they shall see an age
Whiter and holier than the past, and go
Late to their graves. Men shall wear softer hearts,
And shudder at the butcheries of war,
As now at other murders.

Hapless Greece!
Enough of blood has wet thy rocks, and stained
Thy rivers; deep enough thy chains have worn
Their links into thy flesh; the sacrifice
Of thy pure maidens, and thy innocent babes,
And reverend priests, has expiated all
Thy crimes of old. In yonder mingling lights
There is an omen of good days for thee.
Thou shalt arise from midst the dust and sit
Again among the nations. Thine own arm
Shall yet redeem thee. Not in wars like thine
The world takes part. Be it a strife of kings,—
Despot with despot battling for a throne,—
And Europe shall be stirred throughout her realms,
Nations shall put on harness, and shall fall
Upon each other, and in all their bounds
The wailing of the childless shall not cease.
Thine is a war for liberty, and thou
Must fight it single-handed. The old world

Looks coldly on the murderers of thy race,
And leaves thee to the struggle; and the new,—
I fear me thou couldst tell a shameful tale
Of fraud and lust of gain;—thy treasury drained,
And Missolonghi fallen. Yet thy wrongs
Shall put new strength into thy heart and hand,
And God and thy good sword shall yet work out,
For thee, a terrible deliverance.

A Scene on the Banks of the Hudson

Cool shades and dews are round my way,
And silence of the early day;
Mid the dark rocks that watch his bed,
Glitters the mighty Hudson spread,
Unrippled, save by drops that fall
From shrubs that fringe his mountain wall;
And o'er the clear still water swells
The music of the Sabbath bells.
All, save this little nook of land,
Circled with trees, on which I stand;
All, save that line of hills which lie
Suspended in the mimic sky—
Seems a blue void, above, below,
Through which the white clouds come and go;
And from the green world's farthest steep
I gaze into the airy deep.
Loveliest of lovely things are they,
On earth, that soonest pass away.
The rose that lives its little hour
Is prized beyond the sculptured flower.
Even love, long tried and cherished long,
Becomes more tender and more strong
At thought of that insatiate grave
From which its yearnings cannot save.
River! in this still hour thou hast
Too much of heaven on earth to last;
Nor long may thy still waters lie,
An image of the glorious sky.
Thy fate and mine are not repose,
And ere another evening close,
Thou to thy tides shalt turn again,
And I to seek the crowd of men.

A Summer Ramble

The quiet August noon has come;
  A slumberous silence fills the sky,
The fields are still, the woods are dumb,
  In glassy sleep the waters lie.

And mark yon soft white clouds that rest
  Above our vale, a moveless throng;
The cattle on the mountain's breast
  Enjoy the grateful shadow long.

Oh, how unlike those merry hours,
  In early June, when Earth laughs out,
When the fresh winds make love to flowers,
  And woodlands sing and waters shout.

When in the grass sweet voices talk,
  And strains of tiny music swell
From every moss-cup of the rock,
  From every nameless blossom's bell.

But now a joy too deep for sound,
  A peace no other season knows,
Hushes the heavens and wraps the ground,
  The blessing of supreme repose.

Away! I will not be, to-day,
  The only slave of toil and care,
Away from desk and dust! away!
  I'll be as idle as the air.

Beneath the open sky abroad,
  Among the plants and breathing things,
The sinless, peaceful works of God,
  I'll share the calm the season brings.

Come, thou, in whose soft eyes I see
  The gentle meanings of thy heart,
One day amid the woods with me,
  From men and all their cares apart.

And where, upon the meadow's breast,
  The shadow of the thicket lies,
The blue wild-flowers thou gatherest
  Shall glow yet deeper near thine eyes.

Come, and when mid the calm profound,
  I turn, those gentle eyes to seek,
They, like the lovely landscape round,
  Of innocence and peace shall speak.

Rest here, beneath the unmoving shade,
  And on the silent valleys gaze,
Winding and widening, till they fade
  In yon soft ring of summer haze.

The village trees their summits rear
  Still as its spire, and yonder flock
At rest in those calm fields appear
  As chiselled from the lifeless rock.

One tranquil mount the scene o'erlooks—
  There the hushed winds their sabbath keep,
While a near hum from bees and brooks
  Comes faintly like the breath of sleep.

Well may the gazer deem that when,
  Worn with the struggle and the strife,
And heart-sick at the wrongs of men,
  The good forsakes the scene of life;

Like this deep quiet that, awhile,
  Lingers the lovely landscape o'er,
Shall be the peace whose holy smile
  Welcomes him to a happier shore.

The Hunter's Serenade

Thy bower is finished, fairest!
  Fit bower for hunter's bride,
Where old woods overshadow
  The green savanna's side.
I've wandered long, and wandered far,
  And never have I met,
In all this lovely Western land,
  A spot so lovely yet.
But I shall think it fairer
  When thou art come to bless,
With thy sweet smile and silver voice,
  Its silent loveliness.

For thee the wild-grape glistens
  On sunny knoll and tree,
The slim papaya ripens
  Its yellow fruit for thee.
For thee the duck, on glassy stream,
  The prairie-fowl shall die;
My rifle for thy feast shall bring
  The wild-swan from the sky.
The forest's leaping panther,
  Fierce, beautiful, and fleet,
Shall yield his spotted hide to be
  A carpet for thy feet.

I know, for thou hast told me,
  Thy maiden love of flowers;
Ah, those that deck thy gardens
  Are pale compared with ours.
When our wide woods and mighty lawns
  Bloom to the April skies,
The earth has no more gorgeous sight
  To show to human eyes.
In meadows red with blossoms,
  All summer long, the bee
Murmurs, and loads his yellow thighs,
  For thee, my love, and me.

Or wouldst thou gaze at tokens
  Of ages long ago—
Our old oaks stream with mosses,
  And sprout with mistletoe;

And mighty vines, like serpents, climb
The giant sycamore;
And trunks, o'erthrown for centuries,
Cumber the forest floor;
And in the great savanna,
The solitary mound,
Built by the elder world, o'erlooks
The loneliness around.

Come, thou hast not forgotten
Thy pledge and promise quite,
With many blushes murmured,
Beneath the evening light.
Come, the young violets crowd my door,
Thy earliest look to win,
And at my silent window-sill
The jessamine peeps in.
All day the red-bird warbles
Upon the mulberry near,
And the night-sparrow trills her song
All night, with none to hear.

The Hurricane

Lord of the winds! I feel thee nigh,
I know thy breath in the burning sky!
And I wait, with a thrill in every vein,
For the coming of the hurricane!

And lo! on the wing of the heavy gales,
Through the boundless arch of heaven he sails;
Silent and slow, and terribly strong,
The mighty shadow is borne along,
Like the dark eternity to come;
While the world below, dismayed and dumb,
Through the calm of the thick hot atmosphere,
Looks up at its gloomy folds with fear.

They darken fast; and the golden blaze
Of the sun is quenched in the lurid haze,
And he sends through the shade a funeral ray—
A glare that is neither night nor day,
A beam that touches, with hues of death,

The clouds above and the earth beneath.
To its covert glides the silent bird,
While the hurricane's distant voice is heard
Uplifted among the mountains round,
And the forests hear and answer the sound.

He is come! he is come! do ye not behold
His ample robes on the wind unrolled?
Giant of air! we bid thee hail!—
How his gray skirts toss in the whirling gale;
How his huge and writhing arms are bent
To clasp the zone of the firmament,
And fold at length, in their dark embrace,
From mountain to mountain the visible space.

Darker—still darker! the whirlwinds bear
The dust of the plains to the middle air:
And hark to the crashing, long and loud,
Of the chariot of God in the thunder-cloud!
You may trace its path by the flashes that start
From the rapid wheels where'er they dart,
As the fire-bolts leap to the world below,
And flood the skies with a lurid glow.

What roar is that?—'tis the rain that breaks
In torrents away from the airy lakes,
Heavily poured on the shuddering ground,
And shedding a nameless horror round.
Ah! well-known woods, and mountains, and skies,
With the very clouds!—ye are lost to my eyes.
I seek ye vainly, and see in your place
The shadowy tempest that sweeps through space,
A whirling ocean that fills the wall
Of the crystal heaven, and buries all.
And I, cut off from the world, remain
Alone with the terrible hurricane.

The Past

Thou unrelenting Past!
Strong are the barriers round thy dark domain,
And fetters, sure and fast,
Hold all that enter thy unbreathing reign.

Far in thy realm withdrawn,
Old empires sit in sullenness and gloom,
And glorious ages gone
Lie deep within the shadow of thy womb.

Childhood, with all its mirth,
Youth, Manhood, Age that draws us to the ground,
And last, Man's Life on earth,
Glide to thy dim dominions, and are bound.

Thou hast my better years;
Thou hast my earlier friends, the good, the kind,
Yielded to thee with tears—
The venerable form, the exalted mind.

My spirit yearns to bring
The lost ones back—yearns with desire intense,
And struggles hard to wring
Thy bolts apart, and pluck thy captives thence.

In vain; thy gātes deny
All passage save to those who hence depart;
Nor to the streaming eye
Thou giv'st them back—nor to the broken heart.

In thy abysses hide
Beauty and excellence unknown; to thee
Earth's wonder and her pride
Are gathered, as the waters to the sea;

Labors of good to man,
Unpublished charity, unbroken faith,
Love, that midst grief began,
And grew with years, and faltered not in death.

Full many a mighty name
Lurks in thy depths, unuttered, unrevered;
With thee are silent fame,
Forgotten arts, and wisdom disappeared.

Thine for a space are they—
Yet shalt thou yield thy treasures up at last:
Thy gates shall yet give way,
Thy bolts shall fall, inexorable Past!

All that of good and fair
Has gone into thy womb from earliest time,
Shall then come forth to wear
The glory and the beauty of its prime.

They have not perished—no!
Kind words, remembered voices once so sweet,
Smiles, radiant long ago,
And features, the great soul's apparent seat.

All shall come back; each tie
Of pure affection shall be knit again;
Alone shall Evil die,
And Sorrow dwell a prisoner in thy reign.

And then shall I behold
Him, by whose kind paternal side I sprung,
And her, who, still and cold,
Fills the next grave—the beautiful and young.

To Cole, the Painter, Departing for Europe

Thine eyes shall see the light of distant skies;
Yet, Cole! thy heart shall bear to Europe's strand
A living image of our own bright land,
Such as upon thy glorious canvas lies;
Lone lakes—savannas where the bison roves—
Rocks rich with summer garlands—solemn streams—
Skies, where the desert eagle wheels and screams—
Spring bloom and autumn blaze of boundless groves.
Fair scenes shall greet thee where thou goest—fair,
But different—everywhere the trace of men,
Paths, homes, graves, ruins, from the lowest glen
To where life shrinks from the fierce Alpine air.
Gaze on them, till the tears shall dim thy sight,
But keep that earlier, wilder image bright.

The Greek Boy

Gone are the glorious Greeks of old,
Glorious in mien and mind;
Their bones are mingled with the mould,
Their dust is on the wind;
The forms they hewed from living stone
Survive the waste of years, alone,
And, scattered with their ashes, show
What greatness perished long ago.

Yet fresh the myrtles there; the springs
Gush brightly as of yore;
Flowers blossom from the dust of kings,
As many an age before.
There Nature moulds as nobly now,
As e'er of old, the human brow;
And copies still the martial form
That braved Platæa's battle-storm.

Boy! thy first looks were taught to seek
Their heaven in Hellas' skies;
Her airs have tinged thy dusky cheek,
Her sunshine lit thine eyes;
Thine ears have drunk the woodland strains
Heard by old poets, and thy veins
Swell with the blood of demigods,
That slumber in thy country's sods.

Now is thy nation free, though late;
Thy elder brethren broke—
Broke, ere thy spirit felt its weight—
The intolerable yoke.
And Greece, decayed, dethroned, doth see
Her youth-renewed in such as thee:
A shoot of that old vine that made
The nations silent in its shade.

The Evening Wind

Spirit that breathest through my lattice, thou
  That cool'st the twilight of the sultry day,
Gratefully flows thy freshness round my brow;
  Thou hast been out upon the deep at play,
Riding all day the wild blue waves till now,
  Roughening their crests, and scattering high their spray,
And swelling the white sail. I welcome thee
To the scorched land, thou wanderer of the sea!

Nor I alone; a thousand bosoms round
  Inhale thee in the fulness of delight;
And languid forms rise up, and pulses bound
  Livelier, at coming of the wind of night;
And, languishing to hear thy grateful sound,
  Lies the vast inland stretched beyond the sight.
Go forth into the gathering shade; go forth,
God's blessing breathed upon the fainting earth!

Go, rock the little wood-bird in his nest,
  Curl the still waters, bright with stars, and rouse
The wide old wood from his majestic rest,
  Summoning from the innumerable boughs
The strange, deep harmonies that haunt his breast:
  Pleasant shall be thy way where meekly bows
The shutting flower, and darkling waters pass,
And where the o'ershadowing branches sweep the grass.

The faint old man shall lean his silver head
  To feel thee; thou shalt kiss the child asleep,
And dry the moistened curls that overspread
  His temples, while his breathing grows more deep;
And they who stand about the sick man's bed,
  Shall joy to listen to thy distant sweep,
And softly part his curtains to allow
Thy visit, grateful to his burning brow.

Go—but the circle of eternal change,
  Which is the life of Nature, shall restore,
With sounds and scents from all thy mighty range,
  Thee to thy birthplace of the deep once more;
Sweet odors in the sea-air, sweet and strange,
  Shall tell the home-sick mariner of the shore;
And, listening to thy murmur, he shall deem
He hears the rustling leaf and running stream.

To the River Arve

[SUPPOSED TO BE WRITTEN AT A HAMLET NEAR THE FOOT OF MONT BLANC]

Not from the sands or cloven rocks,
  Thou rapid Arve! thy waters flow;
Nor earth, within her bosom, locks
  Thy dark unfathomed wells below.
Thy springs are in the cloud, thy stream
  Begins to move and murmur first
Where ice-peaks feel the noonday beam,
  Or rain-storms on the glacier burst.

Born where the thunder and the blast
  And morning's earliest light are born,
Thou rushest swoln, and loud, and fast,
  By these low homes, as if in scorn:
Yet humbler springs yield purer waves;
  And brighter, glassier streams than thine,
Sent up from earth's unlighted caves,
  With heaven's own beam and image shine.

Yet stay; for here are flowers and trees;
  Warm rays on cottage-roofs are here;
And laugh of girls, and hum of bees,
  Here linger till thy waves are clear.
Thou heedest not—thou hastest on;
  From steep to steep thy torrent falls;
Till, mingling with the mighty Rhone,
  It rests beneath Geneva's walls.

Rush on—but were there one with me
  That loved me, I would light my hearth
Here, where with God's own majesty
  Are touched the features of the earth.
By these old peaks, white, high, and vast,
  Still rising as the tempests beat,
Here would I dwell, and sleep, at last,
  Among the blossoms at their feet.

The Arctic Lover

Gone is the long, long winter night;
  Look, my belovèd one!
How glorious, through his depths of light,
  Rolls the majestic sun!
The willows, waked from winter's death,
Give out a fragrance like thy breath—
  The summer is begun!

Ay, 'tis the long bright summer day:
  Hark to that mighty crash!
The loosened ice-ridge breaks away—
  The smitten waters flash;
Seaward the glittering mountain rides,
While, down its green translucent sides,
  The foamy torrents dash.

See, love, my boat is moored for thee
  By ocean's weedy floor—
The petrel does not skim the sea
  More swiftly than my oar.
We'll go where, on the rocky isles,
Her eggs the screaming sea-fowl piles
  Beside the pebbly shore.

Or, bide thou where the poppy blows,
  With wind-flowers frail and fair,
While I, upon his isle of snow,
  Seek and defy the bear.
Fierce though he be, and huge of frame,
This arm his savage strength shall tame,
  And drag him from his lair.

When crimson sky and flamy cloud
  Bespeak the summer o'er,
And the dead valleys wear a shroud
  Of snows that melt no more,
I'll build of ice thy winter home,
With glistening walls and glassy dome,
  And spread with skins the floor.

The white fox by thy couch shall play;
  And, from the frozen skies,
The meteors of a mimic day

Shall flash upon thine eyes.
And I—for such thy vow—meanwhile
Shall hear thy voice and see thy smile,
Till that long midnight flies.

Hymn of the City

Not in the solitude
Alone may man commune with Heaven, or see,
Only in savage wood
And sunny vale, the present Deity;
Or only hear his voice
Where the winds whisper and the waves rejoice.

Even here do I behold
Thy steps, Almighty!—here, amidst the crowd
Through the great city rolled,
With everlasting murmur deep and loud—
Choking the ways that wind
'Mongst the proud piles, the work of human kind.

Thy golden sunshine comes
From the round heaven, and on their dwellings lies
And lights their inner homes;
For them thou fill'st with air the unbounded skies,
And givest them the stores
Of ocean, and the harvests of its shores.

Thy Spirit is around,
Quickening the restless mass that sweeps along;
And this eternal sound—
Voices and footfalls of the numberless throng—
Like the resounding sea,
Or like the rainy tempest, speaks of Thee.

And when the hour of rest
Comes, like a calm upon the mid-sea brine,
Hushing its billowy breast—
The quiet of that moment too is thine;
It breathes of Him who keeps
The vast and helpless city while it sleeps.

To the Fringed Gentian

Thou blossom bright with autumn dew,
And colored with the heaven's own blue,
That openest when the quiet light
Succeeds the keen and frosty night.

Thou comest not when violets lean
O'er wandering brooks and springs unseen,
Or columbines, in purple dressed,
Nod o'er the ground-bird's hidden nest.

Thou waitest late and com'st alone,
When woods are bare and birds are flown,
And frosts and shortening days portend
The agèd year is near his end.

Then doth thy sweet and quiet eye
Look through its fringes to the sky,
Blue—blue—as if that sky let fall
A flower from its cerulean wall.

I would that thus, when I shall see
The hour of death draw near to me,
Hope, blossoming within my heart,
May look to heaven as I depart.

Song of Marion's Men

Our band is few but true and tried,
  Our leader frank and bold;
The British soldier trembles
  When Marion's name is told.
Our fortress is the good greenwood,
  Our tent the cypress-tree;
We know the forest round us,
  As seamen know the sea.
We know its walls of thorny vines,
  Its glades of reedy grass,
Its safe and silent islands
  Within the dark morass.

Woe to the English soldiery
  That little dread us near!
On them shall light at midnight
  A strange and sudden fear:
When, waking to their tents on fire,
  They grasp their arms in vain,
And they who stand to face us
  Are beat to earth again;
And they who fly in terror deem
  A mighty host behind,
And hear the tramp of thousands
  Upon the hollow wind.

Then sweet the hour that brings release
  From danger and from toil:
We talk the battle over,
  And share the battle's spoil.
The woodland rings with laugh and shout,
  As if a hunt were up,
And woodland flowers are gathered
  To crown the soldier's cup.
With merry songs we mock the wind
  That in the pine-top grieves,
And slumber long and sweetly
  On beds of oaken leaves.

Well knows the fair and friendly moon
  The band that Marion leads—
The glitter of their rifles,
  The scampering of their steeds.
'Tis life to guide the fiery barb

Across the moonlight plain;
'Tis life to feel the night-wind
That lifts the tossing mane.
A moment in the British camp—
A moment—and away
Back to the pathless forest,
Before the peep of day.

Grave men there are by broad Santee,
Grave men with hoary hairs;
Their hearts are all with Marion,
For Marion are their prayers.
And lovely ladies greet our band
With kindliest welcoming,
With smiles like those of summer,
And tears like those of spring.
For them we wear these trusty arms,
And lay them down no more
Till we have driven the Briton,
Forever, from our shore.

The Poems of William Cullen Bryant

III

LATER POEMS

The Editor's Commentary

BRYANT'S LATER POEMS attain a rich sonority and an eloquence which, with the exception of "Thanatopsis," were seldom reached by the earlier work. A breadth of spirit is matched by a full-throated utterance in "America," "Oh Mother of a Mighty Race," "The Death of Slavery," and especially in "The Antiquity of Freedom" with its ringing apostrophe:

> O Freedom! thou are not, as poets dream,
> A fair young girl, with light and delicate limbs.
> . . . Oh, not yet
> Mayst thou unbrace thy corslet, nor lay by
> Thy sword; nor yet, O Freedom! close thy lids
> In slumber; for thine enemy never sleeps,
> And thou must watch and combat, till the day
> Of the new earth and heaven.

But the older Bryant was not tongue-tied when he lowered his voice and relinquished the hortatory note. There is a freshening strain in the unaffected music of "The Snow-Shower," the bucolic tenderness of "The Planting of the Apple Tree," and the young bubbling humor of "Robert of Lincoln."

The lyrical and the militant veins are mingled in "The Green Mountain Boys." Here Bryant does a curious thing: He celebrates the historic expedition of the Vermonters led by Ethan Allen in 1775, an exploit that resulted in the capture of Fort Ticonderoga. But the lines have the lilt of a drinking song, and the last verse is a kind of capitulation. It can no longer resist the rhythm; the bowl is filled and the liquor flows as Bryant, almost against his will, turns into Anacreon.

To the Apennines

Your peaks are beautiful, ye Apennines!
  In the soft light of these serenest skies;
From the broad highland region, black with pines,
  Fair as the hills of Paradise they rise,
Bathed in the tint Peruvian slaves behold
In rosy flushes on the virgin gold.

There, rooted to the aërial shelves that wear
  The glory of a brighter world, might spring
Sweet flowers of heaven to scent the unbreathed air,
  And heaven's fleet messengers might rest the wing
To view the fair earth in its summer sleep,
Silent, and cradled by the glimmering deep.

Below you lie men's sepulchres, the old
  Etrurian tombs, the graves of yesterday;
The herd's white bones lie mixed with human mould,
  Yet up the radiant steeps that I survey
Death never climbed, nor life's soft breath, with pain,
Was yielded to the elements again.

Ages of war have filled these plains with fear;
  How oft the hind has started at the clash
Of spears, and yell of meeting armies here,
  Or seen the lightning of the battle flash
From clouds, that rising with the thunder's sound,
Hung like an earth-born tempest o'er the ground!

Ah me! what armèd nations—Asian horde,
  And Libyan host, the Scythian and the Gaul—
Have swept your base and through your passes poured,
  Like ocean-tides uprising at the call
Of tyrant winds—against your rocky side
The bloody billows dashed, and howled, and died!

How crashed the towers before beleaguering foes,
  Sacked cities smoked and realms were rent in twain;
And commonwealths against their rivals rose,
  Trode out their lives and earned the curse of Cain!
While, in the noiseless air and light that flowed
Round your fair brows, eternal Peace abode.

Here pealed the impious hymn, and altar-flames
  Rose to false gods, a dream-begotten throng,

Jove, Bacchus, Pan, and earlier, fouler names;
While, as the unheeding ages passed along,
Ye, from your station in the middle skies,
Proclaimed the essential Goodness, strong and wise.

In you the heart that sighs for freedom seeks
Her image; there the winds no barrier know,
Clouds come and rest and leave your fairy peaks;
While even the immaterial Mind, below,
And Thought, her wingèd offspring, chained by power,
Pine silently for the redeeming hour.

The Green Mountain Boys

I

Here halt we our march, and pitch our tent
On the rugged forest-ground,
And light our fire with the branches rent
By winds from the beeches round.
Wild storms have torn this ancient wood,
But a wilder is at hand,
With hail of iron and rain of blood,
To sweep and waste the land.

II

How the dark wood rings with our voices shrill,
That startle the sleeping bird!
To-morrow eve must the voice be still,
And the step must fall unheard.
The Briton lies by the blue Champlain,
In Ticonderoga's towers,
And ere the sun rise twice again,
Must they and the lake be ours.

III

Fill up the bowl from the brook that glides
Where the fire-flies light the brake;
A ruddier juice the Briton hides
In his fortress by the lake.
Build high the fire, till the panther leap
From his lofty perch in flight,
And we'll strengthen our weary arms with sleep
For the deeds of to-morrow night.

Seventy-Six

What heroes from the woodland sprung,
  When, through the fresh-awakened land,
The thrilling cry of freedom rung,
And to the work of warfare strung
  The yeoman's iron hand!

Hills flung the cry to hills around,
  And ocean-mart replied to mart,
And streams, whose springs were yet unfound,
Pealed far away the startling sound
  Into the forest's heart.

Then marched the brave from rocky steep,
  From mountain-river swift and cold;
The borders of the stormy deep,
The vales where gathered waters sleep,
  Sent up the strong and bold,—

As if the very earth again
  Grew quick with God's creating breath,
And, from the sods of grove and glen,
Rose ranks of lion-hearted men
  To battle to the death.

The wife, whose babe first smiled that day,
  The fair fond bride of yestereve,
And agèd sire and matron gray,
Saw the loved warriors haste away,
  And deemed it sin to grieve.

Already had the strife begun;
  Already blood, on Concord's plain,
Along the springing grass had run,
And blood had flowed at Lexington,
  Like brooks of April rain.

That death-stain on the vernal sward
  Hallowed to freedom all the shore;
In fragments fell the yoke abhorred—
The footstep of a foreign lord
  Profaned the soil no more.

The Hunter of the Prairies

Ay, this is freedom!—these pure skies
  Were never stained with village smoke:
The fragrant wind, that through them flies,
  Is breathed from wastes by plough unbroke.
Here, with my rifle and my steed,
  And her who left the world for me,
I plant me, where the red deer feed
  In the green desert—and am free.

For here the fair savannas know
  No barriers in the bloomy grass;
Wherever breeze of heaven may blow,
  Or beam of heaven may glance, I pass.
In pastures, measureless as air,
  The bison is my noble game;
The bounding elk, whose antlers tear
  The branches, falls before my aim.

Mine are the river-fowl that scream
  From the long stripe of waving sedge;
The bear that marks my weapon's gleam,
  Hides vainly in the forest's edge;
In vain the she-wolf stands at bay;
  The brinded catamount, that lies
High in the boughs to watch his prey,
  Even in the act of springing, dies.

With what free growth the elm and plane
  Fling their huge arms across my way,
Gray, old, and cumbered with a train
  Of vines, as huge, and old, and gray!
Free stray the lucid streams, and find
  No taint in these fresh lawns and shades;
Free spring the flowers that scent the wind
  Where never scythe has swept the glades.

Alone the Fire, when frost-winds sere
  The heavy herbage of the ground,
Gathers his annual harvest here,
  With roaring like the battle's sound,
And hurrying flames that sweep the plain,
  And smoke-streams gushing up the sky:
I meet the flames with flames again,
  And at my door they cower and die.

Here, from dim woods, the aged past
 Speaks solemnly; and I behold
The boundless future in the vast
 And lonely river, seaward rolled.
Who feeds its founts with rain and dew?
 Who moves, I ask, its gliding mass,
And trains the bordering vines, whose blue
 Bright clusters tempt me as I pass?

Broad are these streams—my steed obeys,
 Plunges, and bears me through the tide.
Wide are these woods—I thread the maze
 Of giant stems, nor ask a guide.
I hunt till day's last glimmer dies
 O'er woody vale and grassy height;
And kind the voice and glad the eyes
 That welcome my return at night.

The Knight's Epitaph

This is the church which Pisa, great and free,
Reared to St. Catharine. How the time-stained walls,
That earthquakes shook not from their poise, appear
To shiver in the deep and voluble tones
Rolled from the organ! Underneath my feet
There lies the lid of a sepulchral vault.
The image of an armèd knight is graven
Upon it, clad in perfect panoply—
Cuishes, and greaves, and cuirass, with barred helm,
Gauntleted hand, and sword, and blazoned shield.
Around, in Gothic characters, worn dim
By feet of worshippers, are traced his name,
And birth, and death, and words of eulogy.
Why should I pore upon them? This old tomb,
This effigy, the strange disusèd form
Of this inscription, eloquently show
His history. Let me clothe in fitting words
The thoughts they breathe, and frame his epitaph:

"He whose forgotten dust for centuries
Has lain beneath this stone, was one in whom
Adventure, and endurance, and emprise,
Exalted the mind's faculties and strung
The body's sinews. Brave he was in fight,
Courteous in banquet, scornful of repose,
And bountiful, and cruel, and devout,
And quick to draw the sword in private feud,
He pushed his quarrels to the death, yet prayed
The saints as fervently on bended knees
As ever shaven cenobite. He loved
As fiercely as he fought. He would have borne
The maid that pleased him from her bower by night
To his hill castle, as the eagle bears
His victim from the fold, and rolled the rocks
On his pursuers. He aspired to see
His native Pisa queen and arbitress
Of cities; earnestly for her he raised
His voice in council, and affronted death
In battle-field, and climbed the galley's deck,
And brought the captured flag of Genoa back,
Or piled upon the Arno's crowded quay
The glittering spoils of the tamed Saracen.
He was not born to brook the stranger's yoke,
But would have joined the exiles that withdrew

Forever, when the Florentine broke in
The gates of Pisa, and bore off the bolts
For trophies—but he died before that day.

"He lived, the impersonation of an age
That never shall return. His soul of fire
Was kindled by the breath of the rude time
He lived in. Now a gentler race succeeds,
Shuddering at blood; the effeminate cavalier,
Turning his eyes from the reproachful past,
And from the hopeless future, gives to ease,
And love, and music, his inglorious life."

"The May Sun Sheds an Amber Light"

The May sun sheds an amber light
On new-leaved woods and lawns between;
But she who, with a smile more bright,
Welcomed and watched the springing green,
Is in her grave,
Low in her grave.

The fair white blossoms of the wood
In groups beside the pathway stand;
But one, the gentle and the good,
Who cropped them with a fairer hand,
Is in her grave,
Low in her grave.

Upon the woodland's morning airs
The small birds' mingled notes are flung;
But she, whose voice, more sweet than theirs,
Once bade me listen while they sung,
Is in her grave,
Low in her grave.

That music of the early year
Brings tears of anguish to my eyes;
My heart aches when the flowers appear;
For then I think of her who lies
Within her grave,
Low in her grave.

A Presentment

"Oh father, let us hence—for hark,
 A fearful murmur shakes the air;
The clouds are coming swift and dark;—
 What horrid shapes they wear!
A wingèd giant sails the sky;
Oh father, father, let us fly!"

"Hush, child; it is a grateful sound,
 That beating of the summer shower;
Here, where the boughs hang close around,
 We'll pass a pleasant hour,
Till the fresh wind, that brings the rain,
Has swept the broad heaven clear again."

"Nay, father, let us haste—for see,
 That horrid thing with hornèd brow—
His wings o'erhang this very tree,
 He scowls upon us now;
His huge black arm is lifted high;
Oh father, father, let us fly!"

"Hush, child"; but, as the father spoke,
 Downward the livid firebolt came,
Close to his ear the thunder broke,
 And, blasted by the flame,
The child lay dead; while dark and still
Swept the grim cloud along the hill.

Earth

A midnight black with clouds is in the sky;
I seem to feel, upon my limbs, the weight
Of its vast brooding shadow. All in vain
Turns the tired eye in search of form; no star
Pierces the pitchy veil; no ruddy blaze,
From dwellings lighted by the cheerful hearth,
Tinges the flowering summits of the grass.
No sound of life is heard, no village hum,
Nor measured tramp of footstep in the path,
Nor rush of wind, while, on the breast of Earth,
I lie and listen to her mighty voice:
A voice of many tones—sent up from streams
That wander through the gloom, from woods unseen
Swayed by the sweeping of the tides of air,
From rocky chasms where darkness dwells all day,
And hollows of the great invisible hills,
And sands that edge the ocean, stretching far
Into the night—a melancholy sound!

O Earth! dost thou too sorrow for the past
Like man thy offspring? Do I hear thee mourn
Thy childhood's unreturning hours, thy springs
Gone with their genial airs and melodies,
The gentle generations of thy flowers,
And thy majestic groves of olden time,
Perished with all their dwellers? Dost thou wail
For that fair age of which the poets tell,
Ere yet the winds grew keen with frost, or fire
Fell with the rains or spouted from the hills,
To blast thy greenness, while the virgin night
Was guiltless and salubrious as the day?
Or haply dost thou grieve for those that die—
For living things that trod thy paths awhile,
The love of thee and heaven—and now they sleep
Mixed with the shapeless dust on which thy herds
Trample and graze? I too must grieve with thee,
O'er loved ones lost. Their graves are far away
Upon thy mountains; yet, while I recline
Alone, in darkness, on thy naked soil,
The mighty nourisher and burial-place
Of man, I feel that I embrace their dust.

Ha! how the murmur deepens! I perceive
And tremble at its dreadful import. Earth
Uplifts a general cry for guilt and wrong,

And heaven is listening. The forgotten graves
Of the heart-broken utter forth their plaint.
The dust of her who loved and was betrayed,
And him who died neglected in his age;
The sepulchres of those who for mankind
Labored, and earned the recompense of scorn;
Ashes of martyrs for the truth, and bones
Of those who, in the strife for liberty,
Were beaten down, their corses given to dogs,
Their names to infamy, all find a voice.
The nook in which the captive, overtoiled,
Lay down to rest at last, and that which holds
Childhood's sweet blossoms, crushed by cruel hands,
Send up a plaintive sound. From battle-fields,
Where heroes madly drave and dashed their hosts
Against each other, rises up a noise,
As if the armèd multitudes of dead
Stirred in their heavy slumber. Mournful tones
Come from the green abysses of the sea—
A story of the crimes the guilty sought
To hide beneath its waves. The glens, the groves,
Paths in the thicket, pools of running brook,
And banks and depths of lake, and streets and lanes
Of cities, now that living sounds are hushed,
Murmur of guilty force and treachery.

Here, where I rest, the vales of Italy
Are round me, populous from early time,
And field of the tremendous warfare waged
'Twixt good and evil. Who, alas! shall dare
Interpret to man's ear the mingled voice
That comes from her old dungeons yawning now
To the black air, her amphitheatres,
Where the dew gathers on the mouldering stones,
And fanes of banished gods, and open tombs,
And roofless palaces, and streets and hearths
Of cities dug from their volcanic graves?
I hear a sound of many languages,
The utterance of nations now no more,
Driven out by mightier, as the days of heaven
Chase one another from the sky. The blood
Of freemen shed by freemen, till strange lords
Came in their hour of weakness, and made fast
The yoke that yet is worn, cries out to heaven.

What then shall cleanse thy bosom, gentle Earth,
From all its painful memories of guilt?
The whelming flood, or the renewing fire,
Or the slow change of time?—that so, at last,
The horrid tale of perjury and strife,
Murder and spoil, which men call history,
May seem a fable, like the inventions told
By poets of the gods of Greece. O thou,
Who sittest far beyond the Atlantic deep,
Among the sources of thy glorious streams,
My native Land of Groves! a newer page
In the great record of the world is thine;
Shall it be fairer? Fear, and friendly Hope,
And Envy, watch the issue, while the lines,
By which thou shalt be judged, are written down.

"Earth's Children Cleave to Earth"

Earth's children cleave to Earth—her frail
Decaying children dread decay.
Yon wreath of mist that leaves the vale
And lessens in the morning ray—
Look, how, by mountain rivulet,
It lingers as it upward creeps,
And clings to fern and copsewood set
Along the green and dewy steeps:
Clings to the flowery kalmia, clings
To precipices fringed with grass,
Dark maples where the wood-thrush sings,
And bowers of fragrant sassafras.
Yet all in vain—it passes still
From hold to hold, it cannot stay,
And in the very beams that fill
The world with glory, wastes away,
Till, parting from the mountain's brow,
It vanishes from human eye,
And that which sprung of earth is now
A portion of the glorious sky.

The Living Lost

Matron! the children of whose love,
  Each to his grave, in youth have passed;
And now the mould is heaped above
  The dearest and the last!
Bride! who dost wear the widow's veil
Before the wedding flowers are pale!
Ye deem the human heart endures
No deeper, bitterer grief than yours.

Yet there are pangs of keener woe,
  Of which the sufferers never speak,
Nor to the world's cold pity show
  The tears that scald the cheek,
Wrung from their eyelids by the shame
And guilt of those they shrink to name,
Whom once they loved with cheerful will,
And love, though fallen and branded, still.

Weep, ye who sorrow for the dead,
  Thus breaking hearts their pain relieve,
And reverenced are the tears they shed,
  And honored ye who grieve.
The praise of those who sleep in earth,
The pleasant memory of their worth,
The hope to meet when life is past,
Shall heal the tortured mind at last.

But ye, who for the living lost
  That agony in secret bear,
Who shall with soothing words accost
  The strength of your despair?
Grief for your sake is scorn for them
Whom ye lament and all condemn;
And o'er the world of spirits lies
A gloom from which ye turn your eyes.

Catterskill Falls

Midst greens and shades the Catterskill leaps,
  From cliffs where the wood-flower clings;
All summer he moistens his verdant steeps,
  With the sweet light spray of the mountain-springs,
And he shakes the woods on the mountain-side,
When they drip with the rains of autumn-tide.

But when, in the forest bare and old,
  The blast of December calls,
He builds, in the starlight clear and cold,
  A palace of ice where his torrent falls,
With turret, and arch, and fretwork fair,
And pillars blue as the summer air.

For whom are those glorious chambers wrought,
  In the cold and cloudless night?
Is there neither spirit nor motion of thought
  In forms so lovely, and hues so bright?
Hear what the gray-haired woodmen tell
Of this wild stream and its rocky dell.

'Twas hither a youth of dreamy mood,
  A hundred winters ago,
Had wandered over the mighty wood,
  When the panther's track was fresh on the snow,
And keen were the winds that came to stir
The long dark boughs of the hemlock-fir.

Too gentle of mien he seemed and fair,
  For a child of those rugged steeps;
His home lay low in the valley where
  The kingly Hudson rolls to the deeps;
But he wore the hunter's frock that day,
And a slender gun on his shoulder lay.

And here he paused, and against the trunk
  Of a tall gray linden leant,
When the broad clear orb of the sun had sunk,
  From his path in the frosty firmament,
And over the round dark edge of the hill
A cold green light was quivering still.

And the crescent moon, high over the green,
  From a sky of crimson shone,

On that icy palace, whose towers were seen
  To sparkle as if with stars of their own,
While the water fell with a hollow sound,
'Twixt the glistening pillars ranged around.

Is that a being of life, that moves
  Where the crystal battlements rise?
A maiden watching the moon she loves,
  At the twilight hour, with pensive eyes?
Was that a garment which seemed to gleam
Betwixt the eye and the falling stream?

'Tis only the torrent tumbling o'er,
  In the midst of those glassy walls,
Gushing, and plunging, and beating the floor
  Of the rocky basin in which it falls.
'Tis only the torrent—but why that start?
Why gazes the youth with a throbbing heart?

He thinks no more of his home afar,
  Where his sire and sister wait.
He heeds no longer how star after star
  Looks forth on the night as the hour grows late.
He heeds not the snow-wreaths, lifted and cast
From a thousand boughs, by the rising blast.

His thoughts are alone of those who dwell
  In the halls of frost and snow,
Who pass where the crystal domes upswell
  From the alabaster floors below,
Where the frost-trees shoot with leaf and spray,
And frost-gems scatter a silvery day.

"And oh that those glorious haunts were mine!"
  He speaks, and throughout the glen
Thin shadows swim in the faint moonshine,
  And take a ghastly likeness of men,
As if the slain by the wintry storms
Came forth to the air in their earthly forms.

There pass the chasers of seal and whale,
  With their weapons quaint and grim,
And bands of warriors in glittering mail,
  And herdsmen and hunters huge of limb;

There are naked arms, with bow and spear,
And furry gauntlets the carbine rear.

There are mothers—and oh how sadly their eyes
On their children's white brows rest!
There are youthful lovers—the maiden lies,
In a seeming sleep, on the chosen breast;
There are fair wan women with moonstruck air,
The snow-stars flecking their long loose hair.

They eye him not as they pass along,
But his hair stands up with dread,
When he feels that he moves with that phantom throng,
Till those icy turrets are over his head,
And the torrent's roar as they enter seems
Like a drowsy murmur heard in dreams.

The glittering threshold is scarcely passed,
When there gathers and wraps him round
A thick white twilight, sullen and vast,
In which there is neither form nor sound;
The phantoms, the glory, vanish all,
With the dying voice of the waterfall.

Slow passes the darkness of that trance,
And the youth now faintly sees
Huge shadows and gushes of light that dance
On a rugged ceiling of unhewn trees,
And walls where the skins of beasts are hung,
And rifles glitter on antlers strung.

On a couch of shaggy skins he lies;
As he strives to raise his head,
Hard-featured woodmen, with kindly eyes,
Come round him and smooth his furry bed,
And bid him rest, for the evening star
Is scarcely set and the day is far.

They had found at eve the dreaming one
By the base of that icy steep,
When over his stiffening limbs begun
The deadly slumber of frost to creep,
And they cherished the pale and breathless form,
Till the stagnant blood ran free and warm.

The White-Footed Deer

It was a hundred years ago,
  When, by the woodland ways,
The traveller saw the wild-deer drink,
  Or crop the birchen sprays.

Beneath a hill, whose rocky side
  O'erbrowed a grassy mead,
And fenced a cottage from the wind,
  A deer was wont to feed.

She only came when on the cliffs
  The evening moonlight lay,
And no man knew the secret haunts
  In which she walked by day.

White were her feet, her forehead showed
  A spot of silvery white,
That seemed to glimmer like a star
  In autumn's hazy night.

And here, when sang the whippoorwill,
  She cropped the sprouting leaves,
And here her rustling steps were heard
  On still October eves.

But when the broad midsummer moon
  Rose o'er that grassy lawn,
Beside the silver-footed deer
  There grazed a spotted fawn.

The cottage dame forbade her son
  To aim the rifle here;
"It were a sin," she said, "to harm
  Or fright that friendly deer.

"This spot has been my pleasant home
  Ten peaceful years and more;
And ever, when the moonlight shines,
  She feeds before our door.

"The red-men say that here she walked
  A thousand moons ago;
They never raise the war-whoop here,
  And never twang the bow.

"I love to watch her as she feeds,
And think that all is well
While such a gentle creature haunts
The place in which we dwell."

The youth obeyed, and sought for game
In forests far away,
Where, deep in silence and in moss,
The ancient woodland lay.

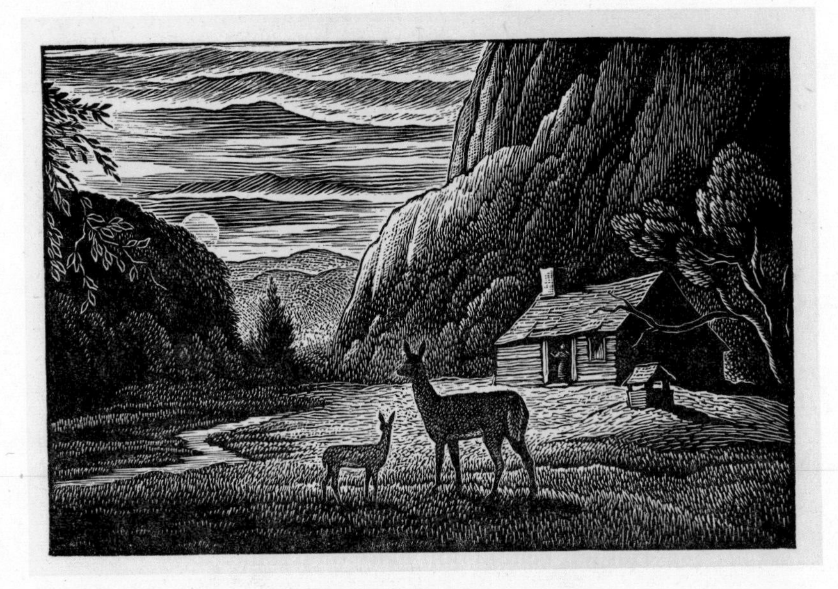

But once, in autumn's golden time
He ranged the wild in vain,
Nor roused the pheasant nor the deer,
And wandered home again.

The crescent moon and crimson eve
Shone with a mingling light;
The deer, upon the grassy mead,
Was feeding full in sight.

He raised the rifle to his eye,
And from the cliffs around
A sudden echo, shrill and sharp,
Gave back its deadly sound.

Away, into the neighboring wood,
The startled creature flew,
And crimson drops at morning lay
Amid the glimmering dew.

Next evening shone the waxing moon
As brightly as before;
The deer upon the grassy mead
Was seen again no more.

But ere that crescent moon was old,
By night the red-men came,
And burnt the cottage to the ground,
And slew the youth and dame.

Now woods have overgrown the mead,
And hid the cliffs from sight;
There shrieks the hovering hawk at noon,
And prowls the fox at night.

In Memory of William Leggett

The earth may ring, from shore to shore,
With echoes of a glorious name,
But he, whose loss our tears deplore,
Has left behind him more than fame.

For when the death-frost came to lie
On Leggett's warm and mighty heart,
And quench his bold and friendly eye,
His spirit did not all depart.

The words of fire that from his pen
Were flung upon the fervid page,
Still move, still shake the hearts of men,
Amid a cold and coward age.

His love of truth, too warm, too strong
For Hope or Fear to chain or chill,
His hate of tyranny and wrong,
Burn in the breasts he kindled still.

The Strange Lady

The summer morn is bright and fresh, the birds are darting by,
As if they loved to breast the breeze that sweeps the cool clear sky;
Young Albert, in the forest's edge, has heard a rustling sound,
An arrow slightly strikes his hand and falls upon the ground.

A dark-haired woman from the wood comes suddenly in sight;
Her merry eye is full and black, her cheek is brown and bright;
Her gown is of the mid-sea blue, her belt with beads is strung,
And yet she speaks in gentle tones, and in the English tongue.

"It was an idle bolt I sent, against the villain crow;
Fair sir, I fear it harmed thy hand; beshrew my erring bow!"
"Ah! would that bolt had not been spent! then, lady, might I wear
A lasting token on my hand of one so passing fair!"

"Thou art a flatterer like the rest, but wouldst thou take with me
A day of hunting in the wild beneath the greenwood tree,
I know where most the pheasants feed, and where the red-deer herd,
And thou shouldst chase the nobler game, and I bring down the bird."

Now Albert in her quiver lays the arrow in its place,
And wonders as he gazes on the beauty of her face:
"Those hunting-grounds are far away, and, lady, 'twere not meet
That night, amid the wilderness, should overtake thy feet."

"Heed not the night; a summer lodge amid the wild is mine—
'Tis shadowed by the tulip-tree, 'tis mantled by the vine;
The wild-plum sheds its yellow fruit from fragrant thickets nigh,
And flowery prairies from the door stretch till they meet the sky.

"There in the boughs that hide the roof the mock-bird sits and sings,
And there the hang-bird's brood within its little hammock swings;
A pebbly brook, where rustling winds among the hopples sweep,
Shall lull thee till the morning sun looks in upon thy sleep."

Away, into the forest depths by pleasant paths they go,
He with his rifle on his arm, the lady with her bow,
Where cornels arch their cool dark boughs o'er beds of wintergreen,
And never at his father's door again was Albert seen.

That night upon the woods came down a furious hurricane,
With howl of winds and roar of streams, and beating of the rain;
The mighty thunder broke and drowned the noises in its crash;
The old trees seemed to fight like fiends beneath the lightning flash.

Next day, within a mossy glen, 'mid mouldering trunks were found
The fragments of a human form upon the bloody ground;
White bones from which the flesh was torn, and locks of glossy hair;
They laid them in the place of graves, yet wist not whose they were.

And whether famished evening wolves had mangled Albert so,
Or that strange dame so gay and fair were some mysterious foe,
Or whether to that forest-lodge, beyond the mountains blue,
He went to dwell with her, the friends who mourned him never knew.

Dante

Who, mid the grasses of the field
   That spring beneath our careless feet,
First found the shining stems that yield
   The grains of life-sustaining wheat:

Who first, upon the furrowed land,
   Strewed the bright grains to sprout, and grow,
And ripen for the reaper's hand—
   We know not, and we cannot know.

But well we know the hand that brought
   And scattered, far as sight can reach,
The seeds of free and living thought
   On the broad field of modern speech.

Mid the white hills that round us lie,
   We cherish that Great Sower's fame,
And, as we pile the sheaves on high,
   With awe we utter Dante's name.

Six centuries, since the poet's birth,
   Have come and flitted o'er our sphere:
The richest harvest reaped on earth
   Crowns the last century's closing year.

Life

Oh Life! I breathe thee in the breeze,
I feel thee bounding in my veins,
I see thee in these stretching trees,
These flowers, this still rock's mossy stains.

This stream of odors flowing by
From clover-field and clumps of pine,
This music, thrilling all the sky,
From all the morning birds, are thine.

Thou fill'st with joy this little one,
That leaps and shouts beside me here,
Where Isar's clay-white rivulets run
Through the dark woods like frighted deer.

Ah! must thy mighty breath, that wakes
Insect and bird, and flower and tree,
From the low-trodden dust, and makes
Their daily gladness, pass from me—

Pass, pulse by pulse, till o'er the ground
These limbs, now strong, shall creep with pain,
And this fair world of sight and sound
Seem fading into night again?

The things, oh Life! thou quickenest, all
Strive upward toward the broad bright sky,
Upward and outward, and they fall
Back to earth's bosom when they die.

All that have borne the touch of death,
All that shall live, lie mingled there,
Beneath that veil of bloom and breath,
That living zone 'twixt earth and air.

There lies my chamber dark and still,
The atoms trampled by my feet
There wait, to take the place I fill
In the sweet air and sunshine sweet.

Well, I have had my turn, have been
Raised from the darkness of the clod,
And for a glorious moment seen
The brightness of the skirts of God;

And knew the light within my breast,
  Though wavering oftentimes and dim,
The power, the will, that never rest,
  And cannot die, were all from him.

Dear child! I know that thou wilt grieve
  To see me taken from thy love,
Wilt seek my grave at Sabbath eve
  And weep, and scatter flowers above.

Thy little heart will soon be healed,
  And being shall be bliss, till thou
To younger forms of life must yield
  The place thou fill'st with beauty now.

When we descend to dust again,
  Where will the final dwelling be
Of thought and all its memories then,
  My love for thee, and thine for me?

The Stream of Life

Oh silvery streamlet of the fields,
  That flowest full and free,
For thee the rains of spring return,
  The summer dews for thee;
And when thy latest blossoms die
  In autumn's chilly showers,
The winter fountains gush for thee,
  Till May brings back the flowers.

Oh Stream of Life! the violet springs
  But once beside thy bed;
But one brief summer, on thy path,
  The dews of heaven are shed.
Thy parent fountains shrink away,
  And close their crystal veins,
And where thy glittering current flowed
  The dust alone remains.

The Hunter's Vision

Upon a rock that, high and sheer,
   Rose from the mountain's breast,
A weary hunter of the deer
   Had sat him down to rest,
And bared to the soft summer air
His hot red brow and sweaty hair.

All dim in haze the mountains lay,
   With dimmer vales between;
And rivers glimmered on their way
   By forests faintly seen;
While ever rose a murmuring sound
From brooks below and bees around.

He listened, till he seemed to hear
   A strain, so soft and low,
That whether in the mind or ear
   The listener scarce might know.
With such a tone, so sweet, so mild,
The watching mother lulls her child.

"Thou weary huntsman," thus it said,
   "Thou faint with toil and heat,
The pleasant land of rest is spread
   Before thy very feet,
And those whom thou wouldst gladly see
Are waiting there to welcome thee."

He looked, and 'twixt the earth and sky,
   Amid the noontide haze,
A shadowy region met his eye,
   And grew beneath his gaze,
As if the vapors of the air
Had gathered into shapes so fair.

Groves freshened as he looked, and flowers
   Showed bright on rocky bank,
And fountains welled beneath the bowers,
   Where deer and pheasant drank.
He saw the glittering streams, he heard
The rustling bough and twittering bird.

And friends, the dead, in boyhood dear
   There lived and walked again,

And there was one who many a year
 Within her grave had lain,
A fair young girl, the hamlet's pride—
His heart was breaking when she died:

Bounding, as was her wont, she came
 Right toward his resting-place,
And stretched her hand and called his name
 With that sweet smiling face.
Forward with fixed and eager eyes,
The hunter leaned in act to rise:

Forward he leaned, and headlong down
 Plunged from that craggy wall;
He saw the rocks, steep, stern, and brown,
 An instant, in his fall;
A frightful instant—and no more,
The dream and life at once were o'er.

The Child's Funeral

Fair is thy sight, Sorrento, green thy shore,
 Black crags behind thee pierce the clear blue skies;
The sea, whose borderers ruled the world of yore,
 As clear and bluer still before thee lies.

Vesuvius smokes in sight, whose fount of fire,
 Outgushing, drowned the cities on his steeps;
And murmuring Naples, spire o'ertopping spire,
 Sits on the slope beyond where Virgil sleeps.

Here doth the earth, with flowers of every hue,
 Prank her green breast when April suns are bright;
Flowers of the morning-red, or ocean-blue,
 Or like the mountain-frost of silvery white.

Currents of fragrance, from the orange-tree,
 And sward of violets, breathing to and fro,
Mingle, and, wandering out upon the sea,
 Refresh the idle boatsman where they blow.

Yet even here, as under harsher climes,
 Tears for the loved and early lost are shed;

That soft air saddens with the funeral-chimes,
  Those shining flowers are gathered for the dead.

Here once a child, a smiling playful one,
  All the day long caressing and caressed,
Died when its little tongue had just begun
  To lisp the names of those it loved the best.

The father strove his struggling grief to quell,
  The mother wept as mothers use to weep,
Two little sisters wearied them to tell
  When their dear Carlo would awake from sleep.

Within an inner room his couch they spread,
  His funeral-couch; with mingled grief and love,
They laid a crown of roses on his head,
  And murmured, "Brighter is his crown above."

They scattered round him, on the snowy sheet,
  Laburnum's strings of sunny-colored gems,
Sad hyacinths, and violets dim and sweet,
  And orange-blossoms on their dark-green stems.

And now the hour is come, the priest is there;
  Torches are lit and bells are tolled; they go,
With solemn rites of blessing and of prayer,
  To lay the little one in earth below.

The door is opened; hark! that quick glad cry;
  Carlo has waked, has waked, and is at play;
The little sisters laugh and leap, and try
  To climb the bed on which the infant lay.

And there he sits alive, and gayly shakes
  In his full hands the blossoms red and white,
And smiles with winking eyes, like one who wakes
  From long deep slumbers at the morning light.

The Battle-Field

Once this soft turf, this rivulet's sands,
Were trampled by a hurrying crowd,
And fiery hearts and armèd hands
Encountered in the battle-cloud.

Ah! never shall the land forget
How gushed the life-blood of her brave—
Gushed, warm with hope and courage yet,
Upon the soil they fought to save.

Now all is calm, and fresh, and still;
Alone the chirp of flitting bird,
And talk of children on the hill,
And bell of wandering kine, are heard.

No solemn host goes trailing by
The black-mouthed gun and staggering wain;
Men start not at the battle-cry,
Oh, be it never heard again!

Soon rested those who fought; but thou
Who minglest in the harder strife
For truths which men receive not now,
Thy warfare only ends with life.

A friendless warfare! lingering long
Through weary day and weary year,
A wild and many-weaponed throng
Hang on thy front, and flank, and rear.

Yet nerve thy spirit to the proof,
And blench not at thy chosen lot.
The timid good may stand aloof,
The sage may frown—yet faint thou not.

Nor heed the shaft too surely cast,
The foul and hissing bolt of scorn;
For with thy side shall dwell, at last,
The victory of endurance born.

Truth, crushed to earth, shall rise again;
Th' eternal years of God are hers;
But Error, wounded, writhes in pain,
And dies among his worshippers.

Yea, though thou lie upon the dust,
When they who helped thee flee in fear,
Die full of hope and manly trust,
Like those who fell in battle here.

Another hand thy sword shall wield,
Another hand the standard wave,
Till from the trumpet's mouth is pealed
The blast of triumph o'er thy grave.

The Death of Lincoln

Oh, slow to smite and swift to spare,
Gentle and merciful and just!
Who, in the fear of God, didst bear
The sword of power, a nation's trust!

In sorrow by thy bier we stand,
Amid the awe that hushes all,
And speak the anguish of a land
That shook with horror at thy fall.

Thy task is done; the bond are free:
We bear thee to an honored grave,
Whose proudest monument shall be
The broken fetters of the slave.

Pure was thy life; its bloody close
Hath placed thee with the sons of light,
Among the noble host of those
Who perished in the cause of Right.

The Winds

I

Ye winds, ye unseen currents of the air,
Softly ye played a few brief hours ago;
Ye bore the murmuring bee; ye tossed the hair
O'er maiden cheeks, that took a fresher glow;
Ye rolled the round white cloud through depths of blue;
Ye shook from shaded flowers the lingering dew;
Before you the catalpa's blossoms flew,
Light blossoms, dropping on the grass like snow.

II

What change is this! Ye take the cataract's sound;
Ye take the whirlpool's fury and its might;
The mountain shudders as ye sweep the ground;
The valley woods lie prone beneath your flight.
The clouds before you shoot like eagles past;
The homes of men are rocking in your blast;
Ye lift the roofs like autumn leaves, and cast,
Skyward, the whirling fragments out of sight.

III

The weary fowls of heaven make wing in vain,
To escape your wrath; ye seize and dash them dead;
Against the earth ye drive the roaring rain;
The harvest-field becomes a river's bed;
And torrents tumble from the hills around,
Plains turn to lakes, and villages are drowned,
And wailing voices, midst the tempest's sound,
Rise, as the rushing waters swell and spread.

IV

Ye dart upon the deep, and straight is heard
A wilder roar, and men grow pale, and pray;
Ye fling its floods around you, as a bird
Flings o'er his shivering plumes the fountain's spray.
See! to the breaking mast the sailor clings;
Ye scoop the ocean to its briny springs,
And take the mountain-billow on your wings,
And pile the wreck of navies round the bay.

V

Why rage ye thus?—no strife for liberty
  Has made you mad; no tyrant, strong through fear,
Has chained your pinions till ye wrench them free,
  And rushed into the unmeasured atmosphere;
For ye were born in freedom where ye blow;
Free o'er the mighty deep to come and go;
Earth's solemn woods were yours, her wastes of snow,
  Her isles where summer blossoms all the year.

VI

O ye wild winds! a mightier Power than yours
  In chains upon the shore of Europe lies;
The sceptred throng whose fetters he endures
  Watch his mute throes with terror in their eyes;
And armèd warriors all around him stand,
And, as he struggles, tighten every band,
And lift the heavy spear, with threatening hand,
  To pierce the victim, should he strive to rise.

VII

Yet oh, when that wronged Spirit of our race
  Shall break, as soon he must, his long-worn chains,
And leap in freedom from his prison-place,
  Lord of his ancient hills and fruitful plains,
Let him not rise, like these mad winds of air,
To waste the loveliness that time could spare,
To fill the earth with woe, and blot her fair
  Unconscious breast with blood from human veins.

VIII

But may he like the spring-time come abroad,
  Who crumbles winter's gyves with gentle might,
When in the genial breeze, the breath of God,
  The unsealed springs come spouting up to light;
Flowers start from their dark prisons at his feet,
The woods, long dumb, awake to hymnings sweet,
And morn and eve, whose glimmerings almost meet,
  Crowd back to narrow bounds the ancient night.

The Old Man's Counsel

Among our hills and valleys, I have known
Wise and grave men, who, while their diligent hands
Tended or gathered in the fruits of earth,
Were reverent learners in the solemn school
Of Nature. Not in vain to them were sent
Seed-time and harvest, or the vernal shower
That darkened the brown tilth, or snow that beat
On the white winter hills. Each brought, in turn,
Some truth, some lesson on the life of man,
Or recognition of the Eternal mind
Who veils his glory with the elements.

One such I knew long since, a white-haired man,
Pithy of speech, and merry when he would;
A genial optimist, who daily drew
From what he saw his quaint moralities.
Kindly he held communion, though so old,
With me a dreaming boy, and taught me much
That books tell not, and I shall ne'er forget.

The sun of May was bright in middle heaven,
And steeped the sprouting forests, the green hills,
And emerald wheat-fields, in his yellow light.
Upon the apple-tree, where rosy buds
Stood clustered, ready to burst forth in bloom,
The robin warbled forth his full clear note
For hours, and wearied not. Within the woods,
Whose young and half transparent leaves scarce cast
A shade, gay circles of anemones
Danced on their stalks; the shad-bush, white with flower,
Brightened the glens; the new-leaved butternut
And quivering poplar to the roving breeze
Gave a balsamic fragrance. In the fields
I saw the pulses of the gentle wind
On the young grass. My heart was touched with joy
At so much beauty, flushing every hour
Into a fuller beauty; but my friend,
The thoughtful ancient, standing at my side,
Gazed on it mildly sad. I asked him why.

"Well mayst thou join in gladness," he replied,
"With the glad earth, her springing plants and flowers,
And this soft wind, the herald of the green
Luxuriant summer. Thou art young like them,

And well mayst thou rejoice. But while the flight
Of seasons fills and knits thy spreading frame,
It withers mine, and thins my hair, and dims
These eyes, whose fading light shall soon be quenched
In utter darkness. Hearest thou that bird?"

I listened, and from midst the depth of woods
Heard the love-signal of the grouse, that wears
A sable ruff around his mottled neck;
Partridge they call him by our northern streams,
And pheasant by the Delaware. He beat
His barred sides with his speckled wings, and made
A sound like distant thunder; slow the strokes
At first, then fast and faster, till at length
They passed into a murmur and were still.

"There hast thou," said my friend, "a fitting type
Of human life. 'Tis an old truth, I know,
But images like these revive the power
Of long familiar truths. Slow pass our days
In childhood, and the hours of light are long
Betwixt the morn and eve; with swifter lapse
They glide in manhood, and in age they fly;
Till days and seasons flit before the mind
As flit the snow-flakes in a winter storm,
Seen rather than distinguished. Ah! I seem
As if I sat within a helpless bark,
By swiftly-running waters hurried on
To shoot some mighty cliff. Along the banks
Grove after grove, rock after frowning rock,
Bare sands and pleasant homes, and flowery nooks,
And isles and whirlpools in the stream, appear
Each after each, but the devoted skiff
Darts by so swiftly that their images
Dwell not upon the mind, or only dwell
In dim confusion; faster yet I sweep
By other banks, and the great gulf is near.

"Wisely, my son, while yet thy days are long,
And this fair change of seasons passes slow,
Gather and treasure up the good they yield—
All that they teach of virtue, of pure thoughts
And kind affections, reverence for thy God
And for thy brethren; so when thou shalt come

Into these barren years, thou mayst not bring
A mind unfurnished and a withered heart."

Long since that white-haired ancient slept—but still,
When the red flower-buds crowd the orchard-bough,
And the ruffed grouse is drumming far within
The woods, his venerable form again
Is at my side, his voice is in my ear.

The Painted Cup

The fresh savannas of the Sangamon
Here rise in gentle swells, and the long grass
Is mixed with rustling hazels. Scarlet tufts
Are glowing in the green, like flakes of fire;
The wanderers of the prairie know them well,
And call that brilliant flower the Painted Cup.

Now, if thou art a poet, tell me not
That these bright chalices were tinted thus
To hold the dew for fairies, when they meet
On moonlight evenings in the hazel-bowers,
And dance till they are thirsty. Call not up,
Amid this fresh and virgin solitude,
The faded fancies of an elder world;
But leave these scarlet cups to spotted moths
Of June, and glistening flies, and humming-birds,
To drink from, when on all these boundless lawns
The morning sun looks hot. Or let the wind
O'erturn in sport their ruddy brims, and pour
A sudden shower upon the strawberry-plant,
To swell the reddening fruit that even now
Breathes a slight fragrance from the sunny slope.

But thou art of a gayer fancy. Well—
Let then the gentle Manitou of flowers,
Lingering amid the bloomy waste he loves,
Though all his swarthy worshippers are gone—
Slender and small, his rounded cheek all brown
And ruddy with the sunshine; let him come
On summer mornings, when the blossoms wake,
And part with little hands the spiky grass,
And touching, with his cherry lips, the edge
Of these bright beakers, drain the gathered dew.

The Fountain

Fountain, that springest on this grassy slope,
Thy quick cool murmur mingles pleasantly,
With the cool sound of breezes in the beech,
Above me in the noontide. Thou dost wear
No stain of thy dark birthplace; gushing up
From the red mould and slimy roots of earth
Thou flashest in the sun. The mountain-air,
In winter, is not clearer, nor the dew
That shines on mountain-blossom. Thus doth God
Bring, from the dark and foul, the pure and bright.

This tangled thicket on the bank above
Thy basin, how thy waters keep it green!
For thou dost feed the roots of the wild-vine
That trails all over it, and to the twigs
Ties fast her clusters. There the spice-bush lifts
Her leafy lances; the viburnum there,
Paler of foliage, to the sun holds up
Her circlet of green berries. In and out
The chipping-sparrow, in her coat of brown,
Steals silently lest I should mark her nest.

Not such thou wert of yore, ere yet the axe
Had smitten the old woods. Then hoary trunks
Of oak, and plane, and hickory, o'er thee held
A mighty canopy. When April winds
Grew soft, the maple burst into a flush
Of scarlet flowers. The tulip-tree, high up,
Opened, in airs of June, her multitude
Of golden chalices to humming-birds
And silken-wingèd insects of the sky.

Frail wood-plants clustered round thy edge in spring;
The liver-leaf put forth her sister blooms
Of faintest blue. Here the quick-footed wolf,
Passing to lap thy waters, crushed the flower
Of sanguinaria, from whose brittle stem
The red drops fell like blood. The deer, too, left
Her delicate footprint in the soft moist mould,
And on the fallen leaves. The slow-paced bear,
In such a sultry summer noon as this,
Stopped at thy stream, and drank, and leaped across.

But thou hast histories that stir the heart
With deeper feeling; while I look on thee
They rise before me. I behold the scene
Hoary again with forests! I behold
The Indian warrior, whom a hand unseen
Has smitten with his death-wound in the woods,
Creep slowly to thy well-known rivulet,
And slake his death-thirst. Hark, that quick fierce cry
That rends the utter silence! 'tis the whoop
Of battle, and a throng of savage men
With naked arms and faces stained like blood,
Fill the green wilderness; the long bare arms
Are heaved aloft, bows twang and arrows stream;
Each makes a tree his shield, and every tree
Sends forth its arrow. Fierce the fight and short,
As is the whirlwind. Soon the conquerors
And conquered vanish, and the dead remain
Mangled by tomahawks. The mighty woods
Are still again, the frighted bird comes back
And plumes her wings; but thy sweet waters run
Crimson with blood. Then, as the sun goes down,
Amid the deepening twilight I descry
Figures of men that crouch and creep unheard,
And bear away the dead. The next day's shower
Shall wash the tokens of the fight away.

I look again—a hunter's lodge is built,
With poles and boughs, beside thy crystal well,
While the meek autumn stains the woods with gold,
And sheds his golden sunshine. To the door
The red-man slowly drags the enormous bear
Slain in the chestnut-thicket, or flings down
The deer from his strong shoulders. Shaggy fells
Of wolf and cougar hang upon the walls,
And loud the black-eyed Indian maidens laugh,
That gather, from the rustling heaps of leaves,
The hickory's white nuts, and the dark fruit
That falls from the gray butternut's long boughs.

So centuries passed by, and still the woods
Blossomed in spring, and reddened when the year
Grew chill, and glistened in the frozen rains
Of winter, till the white man swung the axe

Beside thee—signal of a mighty change.
Then all around was heard the crash of trees,
Trembling awhile and rushing to the ground,
The low of ox, and shouts of men who fired
The brushwood, or who tore the earth with ploughs;
The grain sprang thick and tall, and hid in green
The blackened hill-side; ranks of spiky maize
Rose like a host embattled; the buckwheat
Whitened broad acres, sweetening with its flowers
The August wind. White cottages were seen
With rose-trees at the windows; barns from which
Came loud and shrill the crowing of the cock;
Pastures where rolled and neighed the lordly horse,
And white flocks browsed and bleated. A rich turf
Of grasses brought from far o'ercrept thy bank,
Spotted with the white clover. Blue-eyed girls
Brought pails, and dipped them in thy crystal pool;
And children, ruddy-cheeked and flaxen-haired,
Gathered the glistening cowslip from thy edge.

Since then, what steps have trod thy border! Here
On thy green bank, the woodman of the swamp
Has laid his axe, the reaper of the hill
His sickle, as they stooped to taste thy stream.
The sportsman, tired with wandering in the still
September noon, has bathed his heated brow
In thy cool current. Shouting boys, let loose
For a wild holiday, have quaintly shaped
Into a cup the folded linden-leaf,
And dipped thy sliding crystal. From the wars
Returning, the plumed soldier by thy side
Has sat, and mused how pleasant 'twere to dwell
In such a spot, and be as free as thou,
And move for no man's bidding more. At eve,
When thou wert crimson with the crimson sky,
Lovers have gazed upon thee, and have thought
Their mingled lives should flow as peacefully
And brightly as thy waters. Here the sage,
Gazing into thy self-replenished depth,
Has seen eternal order circumscribe
And bound the motions of eternal change,
And from the gushing of thy simple fount
Has reasoned to the mighty universe.

Is there no other change for thee, that lurks
Among the future ages? Will not man
Seek out strange arts to wither and deform
The pleasant landscape which thou makest green?
Or shall the veins that feed thy constant stream
Be choked in middle earth, and flow no more
For ever, that the water-plants along
Thy channel perish, and the bird in vain
Alight to drink? Haply shall these green hills
Sink, with the lapse of years, into the gulf
Of ocean waters, and thy source be lost
Amidst the bitter brine? Or shall they rise,
Upheaved in broken cliffs and airy peaks,
Haunts of the eagle and the snake, and thou
Gush midway from the bare and barren steep?

The Planting of the Apple-Tree

Come, let us plant the apple-tree.
Cleave the tough greensward with the spade;
Wide let its hollow bed be made;
There gently lay the roots, and there
Sift the dark mould with kindly care,
And press it o'er them tenderly,
As, round the sleeping infant's feet,
We softly fold the cradle-sheet;
So plant we the apple-tree.

What plant we in this apple-tree?
Buds, which the breath of summer days
Shall lengthen into leafy sprays;
Boughs where the thrush, with crimson breast,
Shall haunt and sing and hide her nest;
We plant, upon the sunny lea,
A shadow for the noontide hour,
A shelter from the summer shower,
When we plant the apple-tree.

What plant we in this apple-tree?
Sweets for a hundred flowery springs
To load the May-wind's restless wings,
When, from the orchard-row, he pours
Its fragrance through our open doors;
A world of blossoms for the bee,
Flowers for the sick girl's silent room,
For the glad infant sprigs of bloom,
We plant with the apple-tree.

What plant we in this apple-tree?
Fruits that shall swell in sunny June,
And redden in the August noon,
And drop, when gentle airs come by,
That fan the blue September sky,
While children come, with cries of glee,
And seek them where the fragrant grass
Betrays their bed to those who pass,
At the foot of the apple-tree.

And when, above this apple-tree,
The winter stars are quivering bright,
And winds go howling through the night,
Girls, whose young eyes o'erflow with mirth,

Shall peel its fruit by cottage-hearth,
And guests in prouder homes shall see,
Heaped with the grape of Cintra's vine
And golden orange of the line,
The fruit of the apple-tree.

The fruitage of this apple-tree
Winds and our flag of stripe and star
Shall bear to coasts that lie afar,
Where men shall wonder at the view,
And ask in what fair groves they grew;

And sojourners beyond the sea
Shall think of childhood's careless day,
And long, long hours of summer play,
In the shade of the apple-tree.

Each year shall give this apple-tree
A broader flush of roseate bloom,
A deeper maze of verdurous gloom,
And loosen, when the frost-clouds lower,
The crisp brown leaves in thicker shower.
The years shall come and pass, but we
Shall hear no longer, where we lie,
The summer's songs, the autumn's sigh,
In the boughs of the apple-tree.

And time shall waste this apple-tree.
Oh, when its aged branches throw
Thin shadows on the ground below,
Shall fraud and force and iron will
Oppress the weak and helpless still?
What shall the tasks of mercy be,
Amid the toils, the strifes, the tears
Of those who live when length of years
Is wasting this little apple-tree?

"Who planted this old apple-tree?"
The children of that distant day
Thus to some aged man shall say;
And, gazing on its mossy stem,
The gray-haired man shall answer them:
"A poet of the land was he,
Born in the rude but good old times;
'Tis said he made some quaint old rhymes,
On planting the apple-tree."

An Evening Revery

The summer day is closed—the sun is set:
Well they have done their office, those bright hours,
The latest of whose train goes softly out
In the red west. The green blade of the ground
Has risen, and herds have cropped it; the young twig
Has spread its plaited tissues to the sun;
Flowers of the garden and the waste have blown
And withered; seeds have fallen upon the soil,
From bursting cells, and in their graves await
Their resurrection. Insects from the pools
Have filled the air awhile with humming wings,
That now are still for ever; painted moths
Have wandered the blue sky, and died again;
The mother-bird hath broken for her brood
Their prison shell, or shoved them from the nest,
Plumed for their earliest flight. In bright alcoves,
In woodland cottages with barky walls,
In noisome cells of the tumultuous town,
Mothers have clasped with joy the new-born babe.
Graves by the lonely forest, by the shore
Of rivers and of ocean, by the ways
Of the thronged city, have been hollowed out
And filled, and closed. This day hath parted friends
That ne'er before were parted; it hath knit
New friendships; it hath seen the maiden plight
Her faith, and trust her peace to him who long
Had wooed; and it hath heard, from lips which late
Were eloquent of love, the first harsh word,
That told the wedded one her peace was flown.
Farewell to the sweet sunshine! One glad day
Is added now to Childhood's merry days,
And one calm day to those of quiet Age.
Still the fleet hours run on; and as I lean,
Amid the thickening darkness, lamps are lit,
By those who watch the dead, and those who twine
Flowers for the bride. The mother from the eyes
Of her sick infant shades the painful light,
And sadly listens to his quick-drawn breath.

O thou great Movement of the Universe,
Or Change, or Flight of Time—for ye are one!
That bearest, silently, this visible scene
Into night's shadow and the streaming rays
Of starlight, whither art thou bearing me?

I feel the mighty current sweep me on,
Yet know not whither. Man foretells afar
The courses of the stars; the very hour
He knows when they shall darken or grow bright;
Yet doth the eclipse of Sorrow and of Death
Come unforewarned. Who next, of those I love,
Shall pass from life, or, sadder yet, shall fall
From virtue? Strife with foes, or bitterer strife
With friends, or shame and general scorn of men—
Which who can bear?—or the fierce rack of pain—
Lie they within my path? Or shall the years
Push me, with soft and inoffensive pace,
Into the stilly twilight of my age?
Or do the portals of another life
Even now, while I am glorying in my strength,
Impend around me? Oh! beyond that bourne,
In the vast cycle of being which begins
At that dread threshold, with what fairer forms
Shall the great law of change and progress clothe
Its workings? Gently—so have good men taught—
Gently, and without grief, the old shall glide
Into the new; the eternal flow of things,
Like a bright river of the fields of heaven,
Shall journey onward in perpetual peace.

A Dream

I had a dream—a strange, wild dream—
 Said a dear voice at early light;
And even yet its shadows seem
 To linger in my waking sight.

Earth, green with spring, and fresh with dew,
 And bright with morn, before me stood;
And airs just wakened softly blew
 On the young blossoms of the wood.

Birds sang within the sprouting shade,
 Bees hummed amid the whispering grass,
And children prattled as they played
 Beside the rivulet's dimpling glass.

Fast climbed the sun: the flowers were flown,
 There played no children in the glen;
For some were gone, and some were grown
 To blooming dames and bearded men.

'Twas noon, 'twas summer: I beheld
 Woods darkening in the flush of day,
And that bright rivulet spread and swelled,
 A mighty stream, with creek and bay.

And here was love, and there was strife,
 And mirthful shouts, and wrathful cries,
And strong men, struggling as for life,
 With knotted limbs and angry eyes.

Now stooped the sun—the shades grew thin;
 The rustling paths were piled with leaves,
And sunburnt groups were gathering in,
 From the shorn field, its fruits and sheaves.

The river heaved with sullen sounds;
 The chilly wind was sad with moans;
Black hearses passed, and burial-grounds
 Grew thick with monumental stones.

Still waned the day; the wind that chased
 The jagged clouds blew chiller yet;
The woods were stripped, the fields were waste,
 The wintry sun was near his set.

And of the young, and strong, and fair,
  A lonely remnant, gray and weak,
Lingered, and shivered to the air
  Of that bleak shore and water bleak,

Ah! age is drear, and death is cold!
  I turned to thee, for thou wert near,
And saw thee withered, bowed, and old,
  And woke all faint with sudden fear.

'Twas thus I heard the dreamer say,
  And bade her clear her clouded brow;
"For thou and I, since childhood's day,
  Have walked in such a dream till now.

"Watch we in calmness, as they rise,
  The changes of that rapid dream,
And note its lessons, till our eyes
  Shall open in the morning beam."

Song

These prairies glow with flowers,
  These groves are tall and fair,
The sweet lay of the mocking-bird
  Rings in the morning air;
And yet I pine to see
  My native hill once more,
And hear the sparrow's friendly chirp
  Beside its cottage-door.

And he, for whom I left
  My native hill and brook,
Alas, I sometimes think I trace
  A coldness in his look!
If I have lost his love,
  I know my heart will break;
And haply, they I left for him
  Will sorrow for my sake.

The Return of Youth

My friend, thou sorrowest for thy golden prime,
  For thy fair youthful years too swift of flight;
Thou musest, with wet eyes, upon the time
  Of cheerful hopes that filled the world with light—
Years when thy heart was bold, thy hand was strong,
  And quick the thought that moved thy tongue to speak,
And willing faith was thine, and scorn of wrong
  Summoned the sudden crimson to thy cheek.

Thou lookest forward on the coming days,
  Shuddering to feel their shadow o'er thee creep;
A path, thick-set with changes and decays,
  Slopes downward to the place of common sleep;
And they who walked with thee in life's first stage,
  Leave one by one thy side, and, waiting near,
Thou seest the sad companions of thy age—
  Dull love of rest, and weariness and fear.

Yet grieve thou not, nor think thy youth is gone,
  Nor deem that glorious season e'er could die.
Thy pleasant youth, a little while withdrawn,
  Waits on the horizon of a brighter sky;
Waits, like the morn, that folds her wings and hides
  Till the slow stars bring back her dawning hour;
Waits, like the vanished spring, that slumbering bides
  Her own sweet time to waken bud and flower.

There shall he welcome thee, when thou shalt stand
  On his bright morning hills, with smiles more sweet
Than when at first he took thee by the hand,
  Through the fair earth to lead thy tender feet.
He shall bring back, but brighter, broader still,
  Life's early glory to thine eyes again,
Shall clothe thy spirit with new strength, and fill
  Thy leaping heart with warmer love than then.

Hast thou not glimpses, in the twilight here,
  Of mountains where immortal morn prevails?
Comes there not, through the silence, to thine ear
  A gentle rustling of the morning gales;
A murmur, wafted from that glorious shore,
  Of streams that water banks forever fair,
And voices of the loved ones gone before,
  More musical in that celestial air?

A Hymn of the Sea

The sea is mighty, but a mightier sways
His restless billows. Thou, whose hands have scooped
His boundless gulfs and built his shore, thy breath,
That moved in the beginning o'er his face,
Moves o'er it evermore. The obedient waves
To its strong motion roll, and rise and fall.
Still from that realm of rain thy cloud goes up,
As at the first, to water the great earth,
And keep her valleys green. A hundred realms
Watch its broad shadow warping on the wind,
And in the dropping shower, with gladness hear
Thy promise of the harvest. I look forth
Over the boundless blue, where joyously
The bright crests of innumerable waves
Glance to the sun at once, as when the hands
Of a great multitude are upward flung
In acclamation. I behold the ships
Gliding from cape to cape, from isle to isle,
Or stemming toward far lands, or hastening home
From the Old World. It is thy friendly breeze
That bears them, with the riches of the land,
And treasure of dear lives, till, in the port,
The shouting seaman climbs and furls the sail.

But who shall bide thy tempest, who shall face
The blast that wakes the fury of the sea?
O God! thy justice makes the world turn pale,
When on the armèd fleet, that royally
Bears down the surges, carrying war, to smite
Some city, or invade some thoughtless realm,
Descends the fierce tornado. The vast hulks
Are whirled like chaff upon the waves; the sails
Fly, rent like webs of gossamer; the masts
Are snapped asunder; downward from the decks,
Downward are slung, into the fathomless gulf,
Their cruel engines; and their hosts, arrayed
In trappings of the battle-field, are whelmed
By whirlpools, or dashed dead upon the rocks.
Then stand the nations still with awe, and pause,
A moment, from the bloody work of war.

These restless surges eat away the shores
Of earth's old continents; the fertile plain
Welters in shallows, headlands crumble down,

And the tide drifts the sea-sand in the streets
Of the drowned city. Thou, meanwhile, afar
In the green chambers of the middle sea,
Where broadest spread the waters and the line
Sinks deepest, while no eye beholds thy work,
Creator! thou dost teach the coral-worm
To lay his mighty reefs. From age to age,
He builds beneath the waters, till, at last,
His bulwarks overtop the brine, and check
The long-wave rolling from the southern pole
To break upon Japan. Thou bidd'st the fires,
That smoulder under ocean, heave on high
The new-made mountains, and uplift their peaks,
A place of refuge for the storm-driven bird.
The birds and wafting billows plant the rifts
With herb and tree; sweet fountains gush; sweet airs
Ripple the living lakes that, fringed with flowers,
Are gathered in the hollows. Thou dost look
On thy creation and pronounce it good.
Its valleys, glorious in their summer green,
Praise thee in silent beauty, and its woods,
Swept by the murmuring winds of ocean, join
The murmuring shores in a perpetual hymn.

The Antiquity of Freedom

Here are old trees, tall oaks, and gnarlèd pines,
That stream with gray-green mosses; here the ground
Was never trenched by spade, and flowers spring up
Unsown, and die ungathered. It is sweet
To linger here, among the flitting birds
And leaping squirrels, wandering brooks, and winds
That shake the leaves, and scatter, as they pass,
A fragrance from the cedars, thickly set
With pale-blue berries. In these peaceful shades—
Peaceful, unpruned, immeasurably old—
My thoughts go up the long dim path of years,
Back to the earliest days of liberty.

O Freedom! thou art not, as poets dream,
A fair young girl, with light and delicate limbs,
And wavy tresses gushing from the cap
With which the Roman master crowned his slave
When he took off the gyves. A bearded man,
Armed to the teeth, art thou; one mailèd hand
Grasps the broad shield, and one the sword; thy brow,
Glorious in beauty though it be, is scarred
With tokens of old wars; thy massive limbs
Are strong with struggling. Power at thee has launched
His bolts, and with his lightnings smitten thee;
They could not quench the life thou hast from heaven;
Merciless Power has dug thy dungeon deep,
And his swart armorers, by a thousand fires,
Have forged thy chain; yet, while he deems thee bound,
The links are shivered, and the prison-walls
Fall outward; terribly thou springest forth,
As springs the flame above a burning pile,
And shoutest to the nations, who return
Thy shoutings, while the pale oppressor flies.

Thy birthright was not given by human hands:
Thou wert twin-born with man. In pleasant fields,
While yet our race was few, thou sat'st with him,
To tend the quiet flock and watch the stars,
And teach the reed to utter simple airs.
Thou by his side, amid the tangled wood,
Didst war upon the panther and the wolf,
His only foes; and thou with him didst draw
The earliest furrow on the mountain-side,
Soft with the deluge. Tyranny himself,

Thy enemy, although of reverend look,
Hoary with many years, and far obeyed,
Is later born than thou; and as he meets
The grave defiance of thine elder eye,
The usurper trembles in his fastnesses.

Thou shalt wax stronger with the lapse of years,
But he shall fade into a feebler age—
Feebler, yet subtler. He shall weave his snares,
And spring them on thy careless steps, and clap
His withered hands, and from their ambush call
His hordes to fall upon thee. He shall send
Quaint maskers, wearing fair and gallant forms
To catch thy gaze, and uttering graceful words
To charm thy ear; while his sly imps, by stealth,
Twine round thee threads of steel, light thread on thread,
That grow to fetters; or bind down thy arms
With chains concealed in chaplets. Oh! not yet
Mayst thou unbrace thy corslet, nor lay by
Thy sword; nor yet, O Freedom! close thy lids
In slumber; for thine enemy never sleeps,
And thou must watch and combat till the day
Of the new earth and heaven. But wouldst thou rest
Awhile from tumult and the frauds of men,
These old and friendly solitudes invite
Thy visit. They, while yet the forest-trees
Were young upon the unviolated earth,
And yet the moss-stains on the rock were new,
Beheld thy glorious childhood, and rejoiced.

The Maiden's Sorrow

Seven long years has the desert rain
Dropped on the clods that hide thy face;
Seven long years of sorrow and pain
I have thought of thy burial-place;

Thought of thy fate in the distant West,
Dying with none that loved thee near,
They who flung the earth on thy breast
Turned from the spot without a tear.

There, I think, on that lonely grave,
Violets spring in the soft May shower;
There, in the summer breezes, wave
Crimson phlox and moccasin-flower.

There the turtles alight, and there
Feeds with her fawn the timid doe;
There, when the winter woods are bare,
Walks the wolf on the crackling snow.

Soon wilt thou wipe my tears away;
All my task upon earth is done;
My poor father, old and gray,
Slumbers beneath the churchyard stone.

In the dreams of my lonely bed,
Ever thy form before me seems,
All night long I talk with the dead,
All day long I think of my dreams.

This deep wound that bleeds and aches,
This long pain, a sleepless pain—
When the Father my spirit takes,
I shall feel it no more again.

The Waning Moon

I've watched too late; the morn is near;
  One look at God's broad silent sky!
Oh, hopes and wishes vainly dear,
  How in your very strength ye die!
Even while your glow is on the cheek,
  And scarce the high pursuit begun,
The heart grows faint, the hand grows weak,
  The task of life is left undone.

See where, upon the horizon's brim,
  Lies the still cloud in gloomy bars;
The waning moon, all pale and dim,
  Goes up amid the eternal stars.
Late, in a flood of tender light,
  She floated through the ethereal blue,
A softer sun, that shone all night
  Upon the gathering beads of dew.

And still thou wanest, pallid moon!
  The encroaching shadow grows apace;
Heaven's everlasting watchers soon
  Shall see thee blotted from thy place.
Oh, Night's dethroned and crownless queen!
  Well may thy sad, expiring ray
Be shed on those whose eyes have seen
  Hope's glorious visions fade away.

Shine thou for forms that once were bright,
  For sages in the mind's eclipse,
For those whose words were spells of might,
  But falter now on stammering lips!
In thy decaying beam there lies
  Full many a grave on hill and plain,
Of those who closed their dying eyes
  In grief that they had lived in vain.

Another night, and thou among
  The spheres of heaven shalt cease to shine,
All rayless in the glittering throng
  Whose lustre late was quenched in thine.
Yet soon a new and tender light
  From out thy darkened orb shall beam,
And broaden till it shines all night
  On glistening dew and glimmering stream.

Noon

[FROM AN UNFINISHED POEM]

'Tis noon. At noon the Hebrew bowed the knee
And worshipped, while the husbandmen withdrew
From the scorched field, and the wayfaring man
Grew faint, and turned aside by bubbling fount,
Or rested in the shadow of the palm.

I, too, amid the overflow of day,
Behold the power which wields and cherishes
The frame of Nature. From this brow of rock
That overlooks the Hudson's western marge,
I gaze upon the long array of groves,
The piles and gulfs of verdure drinking in
The grateful heats. They love the fiery sun;
Their broadening leaves grow glossier, and their sprays
Climb as he looks upon them. In the midst,
The swelling river, into his green gulfs,
Unshadowed save by passing sails above,
Takes the redundant glory, and enjoys
The summer in his chilly bed. Coy flowers,
That would not open in the early light,
Push back their plaited sheaths. The rivulet's pool,
That darkly quivered all the morning long
In the cool shade, now glimmers in the sun;
And o'er its surface shoots, and shoots again,
The glittering dragon-fly, and deep within
Run the brown water-beetles to and fro.

A silence, the brief sabbath of an hour,
Reigns o'er the fields; the laborer sits within
His dwelling; he has left his steers awhile,
Unyoked, to bite the herbage, and his dog
Sleeps stretched beside the door-stone in the shade.
Now the gray marmot, with uplifted paws,
No more sits listening by his den, but steals
Abroad, in safety, to the clover-field,
And crops its juicy blossoms. All the while
A ceaseless murmur from the populous town
Swells o'er these solitudes: a mingled sound
Of jarring wheels, and iron hoofs that clash
Upon the stony ways, and hammer-clang,
And creak of engines lifting ponderous bulks,
And calls and cries, and tread of eager feet,
Innumerable, hurrying to and fro.

[NOON]

Noon, in that mighty mart of nations, brings
No pause to toil and care. With early day
Began the tumult, and shall only cease
When midnight, hushing one by one the sounds
Of bustle, gathers the tired brood to rest.

Thus, in his feverish time, when love of gain
And luxury possess the hearts of men,
Thus is it with the noon of human life.
We, in our fervid manhood, in our strength
Of reason, we, with hurry, noise, and care,
Plan, toil, and strive, and pause not to refresh
Our spirits with the calm and beautiful
Of God's harmonious universe, that won
Our youthful wonder; pause not to inquire
Why we are here; and what the reverence
Man owes to man, and what the mystery
That links us to the greater world, beside
Whose borders we but hover for a space.

The Crowded Street

Let me move slowly through the street,
  Filled with an ever-shifting train,
Amid the sound of steps that beat
  The murmuring walks like autumn rain.

How fast the flitting figures come!
  The mild, the fierce, the stony face;
Some bright with thoughtless smiles, and some
  Where secret tears have left their trace.

They pass—to toil, to strife, to rest;
  To halls in which the feast is spread;
To chambers where the funeral guest
  In silence sits beside the dead.

And some to happy homes repair,
  Where children, pressing cheek to cheek,
With mute caresses shall declare
  The tenderness they cannot speak.

And some, who walk in calmness here,
  Shall shudder as they reach the door
Where one who made their dwelling dear,
  Its flower, its light, is seen no more.

Youth, with pale cheek and slender frame,
  And dreams of greatness in thine eye!
Go'st thou to build an early name,
  Or early in the task to die?

Keen son of trade, with eager brow!
  Who is now fluttering in thy snare?
Thy golden fortunes, tower they now,
  Or melt the glittering spires in air?

Who of this crowd to-night shall tread
  The dance till daylight gleam again?
Who sorrow o'er the untimely dead?
  Who writhe in throes of mortal pain?

Some, famine-struck, shall think how long
  The cold dark hours, how slow the light;
And some, who flaunt amid the throng,
  Shall hide in dens of shame to-night.

Each, where his tasks or pleasures call,
They pass, and heed each other not.
There is who heeds, who holds them all,
In His large love and boundless thought.

These struggling tides of life that seem
In wayward, aimless course to tend,
Are eddies of the mighty stream
That rolls to its appointed end.

The Mother's Hymn

Lord, who ordainest for mankind
Benignant toils and tender cares!
We thank Thee for the ties that bind
The mother to the child she bears.

We thank Thee for the hopes that rise,
Within her heart, as, day by day,
The dawning soul, from those young eyes,
Looks, with a clearer, steadier ray.

And grateful for the blessing given
With that dear infant on her knee,
She trains the eye to look to heaven,
The voice to lisp a prayer to Thee.

Such thanks the blessed Mary gave,
When, from her lap, the Holy Child,
Sent from on high to seek and save
The lost of earth, looked up and smiled.

All-Gracious! grant, to those that bear
A mother's charge, the strength and light
To lead the steps that own their care
In ways of Love, and Truth, and Right.

My Autumn Walk

On woodlands ruddy with autumn
  The amber sunshine lies;
I look on the beauty round me,
  And tears come into my eyes.
For the wind that sweeps the meadows
  Blows out of the far Southwest,
Where our gallant men are fighting,
  And the gallant dead are at rest.

The golden-rod is leaning,
  And the purple aster waves
In a breeze from the land of battles,
  A breath from the land of graves.
Full fast the leaves are dropping
  Before that wandering breath;
As fast, on the field of battle,
  Our brethren fall in death.

Beautiful over my pathway
  The forest spoils are shed;
They are spotting the grassy hillocks
  With purple and gold and red.
Beautiful is the death-sleep
  Of those who bravely fight
In their country's holy quarrel,
  And perish for the Right.

But who shall comfort the living,
The light of whose homes is gone:
The bride that, early widowed,
Lives broken-hearted on;
The matron whose sons are lying
In graves on a distant shore;
The maiden, whose promised husband
Comes back from the war no more?

I look on the peaceful dwellings
Whose windows glimmer in sight,
With croft and garden and orchard,
That bask in the mellow light;
And I know that, when our couriers
With news of victory come,
They will bring a bitter message
Of hopeless grief to some.

Again I turn to the woodlands,
And shudder as I see
The mock-grape's blood-red banner
Hung out on the cedar-tree;
And I think of days of slaughter,
And the night-sky red with flames,
On the Chattahoochee's meadows,
And the wasted banks of the James.

Oh, for the fresh spring-season,
When the groves are in their prime;
And far away in the future
Is the frosty autumn-time!
Oh, for that better season,
When the pride of the foe shall yield,
And the hosts of God and Freedom
March back from the well-won field;

And the matron shall clasp her first-born
With tears of joy and pride;
And the scarred and war-worn lover
Shall claim his promised bride!
The leaves are swept from the branches;
But the living buds are there,
With folded flower and foliage,
To sprout in a kinder air.

The Conqueror's Grave

Within this lowly grave a Conqueror lies,
   And yet the monument proclaims it not,
Nor round the sleeper's name hath chisel wrought
   The emblems of a fame that never dies,—
Ivy and amaranth, in a graceful sheaf,
Twined with the laurel's fair, imperial leaf.
         A simple name alone,
         To the great world unknown,
Is graven here, and wild-flowers, rising round,
Meek meadow-sweet and violets of the ground,
   Lean lovingly against the humble stone.

Here, in the quiet earth, they laid apart
   No man of iron mould and bloody hands,
Who sought to wreak upon the cowering lands
   The passions that consumed his restless heart;
But one of tender spirit and delicate frame,
         Gentlest, in mien and mind,
         Of gentle womankind,
Timidly shrinking from the breath of blame:
One in whose eyes the smile of kindness made
   Its haunt, like flowers by sunny brooks in May,
Yet, at the thought of others' pain, a shade
Of sweeter sadness chased the smile away.

Nor deem that when the hand that moulders here
Was raised in menace, realms were chilled with fear,
   And armies mustered at the sign, as when
Clouds rise on clouds before the rainy East—
   Gray captains leading bands of veteran men
And fiery youths to be the vulture's feast.
Not thus were waged the mighty wars that gave
The victory to her who fills this grave:
         Alone her task was wrought,
         Alone the battle fought;
Through that long strike her constant hope was staid
On God alone, nor looked for other aid.

She met the hosts of Sorrow with a look
   That altered not beneath the frown they wore,
And soon the lowering brood were tamed, and took,
   Meekly, her gentle rule, and frowned no more.
Her soft hand put aside the assaults of wrath,

And calmly broke in twain
The fiery shafts of pain,
And rent the nets of passion from her path.
By that victorious hand despair was slain.
With love she vanquished hate and overcame
Evil with good, in her Great Master's name.

Her glory is not of this shadowy state,
Glory that with the fleeting season dies;
But when she entered at the sapphire gate
What joy was radiant in celestial eyes!
How heaven's bright depths with sounding welcomes rung
And flowers of heaven by shining hands were flung!
And He who, long before,
Pain, scorn, and sorrow bore,
The Mighty Sufferer, with aspect sweet,
Smiled on the timid stranger from his seat;
He who returning, glorious, from the grave,
Dragged Death, disarmed, in chains, a crouching slave.

See, as I linger here, the sun grows low;
Cool airs are murmuring that the night is near.
Oh, gentle sleeper, from thy grave I go
Consoled though sad, in hope and yet in fear.
Brief is the time, I know,
The warfare scarce begun;
Yet all may win the triumphs thou hast won.
Still flows the fount whose waters strengthened thee,
The victors' names are yet too few to fill
Heaven's mighty roll; the glorious armory,
That ministered to thee, is open still.

A Rain-Dream

These strifes, these tumults of the noisy world,
Where Fraud, the coward, tracks his prey by stealth,
And Strength, the ruffian, glories in his guilt,
Oppress the heart with sadness. Oh, my friend,
In what serener mood we look upon
The gloomiest aspects of the elements
Among the woods and fields! Let us awhile,
As the slow wind is rolling up the storm,
In fancy leave this maze of dusty streets,
Forever shaken by the importunate jar
Of commerce, and upon the darkening air
Look from the shelter of our rural home.
Who is not awed that listens to the Rain,
Sending his voice before him? Mighty Rain!
The upland steeps are shrouded by thy mists;
Thy shadow fills the hollow vale; the pools
No longer glimmer, and the silver streams
Darken to veins of lead at thy approach.
O mighty Rain; already thou art here;
And every roof is beaten by thy streams,
And, as thou passest, every glassy spring
Grows rough, and every leaf in all the woods
Is struck, and quivers. All the hill-tops slake
Their thirst from thee; a thousand languishing fields,
A thousand fainting gardens, are refreshed;
A thousand idle rivulets start to speed,
And with the graver murmur of the storm
Blend their light voices as they hurry on.
Thou fill'st the circle of the atmosphere
Alone; there is no living thing abroad,
No bird to wing the air nor beast to walk
The field; the squirrel in the forest seeks
His hollow tree; the marmot of the field
Has scampered to his den; the butterfly
Hides under her broad leaf; the insect crowds,
That made the sunshine populous, lie close
In their mysterious shelters, whence the sun
Will summon them again. The mighty Rain
Holds the vast empire of the sky alone.
I shut my eyes, and see, as in a dream,
The friendly clouds drop down spring violets
And summer columbines, and all the flowers
That tuft the woodland floor, or overarch
The streamlet:—spiky grass for genial June,

Brown harvests for the waiting husbandman,
And for the woods a deluge of fresh leaves.
I see these myriad drops that slake the dust,
Gathered in glorious streams, or rolling blue
In billows on the lake or on the deep,
And bearing navies. I behold them change
To threads of crystal as they sink in earth
And leave its stains behind, to rise again
In pleasant nooks of verdure, where the child,
Thirsty with play, in both his little hands
Shall take the cool, clear water, raising it
To wet his pretty lips. To-morrow noon
How proudly will the water-lily ride
The brimming pool, o'erlooking, like a queen
Her circle of broad leaves! In lonely wastes,
When next the sunshine makes them beautiful,
Gay troops of butterflies shall light to drink
At the replenished hollows of the rock.
Now slowly falls the dull blank night, and still,
All through the starless hours, the mighty Rain
Smites with perpetual sound the forest-leaves,
And beats the matted grass, and still the earth
Drinks the unstinted bounty of the clouds—
Drinks for her cottage wells, her woodland brooks—
Drinks for the springing trout, the toiling bee,
And brooding bird—drinks for her tender flowers,
Tall oaks, and all the herbage of her hills.
A melancholy sound is in the air,
A deep sigh in the distance, a shrill wail
Around my dwelling. 'Tis the Wind of night;
A lonely wanderer between earth and cloud,
In the black shadow and the chilly mist,
Along the streaming mountain-side, and through
The dripping woods, and o'er the plashy fields,
Roaming and sorrowing still, like one who makes
The journey of life alone, and nowhere meets
A welcome or a friend, and still goes on
In darkness. Yet a while, a little while,
And he shall toss the glittering leaves in play,
And dally with the flowers, and gayly lift
The slender herbs, pressed low by weight of rain,
And drive, in joyous triumph, through the sky,
White clouds, the laggard remnants of the storm.

An Invitation to the Country

Already, close by our summer dwelling,
  The Easter sparrow repeats her song;
A merry warbler, she chides the blossoms—
  The idle blossoms that sleep so long.

The bluebird chants, from the elm's long branches,
  A hymn to welcome the budding year.
The south wind wanders from field to forest,
  And softly whispers, "The Spring is here."

Come, daughter mine, from the gloomy city,
  Before those lays from the elm have ceased;
The violet breathes, by our door, as sweetly
  As in the air of her native East.

Though many a flower in the wood is waking,
  The daffodil is our doorside queen;
She pushes upward the sward already,
  To spot with sunshine the early green.

No lays so joyous as these are warbled
  From wiry prison in maiden's bower;
No pampered bloom of the green-house chamber
  Has half the charm of the lawn's first flower.

Yet these sweet sounds of the early season,
  And these fair sights of its sunny days,
Are only sweet when we fondly listen,
  And only fair when we fondly gaze.

There is no glory in star or blossom
  Till looked upon by a loving eye;
There is no fragrance in April breezes
  Till breathed with joy as they wander by.

Come, Julia dear, for the sprouting willows,
  The opening flowers, and the gleaming brooks,
And hollows, green in the sun, are waiting
  Their dower of beauty from thy glad looks.

The Wind and Stream

A brook came stealing from the ground;
  You scarcely saw its silvery gleam
Among the herbs that hung around
  The borders of the winding stream,
The pretty stream, the placid stream,
The softly-gliding, bashful stream.

A breeze came wandering from the sky,
  Light as the whispers of a dream;
He put the o'erhanging grasses by,
  And softly stooped to kiss the stream,
The pretty stream, the flattered stream,
The shy, yet unreluctant stream.

The water, as the wind passed o'er,
  Shot upward many a glancing beam,
Dimpled and quivered more and more,
  And tripped along, a livelier stream,
The flattered stream, the simpering stream,
The fond, delighted, silly stream.

Away the airy wanderer flew
  To where the fields with blossoms teem,
To sparkling springs and rivers blue,
  And left alone that little stream,
The flattered stream, the cheated stream,
The sad, forsaken, lonely stream.

That careless wind came never back;
  He wanders yet the fields, I deem,
But, on its melancholy track,
  Complaining went that little stream,
The cheated stream, the hopeless stream,
The ever-murmuring, mourning stream.

A Song for New-Year's Eve

Stay yet, my friends, a moment stay—
Stay till the good old year,
So long companion of our way,
Shakes hands, and leaves us here.
Oh stay, oh stay,
One little hour, and then away.

The year, whose hopes were high and strong,
Has now no hopes to wake;
Yet one hour more of jest and song
For his familiar sake.
Oh stay, oh stay,
One mirthful hour, and then away.

The kindly year, his liberal hands
Have lavished all his store.
And shall we turn from where he stands,
Because he gives no more?
Oh stay, oh stay,
One grateful hour, and then away.

Days brightly came and calmly went,
While yet he was our guest;
How cheerfully the week was spent!
How sweet the seventh day's rest!
Oh stay, oh stay,
One golden hour, and then away.

Dear friends were with us, some who sleep
Beneath the coffin-lid:
What pleasant memories we keep
Of all they said and did!
Oh stay, oh stay,
One tender hour, and then away.

Even while we sing, he smiles his last,
And leaves our sphere behind.
The good old year is with the past;
Oh be the new as kind!
Oh stay, oh stay,
One parting strain, and then away.

A Sick-Bed

Long hast thou watched my bed,
And smoothed the pillow oft
For this poor, aching head,
With touches kind and soft.

Oh! smooth it yet again,
As softly as before;
Once—only once—and then
I need thy hand no more.

Yet here I may not stay,
Where I so long have lain,
Through many a restless day
And many a night of pain.

But bear me gently forth
Beneath the open sky,
Where, on the pleasant earth,
Till night the sunbeams lie.

There, through the coming days,
I shall not look to thee
My weary side to raise,
And shift it tenderly.

There sweetly shall I sleep;
Nor wilt thou need to bring
And put to my hot lip
Cool water from the spring;

Nor wet the kerchief laid
Upon my burning brow;
Nor from my eyeballs shade
The light that wounds them now;

Nor watch that none shall tread,
With noisy footstep, nigh;
Nor listen by my bed,
To hear my faintest sigh,

And feign a look of cheer,
And words of comfort speak,
Yet turn to hide the tear
That gathers on thy cheek.

[A SICK-BED]

Beside me, where I rest,
  Thy loving hands will set
The flowers that please me best—
  Moss-rose and violet.

Then to the sleep I crave
  Resign me, till I see
The face of Him who gave
  His life for thee and me.

Yet, with the setting sun,
  Come, now and then, at eve,
And think of me as one
  For whom thou shouldst not grieve;

Who, when the kind release
  From sin and suffering came,
Passed to the appointed peace
  In murmuring thy name.

Leave at my side a space,
  Where thou shalt come, at last,
To find a resting-place,
  When many years are past.

The New and the Old

New are the leaves on the oaken spray,
  New the blades of the silky grass;
Flowers, that were buds but yesterday,
  Peep from the ground where'er I pass.

These gay idlers, the butterflies,
  Broke, to-day, from their winter shroud;
These light airs, that winnow the skies,
  Blow, just born, from the soft, white cloud.

Gushing fresh in the little streams,
  What a prattle the waters make!
Even the sun, with his tender beams,
  Seems as young as the flowers they wake.

Children are wading, with cheerful cries,
  In the shoals of the sparkling brook;
Laughing maidens, with soft, young eyes,
  Walk or sit in the shady nook.

What am I doing, thus alone,
  In the glory of Nature here,
Silver-haired, like a snow-flake thrown
  On the greens of the springing year?

Only for brows unploughed by care,
  Eyes that glisten with hope and mirth,
Cheeks unwrinkled, and unblanched hair,
  Shines this holiday of the earth.

Under the grass, with the clammy clay,
  Lie in darkness the last year's flowers,
Born of a light that has passed away,
  Dews long dried and forgotten showers.

"Under the grass is the fitting home,"
  So they whisper, "for such as thou,
When the winter of life is come,
  Chilling the blood, and frosting the brow."

Robert of Lincoln

Merrily swinging on brier and weed,
   Near to the nest of his little dame,
Over the mountain-side or mead,
   Robert of Lincoln is telling his name:
      Bob-o'-link, bob-o'-link,
      Spink, spank, spink;
Snug and safe is that nest of ours,
Hidden among the summer flowers.
         Chee, chee, chee.

Robert of Lincoln is gayly drest,
   Wearing a bright black wedding-coat;
White are his shoulders and white his crest.
   Hear him call in his merry note:
      Bob-o'-link, bob-o'-link,
      Spink, spank, spink;
Look, what a nice new coat is mine,
Sure there was never a bird so fine.
         Chee, chee, chee.

Robert of Lincoln's Quaker wife,
   Pretty and quiet, with plain brown wings,
Passing at home a patient life,
   Broods in the grass while her husband sings:
      Bob-o'-link, bob-o'-link,
      Spink, spank, spink;
Brood, kind creature; you need not fear
Thieves and robbers while I am here.
         Chee, chee, chee.

Modest and shy as a nun is she;
   One weak chirp is her only note.
Braggart and prince of braggarts is he,
   Pouring boasts from his little throat:
      Bob-o'-link, bob-o'-link,
      Spink, spank, spink;
Never was I afraid of man;
Catch me, cowardly knaves, if you can!
         Chee, chee, chee.

Six white eggs on a bed of hay,
   Flecked with purple, a pretty sight!
There as the mother sits all day,
   Robert is singing with all his might:

Bob-o'-link, bob-o'-link,
Spink, spank, spink;
Nice good wife, that never goes out,
Keeping house while I frolic about.
Chee, chee, chee.

Soon as the little ones chip the shell,
Six wide mouths are open for food;
Robert of Lincoln bestirs him well,
Gathering seeds for the hungry brood.
Bob-o'-link, bob-o'-link,
Spink, spank, spink;
This new life is likely to be
Hard for a gay young fellow like me.
Chee, chee, chee.

Robert of Lincoln at length is made
Sober with work, and silent with care;
Off is his holiday garment laid,
Half forgotten that merry air:
Bob-o'-link, bob-o'-link,
Spink, spank, spink;
Nobody knows but my mate and I
Where our nest and our nestlings lie.
Chee, chee, chee.

Summer wanes; the children are grown;
  Fun and frolic no more he knows;
Robert of Lincoln's a humdrum crone;
  Off he flies, and we sing as he goes:
      Bob-o'-link, bob-o'-link,
      Spink, spank, spink;
When you can pipe that merry old strain,
Robert of Lincoln, come back again.
            Chee, chee, chee.

"*Oh Mother of a Mighty Race*"

Oh mother of a mighty race,
Yet lovely in thy youthful grace!
The elder dames, thy haughty peers,
Admire and hate thy blooming years.
With words of shame
And taunts of scorn they join thy name.

For on thy cheeks the glow is spread
That tints thy morning hills with red;
Thy step—the wild-deer's rustling feet
Within thy woods are not more fleet;
Thy hopeful eye
Is bright as thine own sunny sky.

Ay, let them rail—those haughty ones,
While safe thou dwellest with thy sons.
They do not know how loved thou art,
How many a fond and fearless heart
Would rise to throw
Its life between thee and the foe.

They know not, in their hate and pride,
What virtues with thy children bide;
How true, how good, thy graceful maids
Make bright, like flowers, the valley-shades;
What generous men
Spring, like thine oaks, by hill and glen;—

What cordial welcomes greet the guest
By thy lone rivers of the West;
How faith is kept, and truth revered,
And man is loved, and God is feared,
In woodland homes,
And where the ocean border foams.

There's freedom at thy gates and rest
For Earth's down-trodden and opprest,
A shelter for the hunted head,
For the starved laborer toil and bread.
Power, at thy bounds,
Stops and calls back his baffled hounds.

Oh, fair young mother! on thy brow
Shall sit a nobler grace than now.

["OH MOTHER OF A MIGHTY RACE"]

Deep in the brightness of the skies
The thronging years in glory rise,
And, as they fleet,
Drop strength and riches at thy feet.

Thine eye, with every coming hour,
Shall brighten, and thy form shall tower;
And when thy sisters, elder born,
Would brand thy name with words of scorn,
Before thine eye,
Upon their lips the taunt shall die.

The Unknown Way

A burning sky is o'er me,
  The sands beneath me glow,
As onward, onward, wearily,
  In the sultry morn I go.

From the dusty path there opens,
  Eastward, an unknown way;
Above its windings, pleasantly,
  The woodland branches play.

A silvery brook comes stealing
  From the shadow of its trees,
Where slender herbs of the forest stoop
  Before the entering breeze.

Along those pleasant windings
  I would my journey lay,
Where the shade is cool and the dew of night
  Is not yet dried away.

Path of the flowery woodland!
  Oh whither dost thou lead,
Wandering by grassy orchard-grounds,
  Or by the open mead?

Goest thou by nestling cottage?
  Goest thou by stately hall,
Where the broad elm droops, a leafy dome,
  And woodbines flaunt on the wall?

By steeps where children gather
  Flowers of the yet fresh year?
By lonely walks where lovers stray
  Till the tender stars appear?

Or haply dost thou linger
  On barren plains and bare,
Or clamber the bald mountain-side
  Into the thinner air?—

Where they who journey upward
  Walk in a weary track,
And oft upon the shady vale
  With longing eyes look back?

[THE UNKNOWN WAY]

I hear a solemn murmur,
  And, listening to the sound,
I know the voice of the mighty Sea,
  Beating his pebbly bound.

Dost thou, oh path of the woodland!
  End where those waters roar,
Like human life, on a trackless beach,
  With a boundless Sea before?

The Voice of Autumn

There comes, from yonder height,
  A soft repining sound,
Where forest-leaves are bright,
And fall, like flakes of light,
      To the ground.

It is the autumn breeze,
  That, lightly floating on,
Just skims the weedy leas,
Just stirs the glowing trees,
      And is gone.

He moans by sedgy brook,
  And visits, with a sigh,
The last pale flowers that look,
From out their sunny nook,
      At the sky.

O'er shouting children flies
  That light October wind,
And, kissing cheeks and eyes,
He leaves their merry cries
      Far behind,

And wanders on to make
  That soft uneasy sound
By distant wood and lake,
Where distant fountains break
      From the ground.

No bower where maidens dwell
  Can win a moment's stay;
Nor fair untrodden dell;
He sweeps the upland swell,
      And away!

Mourn'st thou thy homeless state?
  O soft, repining wind!
That early seek'st and late
The rest it is thy fate
      Not to find.

Not on the mountain's breast,
  Not on the ocean's shore,

In all the East and West:
The wind that stops to rest
Is no more.

By valleys, woods, and springs,
No wonder thou shouldst grieve
For all the glorious things
Thou touchest with thy wings
And must leave.

The Snow-Shower

Stand here by my side and turn, I pray,
  On the lake below thy gentle eyes;
The clouds hang over it, heavy and gray,
  And dark and silent the water lies;
And out of that frozen mist the snow
In wavering flakes begins to flow;
          Flake after flake
They sink in the dark and silent lake.

See how in a living swarm they come
  From the chambers beyond that misty veil;
Some hover awhile in air, and some
  Rush prone from the sky like summer hail.
All, dropping swiftly or settling slow,
Meet, and are still in the depths below;
          Flake after flake
Dissolved in the dark and silent lake.

Here delicate snow-stars, out of the cloud,
  Come floating downward in airy play,
Like spangles dropped from the glistening crowd
  That whiten by night the milky way;
There broader and burlier masses fall;
The sullen water buries them all—
          Flake after flake—
All drowned in the dark and silent lake.

And some, as on tender wings they glide
  From their chilly birth-cloud, dim and gray,
Are joined in their fall, and, side by side,
  Come clinging along their unsteady way;
As friend with friend, or husband with wife,
Makes hand in hand the passage of life;
          Each mated flake
Soon sinks in the dark and silent lake.

Lo! while we are gazing, in swifter haste
  Stream down the snows, till the air is white,
As, myriads by myriads madly chased,
  They fling themselves from their shadowy height.
The fair, frail creatures of middle sky,
What speed they make, with their grave so nigh;
          Flake after flake,
To lie in the dark and silent lake!

I see in thy gentle eyes a tear;
  They turn to me in sorrowful thought;
Thou thinkest of friends, the good and dear,
  Who were for a time, and now are not;
Like these fair children of cloud and frost,
That glisten a moment and then are lost,
          Flake after flake—
All lost in the dark and silent lake.

Yet look again, for the clouds divide;
  A gleam of blue on the water lies;
And far away, on the mountain-side,
  A sunbeam falls from the opening skies,
But the hurrying host that flew between
The cloud and the water, no more is seen;
          Flake after flake,
At rest in the dark and silent lake.

The Twenty-Seventh of March

Oh, gentle one, thy birthday sun should rise
Amid a chorus of the merriest birds
That ever sang the stars out of the sky
In a June morning. Rivulets should send
A voice of gladness from their winding paths,
Deep in o'erarching grass, where playful winds,
Stirring the loaded stems, should shower the dew
Upon the grassy water. Newly-blown
Roses, by thousands, to the garden-walks
Should tempt the loitering moth and diligent bee.
The longest, brightest day in all the year
Should be the day on which thy cheerful eyes
First opened on the earth, to make thy haunts
Fairer and gladder for thy kindly looks.

Thus might a poet say; but I must bring
A birthday offering of an humbler strain,
And yet it may not please thee less. I hold
That 'twas the fitting season for thy birth
When March, just ready to depart, begins
To soften into April. Then we have
The delicatest and most welcome flowers,
And yet they take least heed of bitter wind
And lowering sky. The periwinkle then,
In an hour's sunshine, lifts her azure blooms
Beside the cottage-door; within the woods
Tufts of ground-laurel, creeping underneath
The leaves of the last summer, send their sweets
Up to the chilly air, and, by the oak,
The squirrel-cups, a graceful company,
Hide in their bells, a soft aërial blue—
Sweet flowers, that nestle in the humblest nooks,
And yet within whose smallest bud is wrapped
A world of promise! Still the north wind breathes
His frost, and still the sky sheds snow and sleet;
Yet ever, when the sun looks forth again,
The flowers smile up to him from their low seats.

Well hast thou borne the bleak March day of life.
Its storms and its keen winds to thee have been
Most kindly tempered, and through all its gloom
There has been warmth and sunshine in thy heart;
The griefs of life to thee have been like snows,
That light upon the fields in early spring,

Making them greener. In its milder hours,
The smile of this pale season, thou hast seen
The glorious bloom of June, and in the note
Of early bird, that comes a messenger
From climes of endless verdure, thou hast heard
The choir that fills the summer woods with song.

Now be the hours that yet remain to thee
Stormy or sunny, sympathy and love,
That inextinguishably dwell within
Thy heart, shall give a beauty and a light
To the most desolate moments, like the glow
Of a bright fireside in the wildest day;
And kindly words and offices of good
Shall wait upon thy steps, as thou goest on,
Where God shall lead thee, till thou reach the gates
Of a more genial season, and thy path
Be lost to human eye among the bowers
And living fountains of a brighter land.

The Night Journey of a River

Oh River, gentle River! gliding on
In silence underneath the starless sky!
Thine is a ministry that never rests
Even while the living slumber. For a time
The meddler, man, hath left the elements
In peace; the ploughman breaks the clods no more;
The miner labors not, with steel and fire,
To rend the rock, and he that hews the stone,
And he that fells the forest, he that guides
The loaded wain, and the poor animal
That drags it, have forgotten, for a time,
Their toils, and share the quiet of the earth.

Thou pausest not in thine allotted task,
Oh darkling River! Through the night I hear
Thy wavelets rippling on the pebbly beach;
I hear thy current stir the rustling sedge,
That skirts thy bed; thou intermittest not
Thine everlasting journey, drawing on
A silvery train from many a woodland spring
And mountain-brook. The dweller by thy side,
Who moored his little boat upon thy beach,
Though all the waters that upbore it then
Have slid away o'er night, shall find, at morn,
Thy channel filled with waters freshly drawn
From distant cliffs, and hollows where the rill
Comes up amid the water-flags. All night
Thou givest moisture to the thirsty roots
Of the lithe willow and o'erhanging plane,
And cherishest the herbage of thy bank,
Spotted with little flowers, and sendest up
Perpetually the vapors from thy face,
To steep the hills with dew, or darken heaven
With drifting clouds, that trail the shadowy shower.

Oh River! darkling River! what a voice
Is that thou utterest while all else is still—
The ancient voice that, centuries ago,
Sounded between thy hills, while Rome was yet
A weedy solitude by Tiber's stream!
How many, at this hour, along thy course,
Slumber to thine eternal murmurings,
That mingle with the utterance of their dreams!
At dead of night the child awakes and hears

Thy soft, familiar dashings, and is soothed,
And sleeps again. An airy multitude
Of little echoes, all unheard by day,
Faintly repeat, till morning, after thee,
The story of thine endless goings forth.

Yet there are those who lie beside thy bed
For whom thou once didst rear the bowers that screen
Thy margin, and didst water the green fields;
And now there is no night so still that they
Can hear thy lapse; their slumbers, were thy voice
Louder than Ocean's, it could never break.
For them the early violet no more
Opens upon thy bank, nor, for their eyes,
Glitter the crimson pictures of the clouds,
Upon thy bosom, when the sun goes down.
Their memories are abroad, the memories
Of those who last were gathered to the earth,
Lingering within the homes in which they sat,
Hovering above the paths in which they walked,
Haunting them like a presence. Even now
They visit many a dreamer in the forms
They walked in, ere at last they wore the shroud.
And eyes there are which will not close to dream,
For weeping and for thinking of the grave,
The new-made grave, and the pale one within.
These memories and these sorrows all shall fade,
And pass away, and fresher memories
And newer sorrows come and dwell awhile
Beside thy borders, and, in turn, depart.

On glide thy waters, till at last they flow
Beneath the windows of the populous town,
And all night long give back the gleam of lamps,
And glimmer with the trains of light that stream
From halls where dancers whirl. A dimmer ray
Touches thy surface from the silent room
In which they tend the sick, or gather round
The dying; and a slender, steady beam
Comes from the little chamber, in the roof
Where, with a feverous crimson on her cheek,
The solitary damsel, dying, too,
Plies the quick needle till the stars grow pale.
There, close beside the haunts of revel, stand

The blank, unlighted windows, where the poor,
In hunger and in darkness, wake till morn.
There, drowsily, on the half-conscious ear
Of the dull watchman, pacing on the wharf,
Falls the soft ripple of the waves that strike
On the moored bark; but guiltier listeners
Are nigh, the prowlers of the night, who steal
From shadowy nook to shadowy nook, and start
If other sounds than thine are in the air.

Oh, glide away from those abodes, that bring
Pollution to thy channel and make foul
Thy once clear current; summon thy quick waves
And dimpling eddies; linger not, but haste,
With all thy waters, haste thee to the deep,
There to be tossed by shifting winds and rocked
By that mysterious force which lives within
The sea's immensity, and wields the weight
Of its abysses, swaying to and fro
The billowy mass, until the stain, at length,
Shall wholly pass away, and thou regain
The crystal brightness of thy mountain-springs.

The Life That Is

Thou, who so long hast pressed the couch of pain,
Oh welcome, welcome back to life's free breath—
To life's free breath and day's sweet light again,
From the chill shadows of the gate of death!

For thou hadst reached the twilight bound between
The world of spirits and this grosser sphere;
Dimly by thee the things of earth were seen,
And faintly fell earth's voices on thine ear.

And now, how gladly we behold, at last,
The wonted smile returning to thy brow!
The very wind's low whisper, breathing past,
In the light leaves, is music to thee now.

Thou wert not weary of thy lot; the earth
Was ever good and pleasant in thy sight;
Still clung thy loves about the household hearth,
And sweet was every day's returning light.

Then welcome back to all thou wouldst not leave,
To this grand march of seasons, days, and hours;
The glory of the morn, the glow of eve,
The beauty of the streams, and stars, and flowers;

To eyes on which thine own delight to rest;
To voices which it is thy joy to hear;
To the kind toils that ever pleased thee best,
The willing tasks of love, that made life dear.

Welcome to grasp of friendly hands; to prayers
Offered where crowds in reverent worship come,
Or softly breathed amid the tender cares
And loving inmates of thy quiet home.

Thou bring'st no tidings of the better land,
Even from its verge; the mysteries opened there
Are what the faithful heart may understand
In its still depths, yet words may not declare.

And well I deem, that, from the brighter side
Of life's dim border, some o'erflowing rays
Streamed from the inner glory, shall abide
Upon thy spirit through the coming days.

Twice wert thou given me; once in thy fair prime,
Fresh from the fields of youth, when first we met,
And all the blossoms of that hopeful time
Clustered and glowed where'er thy steps were set.

And now, in thy ripe autumn, once again
Given back to fervent prayers and yearnings strong,
From the drear realm of sickness and of pain
When we had watched, and feared, and trembled long.

Now may we keep thee from the balmy air
And radiant walks of heaven a little space,
Where He, who went before thee to prepare
For His meek followers, shall assign thy place.

The Song of the Sower

I

The maples redden in the sun;
  In autumn gold the beeches stand;
Rest, faithful plough, thy work is done
  Upon the teeming land.
Bordered with trees whose gay leaves fly
On every breath that sweeps the sky,
The fresh dark acres furrowed lie,
  And ask the sower's hand.
Loose the tired steer and let him go
To pasture where the gentians blow,
And we, who till the grateful ground,
Fling we the golden shower around.

II

Fling wide the generous grain; we fling
O'er the dark mould the green of spring.
For thick the emerald blades shall grow,
When first the March winds melt the snow,
And to the sleeping flowers, below,
    The early bluebirds sing.
Fling wide the grain; we give the fields
  The ears that nod in summer's gale,
The shining stems that summer gilds,
  The harvest that o'erflows the vale,
And swells, an amber sea, between
The full-leaved woods, its shores of green.
Hark! from the murmuring clods I hear
Glad voices of the coming year;
The song of him who binds the grain,
The shout of those that load the wain,
And from the distant grange there comes
  The clatter of the thresher's flail,
And steadily the millstone hums
  Down in the willowy vale.

III

Fling wide the golden shower; we trust
The strength of armies to the dust.
This peaceful lea may haply yield
Its harvest for the tented field.
Ha! feel ye not your fingers thrill,
  As o'er them, in the yellow grains,
Glide the warm drops of blood that fill,

For mortal strife, the warrior's veins;
Such as, on Solferino's day,
Slaked the brown sand and flowed away—
Flowed till the herds, on Mincio's brink,
Snuffed the red stream and feared to drink;—
Blood that in deeper pools shall lie,
On the sad earth, as time grows gray,
When men by deadlier arts shall die,
And deeper darkness blot the sky
Above the thundering fray;
And realms, that hear the battle-cry,
Shall sicken with dismay;
And chieftains to the war shall lead
Whole nations, with the tempest's speed,
To perish in a day;—
Till man, by love and mercy taught,
Shall rue the wreck his fury wrought,
And lay the sword away!
Oh strew, with pausing, shuddering hand,
The seed upon the helpless land,
As if, at every step, ye cast
The pelting hail and riving blast.

IV

Nay, strew, with free and joyous sweep,
The seed upon the expecting soil;
For hence the plenteous year shall heap
The garners of the men who toil.
Strew the bright seed for those who tear
The matted sward with spade and share,
And those whose sounding axes gleam
Beside the lonely forest-stream,
Till its broad banks lie bare;
And him who breaks the quarry-ledge,
With hammer-blows, plied quick and strong,
And him who, with the steady sledge,
Smites the shrill anvil all day long.
Sprinkle the furrow's even trace
For those whose toiling hands uprear
The roof-trees of our swarming race,
By grove and plain, by stream and mere;
Who forth, from crowded city, lead
The lengthening street, and overlay

Green orchard-plot and grassy mead
  With pavement of the murmuring way.
Cast, with full hands the harvest cast,
For the brave men that climb the mast,
When to the billow and the blast
  It swings and stoops, with fearful strain,
And bind the fluttering mainsail fast,
  Till the tossed bark shall sit, again,
  Safe as a sea-bird on the main.

V

Fling wide the grain for those who throw
The clanking shuttle to and fro,
In the long row of humming rooms,
  And into ponderous masses wind
The web that, from a thousand looms,
  Comes forth to clothe mankind.
Strew, with free sweep, the grain for them,
  By whom the busy thread
Along the garment's even hem
  And winding seam is led;
A pallid sisterhood, that keep
  The lonely lamp alight,
In strife with weariness and sleep,
  Beyond the middle night.
Large part be theirs in what the year
Shall ripen for the reaper here.

VI

Still, strew, with joyous hand, the wheat
On the soft mould beneath our feet,
    For even now I seem
To hear a sound that lightly rings
From murmuring harp and viol's strings,
    As in a summer dream.
The welcome of the wedding-guest,
  The bridegroom's look of bashful pride,
  The faint smile of the pallid bride,
And bridemaid's blush at matron's jest,
And dance and song and generous dower,
Are in the shining grains we shower.

VII

Scatter the wheat for shipwrecked men,
Who, hunger-worn, rejoice again
    In the sweet safety of the shore,
And wanderers, lost in woodlands drear,
Whose pulses bound with joy to hear
    The herd's light bell once more.
    Freely the golden spray be shed
For him whose heart, when night comes down
On the close alleys of the town,
    Is faint for lack of bread.

In chill roof-chambers, bleak and bare,
Or the damp cellar's stifling air,
She who now sees, in mute despair,
        Her children pine for food,
Shall feel the dews of gladness start
To lids long tearless, and shall part
The sweet loaf with a grateful heart,
        Among her thin pale brood.
Dear, kindly Earth, whose breast we till!
Oh, for thy famished children, fill,

Where'er the sower walks,
Fill the rich ears that shade the mould
With grain for grain, a hundredfold,
To bend the sturdy stalks.

VIII

Strew silently the fruitful seed,
As softly o'er the tilth ye tread,
For hands that delicately knead
The consecrated bread—
The mystic loaf that crowns the board,
When, round the table of their Lord,
Within a thousand temples set,
In memory of the bitter death
Of Him who taught at Nazareth,
His followers are met,
And thoughtful eyes with tears are wet,
As of the Holy One they think,
The glory of whose rising yet
Makes bright the grave's mysterious brink.

IX

Brethren, the sower's task is done.
The seed is in its winter bed.
Now let the dark-brown mould be spread,
To hide it from the sun,
And leave it to the kindly care
Of the still earth and brooding air,
As when the mother, from her breast,
Lays the hushed babe apart to rest,
And shades its eyes, and waits to see
How sweet its waking smile will be.
The tempest now may smite, the sleet
All night on the drowned furrow beat,
And winds that, from the cloudy hold,
Of winter breathe the bitter cold,
Stiffen to stone the mellow mould,
Yet safe shall lie the wheat;
Till, out of heaven's unmeasured blue,
Shall walk again the genial year,
To wake with warmth and nurse with dew
The germs we lay to slumber here.

X

Oh blessed harvest yet to be!
  Abide thou with the Love that keeps,
In its warm bosom, tenderly,
  The Life which wakes and that which sleeps.
The Love that leads the willing spheres
Along the unending track of years,
And watches o'er the sparrow's nest,
Shall brood above thy winter rest,
And raise thee from the dust, to hold
  Light whisperings with the winds of May,
And fill thy spikes with living gold,
  From summer's yellow ray;
Then, as thy garners give thee forth,
  On what glad errands shalt thou go,
Wherever, o'er the waiting earth,
  Roads wind and rivers flow!
The ancient East shall welcome thee
To mighty marts beyond the sea,
And they who dwell where palm-groves sound
To summer winds the whole year round,
Shall watch, in gladness, from the shore,
The sails that bring thy glistening store.

The Cloud on the Way

See, before us, in our journey, broods a mist upon the ground;
Thither leads the path we walk in, blending with that gloomy bound.
Never eye hath pierced its shadows to the mystery they screen;
Those who once have passed within it never more on earth are seen.
Now it seems to stoop beside us, now at seeming distance lowers,
Leaving banks that tempt us onward bright with summer-green and
flowers.
Yet it blots the way forever; there our journey ends at last;
Into that dark cloud we enter, and are gathered to the past.
Thou who, in this flinty pathway, leading through a stranger-land,
Passest down the rocky valley, walking with me hand in hand,
Which of us shall be the soonest folded to that dim Unknown?
Which shall leave the other walking in this flinty path alone?
Even now I see thee shudder, and thy cheek is white with fear,
And thou clingest to my side as comes that darkness sweeping near.
"Here," thou sayst, "the path is rugged, sown with thorns that wound
the feet;
But the sheltered glens are lovely, and the rivulet's song is sweet;
Roses breathe from tangled thickets; lilies bend from ledges brown;
Pleasantly between the pelting showers the sunshine gushes down;
Dear are those who walk beside us, they whose looks and voices make
All this rugged region cheerful, till I love it for their sake.
Far be yet the hour that takes me where that chilly shadow lies,
From the things I know and love, and from the sight of loving eyes!"
So thou murmurest, fearful one; but see, we tread a rougher way;
Fainter glow the gleams of sunshine that upon the dark rocks play;
Rude winds strew the faded flowers upon the crags o'er which we pass;
Banks of verdure, when we reach them, hiss with tufts of withered
grass.
One by one we miss the voices which we loved so well to hear;
One by one the kindly faces in that shadow disappear.
Yet upon the mist before us fix thine eyes with closer view;
See, beneath its sullen skirts, the rosy morning glimmers through.
One whose feet the thorns have wounded passed that barrier and came
back,
With a glory on His footsteps lighting yet the dreary track.
Boldly enter where He entered; all that seems but darkness here,
When thou once hast passed beyond it, haply shall be crystal clear.
Viewed from that serener realm, the walks of human life may lie,
Like the page of some familiar volume, open to thine eye;
Haply, from the o'erhanging shadow, thou mayst stretch an unseen
hand,
To support the wavering steps that print with blood the rugged land.
Haply, leaning o'er the pilgrim, all unweeting thou art near,

Thou mayst whisper words of warning or of comfort in his ear
Till, beyond the border where that brooding mystery bars the sight,
Those whom thou hast fondly cherished stand with thee in peace and
light.

The Third of November, 1861

Softly breathes the west-wind beside the ruddy forest,
Taking leaf by leaf from the branches where he flies.
Sweetly streams the sunshine, this third day of November,
Through the golden haze of the quiet autumn skies.

Tenderly the season has spared the grassy meadows,
Spared the petted flowers that the old world gave the new,
Spared the autumn-rose and the garden's group of pansies,
Late-blown dandelions and periwinkles blue.

On my cornice linger the ripe black grapes ungathered;
Children fill the groves with the echoes of their glee,
Gathering tawny chestnuts, and shouting when beside them
Drops the heavy fruit of the tall black-walnut tree.

Glorious are the woods in their latest gold and crimson,
Yet our full-leaved willows are in their freshest green.
Such a kindly autumn, so mercifully dealing
With the growths of summer, I never yet have seen.

Like this kindly season may life's decline come o'er me;
Past is manhood's summer, the frosty months are here;
Yet be genial airs and a pleasant sunshine left me,
Leaf, and fruit, and blossom, to mark the closing year!

Dreary is the time when the flowers of earth are withered;
Dreary is the time when the woodland leaves are cast—
When, upon the hillside, all hardened into iron,
Howling, like a wolf, flies the famished northern blast.

Dreary are the years when the eye can look no longer
With delight on Nature, or hope on human kind;
Oh, may those that whiten my temples, as they pass me,
Leave the heart unfrozen, and spare the cheerful mind!

The Tides

The moon is at her full, and, riding high,
    Floods the calm fields with light;
The airs that hover in the summer-sky
    Are all asleep to-night.
There comes no voice from the great woodlands round
    That murmured all the day;
Beneath the shadow of their boughs the ground
    Is not more still than they.

But ever heaves and moans the restless Deep;
    His rising tides I hear,
Afar I see the glimmering billows leap;
    I see them breaking near.
Each wave springs upward, climbing toward the fair
    Pure light that sits on high—
Springs eagerly, and faintly sinks, to where
    The mother-waters lie.

Upward again it swells; the moonbeams show
    Again its glimmering crest;
Again it feels the fatal weight below,
    And sinks, but not to rest.
Again and yet again; until the Deep
    Recalls his brood of waves;
And, with a sullen moan, abashed, they creep
    Back to his inner caves.

Brief respite! they shall rush from that recess
    With noise and tumult soon,
And fling themselves, with unavailing stress,
    Up toward the placid moon.
O restless Sea, that, in thy prison here,
    Dost struggle and complain;
Through the slow centuries yearning to be near
    To that fair orb in vain;

The glorious source of light and heat must warm
    Thy billows from on high,
And change them to the cloudy trains that form
    The curtain of the sky.
Then only may they leave the waste of brine
    In which they welter here,
And rise above the hills of earth, and shine
    In a serener sphere.

Italy

Voices from the mountains speak,
  Apennines to Alps reply;
Vale to vale and peak to peak
  Toss an old-remembered cry:
    "Italy
    Shall be free!"
Such the mighty shout that fills
All the passes of her hills.

All the old Italian lakes
  Quiver at that quickening word;
Como with a thrill awakes;
  Garda to her depths is stirred;
    Mid the steeps
    Where he sleeps,
Dreaming of the elder years,
Startled Thrasymenus hears.

Sweeping Arno, swelling Po,
  Murmur freedom to their meads.
Tiber swift and Liris slow
  Send strange whispers from their reeds.
    "Italy
    Shall be free!"
Sing the glittering brooks that slide,
Toward the sea, from Etna's side.

Long ago was Gracchus slain;
  Brutus perished long ago;
Yet the living roots remain
  Whence the shoots of greatness grow;
    Yet again,
    Godlike men,
Sprung from that heroic stem,
Call the land to rise with them.

They who haunt the swarming street,
  They who chase the mountain-boar,
Or, where cliff and billow meet,
  Prune the vine or pull the oar,
    With a stroke
    Break their yoke;
Slaves but yestereve were they—
Freemen with the dawning day.

Looking in his children's eyes,
While his own with gladness flash,
"These," the Umbrian father cries,
"Ne'er shall crouch beneath the lash!
These shall ne'er
Brook to wear
Chains whose cruel links are twined
Round the crushed and withering mind."

Monarchs! ye whose armies stand
Harnessed for the battle-field!
Pause, and from the lifted hand
Drop the bolts of war ye wield.
Stand aloof
While the proof
Of the people's might is given;
Leave their kings to them and Heaven!

Stand aloof, and see the oppressed
Chase the oppressor, pale with fear,
As the fresh winds of the west
Blow the misty valleys clear.
Stand and see
Italy
Cast the gyves she wears no more
To the gulfs that steep her shore.

Among the Trees

Oh ye who love to overhang the springs,
And stand by running waters, ye whose boughs
Make beautiful the rocks o'er which they play,
Who pile with foliage the great hills, and rear
A paradise upon the lonely plain,
Trees of the forest, and the open field!
Have ye no sense of being? Does the air,
The pure air, which I breathe with gladness, pass
In gushes o'er your delicate lungs, your leaves,
All unenjoyed? When on your winter's sleep
The sun shines warm, have ye no dreams of spring?
And when the glorious spring-time comes at last,
Have ye no joy of all your bursting buds,
And fragrant blooms, and melody of birds
To which your young leaves shiver? Do ye strive
And wrestle with the wind, yet know it not?
Feel ye no glory in your strength when he,
The exhausted Blusterer, flies beyond the hills,
And leaves you stronger yet? Or have ye not
A sense of loss when he has stripped your leaves,
Yet tender, and has splintered your fair boughs?
Does the loud bolt that smites you from the cloud
And rends you, fall unfelt? Do there not run
Strange shudderings through your fibres when the axe
Is raised against you, and the shining blade
Deals blow on blow, until, with all their boughs,
Your summits waver and ye fall to earth?
Know ye no sadness when the hurricane
Has swept the wood and snapped its sturdy stems
Asunder, or has wrenched, from out the soil,
The mightiest with their circles of strong roots,
And piled the ruin all along his path?

Nay, doubt we not that under the rough rind,
In the green veins of these fair growths of earth,
There dwells a nature that receives delight
From all the gentle processes of life,
And shrinks from loss of being. Dim and faint
May be the sense of pleasure and of pain,
As in our dreams; but, haply, real still.

Our sorrows touch you not. We watch beside
The beds of those who languish or who die,
And minister in sadness, while our hearts

Offer perpetual prayer for life and ease
And health to the belovèd sufferers.
But ye, while anxious fear and fainting hope
Are in our chambers, ye rejoice without.
The funeral goes forth; a silent train
Moves slowly from the desolate home; our hearts
Are breaking as we lay away the loved,
Whom we shall see no more, in their last rest,
Their little cells within the burial-place.
Ye have no part in this distress; for still
The February sunshine steeps your boughs
And tints the buds and swells the leaves within;
While the song-sparrow, warbling from her perch,
Tells you that spring is near. The wind of May
Is sweet with breath of orchards, in whose boughs
The bees and every insect of the air
Make a perpetual murmur of delight,
And by whose flowers the humming-bird hangs poised
In air, and draws their sweets and darts away.
The linden, in the fervors of July,
Hums with a louder concert. When the wind
Sweeps the broad forest in its summer prime,
As when some master-hand exulting sweeps
The keys of some great organ, ye give forth
The music of the woodland depths, a hymn
Of gladness and of thanks. The hermit-thrust
Pipes his sweet note to make your arches ring;
The faithful robin, from the wayside elm,
Carols all day to cheer his siting mate;
And when the autumn comes, the kings of earth,
In all their majesty, are not arrayed
As ye are, clothing the broad mountain-side
And spotting the smooth vales with red and gold;
While, swaying to the sudden breeze, ye fling
Your nuts to earth, and the brisk squirrel comes
To gather them, and barks with childish glee,
And scampers with them to his hollow oak.

Thus, as the seasons pass, ye keep alive
The cheerfulness of Nature, till in time
The constant misery which wrings the heart
Relents, and we rejoice with you again,
And glory in your beauty; till once more
We look with pleasure on your varnished leaves,

That gayly glance in sunshine, and can hear,
Delighted, the soft answer which your boughs
Utter in whispers to the babbling brook.

Ye have no history. I cannot know
Who, when the hillside trees were hewn away,
Haply two centuries since, bade spare this oak,
Leaning to shade, with his irregular arms,
Low-bent and long, the fount that from his roots
Slips through a bed of cresses toward the bay—
I know not who, but thank him that he left
The tree to flourish where the acorn fell,
And join these later days to that far time
While yet the Indian hunter drew the bow
In the dim woods, and the white woodman first
Opened these fields to sunshine, turned the soil
And strewed the wheat. An unremembered Past
Broods, like a presence, mid the long gray boughs
Of this old tree, which has outlived so long
The flitting generations of mankind.

Ye have no history. I ask in vain
Who planted on the slope this lofty group
Of ancient pear-trees that with spring-time burst
Into such breadth of bloom. One bears a scar
Where the quick lightning scored its trunk, yet still

It feels the breath of Spring, and every May
Is white with blossoms. Who it was that laid
Their infant roots in earth, and tenderly
Cherished the delicate sprays, I ask in vain,
Yet bless the unknown hand to which I owe
This annual festival of bees, these songs
Of birds within their leafy screen, these shouts
Of joy from children gathering up the fruit
Shaken in August from the willing boughs.

Ye that my hands have planted, or have spared,
Beside the way, or in the orchard-ground,
Or in the open meadow, ye whose boughs
With every summer spread a wider shade,
Whose herd in coming years shall lie at rest
Beneath your noontide shelter? who shall pluck
Your ripened fruit? who grave, as was the wont
Of simple pastoral ages, on the rind
Of my smooth beeches some belovèd name?
Idly I ask; yet may the eyes that look
Upon you, in your later, nobler growth,
Look also on a nobler age than ours;
An age when, in the eternal strife between
Evil and Good, the Power of Good shall win
A grander mastery; when kings no more
Shall summon millions from the plough to learn
The trade of slaughter, and of populous realms
Make camps of war; when in our younger land
The hand of ruffian Violence, that now
Is insolently raised to smite, shall fall
Unnerved before the calm rebuke of Law,
And Fraud, his sly confederate, shrink, in shame,
Back to his covert, and forego his prey.

A Day-Dream

A day-dream by the dark-blue deep;
  Was it a dream, or something more?
I sat where Posilippo's steep,
  With its gray shelves, o'erhung the shore.

On ruined Roman walls around
  The poppy flaunted, for 'twas May;
And at my feet, with gentle sound,
  Broke the light billows of the bay.

I sat and watched the eternal flow
  Of those smooth billows toward the shore,
While quivering lines of light below
  Ran with them on the ocean-floor:

Till, from the deep, there seemed to rise
  White arms upon the waves outspread,
Young faces, lit with soft blue eyes,
  And smooth, round cheeks, just touched with red.

Their long, fair tresses, tinged with gold,
  Lay floating on the ocean-streams,
And such their brows as bards behold—
  Love-stricken bards—in morning dreams.

Then moved their coral lips; a strain
  Low, sweet and sorrowful, I heard,
As if the murmurs of the main
  Were shaped to syllable and word.

"The sight thou dimly dost behold,
  Oh, stranger from a distant sky!
Was often, in the days of old,
  Seen by the clear, believing eye.

"Then danced we on the wrinkled sand,
  Sat in cool caverns by the sea,
Or wandered up the bloomy land,
  To talk with shepherds on the lea.

"To us, in storms, the seaman prayed,
  And where our rustic altars stood,
His little children came and laid
  The fairest flowers of field and wood.

"Oh woe, a long, unending woe!
  For who shall knit the ties again
That linked the sea-nymphs, long ago,
  In kindly fellowship with men?

"Earth rears her flowers for us no more;
  A half-remembered dream are we;
Unseen we haunt the sunny shore,
  And swim, unmarked, the glassy sea.

"And we have none to love or aid,
  But wander, heedless of mankind,
With shadows by the cloud-rack made,
  With moaning wave and sighing wind.

"Yet sometimes, as in elder days,
  We come before the painter's eye,
Or fix the sculptor's eager gaze,
  With no profaner witness nigh.

"And then the words of men grow warm
  With praise and wonder, asking where
The artist saw the perfect form
  He copied forth in lines so fair."

As thus they spoke, with wavering sweep
  Floated the graceful forms away;
Dimmer and dimmer, through the deep,
  I saw the white arms gleam and play.

Fainter and fainter, on mine ear,
  Fell the soft accents of their speech,
Till I, at last, could only hear
  The waves run murmuring up the beach.

Not Yet

Oh country, marvel of the earth!
  Oh realm to sudden greatness grown!
The age that gloried in thy birth,
  Shall it behold thee overthrown?
Shall traitors lay that greatness low?
No, land of Hope and Blessing, No!
And we, who wear thy glorious name,
  Shall we, like cravens, stand apart,
When those whom thou hast trusted aim
  The death-blow at thy generous heart?
Forth goes the battle-cry, and lo!
Hosts rise in harness, shouting, No!
And they who founded, in our land,
  The power that rules from sea to sea,
Bled they in vain, or vainly planned
  To leave their country great and free?
Their sleeping ashes, from below,
Send up the thrilling murmur, No!

Knit they the gentle ties which long
  These sister States were proud to wear,
And forged the kindly links so strong
  For idle hands in sport to tear?
For scornful hands aside to throw?
No, by our fathers' memory, No!
Our humming marts, our iron ways,
  Our wind-tossed woods on mountain-crest,
The hoarse Atlantic, with its bays,
  The calm, broad Ocean of the West,
And Mississippi's torrent-flow,
And loud Niagara, answer, No!
Not yet the hour is nigh when they
  Who deep in Eld's dim twilight sit,
Earth's ancient kings, shall rise and say,
  "Proud country, welcome to the pit!
So soon art thou, like us, brought low!"
No, sullen group of shadows, No!

For now, behold, the arm that gave
  The victory in our fathers' day,
Strong, as of old, to guard and save—
  That mighty arm which none can stay—
On clouds above and fields below,
Writes, in men's sight, the answer, No!

Our Country's Call

Lay down the axe; fling by the spade;
   Leave in its track the toiling plough;
The rifle and the bayonet-blade
   For arms like yours were fitter now;
And let the hands that ply the pen
   Quit the light task, and learn to wield
The horseman's crooked brand, and rein
   The charger on the battle-field.

Our country calls; away! away!
   To where the blood-stream blots the green.
Strike to defend the gentlest sway
   That Time in all his course has seen.
See, from a thousand coverts—see,
   Spring the armed foes that haunt her track;
They rush to smite her down, and we
   Must beat the banded traitors back.

Ho! sturdy as the oaks ye cleave,
   And moved as soon to fear and flight,
Men of the glade and forest! leave
   Your woodcraft for the field of fight.
The arms that wield the axe must pour
   An iron tempest on the foe;
His serried ranks shall reel before
   The arm that lays the panther low.

And ye, who breast the mountain-storm
   By grassy steep or highland lake,
Come, for the land ye love, to form
   A bulwark that no foe can break.
Stand, like your own gray cliffs that mock
   The whirlwind, stand in her defence;
The blast as soon shall move the rock
   As rushing squadrons bear ye thence.

And ye, whose homes are by her grand
   Swift rivers, rising far away,
Come from the depth of her green land,
   As mighty in your march as they;
As terrible as when the rains
   Have swelled them over bank and bourne,
With sudden floods to drown the plains
   And sweep along the woods uptorn.

And ye, who throng, beside the deep,
  Her ports and hamlets of the strand,
In number like the waves that leap
  On his long-murmuring marge of sand—
Come like that deep, when, o'er his brim,
  He rises, all his floods to pour,
And flings the proudest barks that swim,
  A helpless wreck, against the shore!

Few, few were they whose swords of old
  Won the fair land in which we dwell;
But we are many, we who hold
  The grim resolve to guard it well.
Strike, for that broad and goodly land,
  Blow after blow, till men shall see
That Might and Right move hand in hand,
  And glorious must their triumph be!

The Constellations

O Constellations of the early night,
That sparkled brighter as the twilight died,
And made the darkness glorious! I have seen
Your rays grow dim upon the horizon's edge,
And sink behind the mountains. I have seen
The great Orion, with his jewelled belt,
That large-limbed warrior of the skies, go down
Into the gloom. Beside him sank a crowd
Of shining ones. I look in vain to find
The group of sister-stars, which mothers love
To show their wondering babes, the gentle Seven.
Along the desert space mine eyes in vain
Seek the resplendent cressets which the Twins
Uplifted in their ever-youthful hands.
The streaming tresses of the Egyptian Queen
Spangle the heavens no more. The Virgin trails
No more her glittering garments through the blue.
Gone! all are gone! and the forsaken Night,
With all her winds, in all her dreary wastes,
Sighs that they shine upon her face no more.
  Now only here and there a little star
Looks forth alone. Ah me! I know them not,
Those dim successors of the numberless host
That filled the heavenly fields, and flung to earth
Their quivering fires. And now the middle watch
Betwixt the eve and morn is past, and still
The darkness gains upon the sky, and still
It closes round my way. Shall, then, the Night
Grow starless in her later hours? Have these
No train of flaming watchers, that shall mark
Their coming and farewell? O Sons of Light!
Have ye then left me ere the dawn of day
To grope along my journey sad and faint?
  Thus I complained, and from the darkness round
A voice replied—was it indeed a voice,
Or seeming accents of a waking dream
Heard by the inner ear? But thus it said:
O Traveller of the Night! thine eyes are dim
With watching; and the mists, that chill the vale
Down which thy feet are passing, hide from view
The ever-burning stars. It is thy sight
That is so dark, and not the heavens. Thine eyes,
Were they but clear, would see a fiery host
Above thee; Hercules, with flashing mace,

The Lyre with silver chords, the Swan uppoised
On gleaming wings, the Dolphin gliding on
With glistening scales, and that poetic steed,
With beamy mane, whose hoof struck out from earth
The fount of Hippocrene, and many more,
Fair clustered splendors, with whose rays the Night
Shall close her march in glory, ere she yield,
To the young Day, the great earth steeped in dew.
So spake the monitor, and I perceived
How vain were my repinings, and my thought
Went backward to the vanished years and all
The good and great who came and passed with them,
And knew that ever would the years to come
Bring with them, in their course, the good and great,
Lights of the world, though, to my clouded sight,
Their rays might seem but dim, or reach me not.

A Legend of the Delawares

The air is dark with cloud on cloud,
   And, through the leaden-colored mass,
With thunder-crashes quick and loud,
   A thousand shafts of lightning pass.

And to and fro they glance and go,
   Or, darting downward, smite the ground.
What phantom arms are those that throw
   The shower of fiery arrows round?

A louder crash! a mighty oak
   Is smitten from that stormy sky.
Its stem is shattered by the stroke;
   Around its root the branches lie.

Fresh breathes the wind; the storm is o'er;
   The piles of mist are swept away;
And from the open sky, once more,
   Streams gloriously the golden day.

A dusky hunter of the wild
   Is passing near, and stops to see
The wreck of splintered branches piled
   About the roots of that huge tree.

Lo, quaintly shaped and fairly strung,
   Wrought by what hand he cannot know,
On that drenched pile of boughs, among
   The splinters, lies a polished bow.

He lifts it up; the drops that hang
   On the smooth surface glide away:
He tries the string, no sharper twang
   Was ever heard on battle-day.

Homeward Onetho bears the prize:
   Who meets him as he turns to go?
An agèd chief, with quick, keen eyes,
   And bending frame, and locks of snow.

"See, what I bring, my father, see
   This goodly bow which I have found
Beneath a thunder-riven tree,
   Dropped with the lightning to the ground."

"Beware, my son; it is not well"—
   The white-haired chieftain makes reply—
"That we who in the forest dwell
   Should wield the weapons of the sky.

"Lay back that weapon in its place;
   Let those who bore it bear it still,
Lest thou displease the ghostly race
   That float in mist from hill to hill."

"My father, I will only try
   How well it sends a shaft, and then,
Be sure, this goodly bow shall lie
   Among the splintered boughs again."

So to the hunting-ground he hies,
   To chase till eve the forest-game,
And not a single arrow flies,
   From that good bow, with erring aim.

And then he deems that they, who swim
   In trains of cloud the middle air,
Perchance had kindly thoughts of him
   And dropped the bow for him to bear.

He bears it from that day, and soon
  Becomes the mark of every eye,
And wins renown with every moon
  That fills its circle in the sky.

None strike so surely in the chase;
  None bring such trophies from the fight;
And, at the council-fire, his place
  Is with the wise and men of might.

And far across the land is spread,
  Among the hunter tribes, his fame;
Men name the bowyer-chief with dread
  Whose arrows never miss their aim.

See next his broad-roofed cabin rise
  On a smooth river's pleasant side,
And she who has the brightest eyes
  Of all the tribe becomes his bride.

A year has passed; the forest sleeps
  In early autumn's sultry glow;
Onetho, on the mountain-steeps,
  Is hunting with that trusty bow.

But they, who by the river dwell,
  See the dim vapors thickening o'er
Long mountain-range and severing dell,
  And hear the thunder's sullen roar.

Still darker grows the spreading cloud
  From which the booming thunders sound,
And stoops and hangs a shadowy shroud
  Above Onetho's hunting-ground.

Then they who, from the river-vale,
  Are gazing on the distant storm,
See in the mists that ride the gale
  Dim shadows of the human form—

Tall warriors, plumed, with streaming hair
  And lifted arms that bear the bow,
And send athwart the murky air
  The arrowy lightnings to and fro.

Loud is the tumult of an hour—
Crash of torn boughs and howl of blast,
And thunder-peal and pelting shower,
And then the storm is overpast.

Where is Onetho? what delays
His coming? why should he remain
Among the plashy woodland ways,
Swoln brooks and boughs that drip with rain?

He comes not, and the younger men
Go forth to search the forest round.
They track him to a mountain-glen,
And find him lifeless on the ground.

The goodly bow that was his pride
Is gone, but there the arrows lie;
And now they know the death he died,
Slain by the lightnings of the sky.

They bear him thence in awe and fear
Back to the vale with stealthy tread;
There silently, from far and near,
The warriors gather round the dead.

But in their homes the women bide;
Unseen they sit and weep apart,
And, in her bower, Onetho's bride
Is sobbing with a broken heart.

They lay in earth their bowyer-chief,
And at his side their hands bestow
His dreaded battle-axe and sheaf
Of arrows, but without a bow.

"Too soon he died; it is not well"—
The old men murmured, standing nigh—
"That we, who in the forest dwell,
Should wield the weapons of the sky."

The Poet

Thou, who wouldst wear the name
  Of poet mid thy brethren of mankind,
And clothe in words of flame
  Thoughts that shall live within the general mind!
Deem not the framing of a deathless lay
The pastime of a drowsy summer day.

But gather all thy powers,
  And wreak them on the verse that thou dost weave,
And in thy lonely hours,
  At silent morning or at wakeful eve,
While the warm current tingles through thy veins
Set forth the burning words in fluent strains.

No smooth array of phrase,
  Artfully sought and ordered though it be,
Which the cold rhymer lays
  Upon his page with languid industry,
Can wake the listless pulse to livelier speed,
Or fill with sudden tears the eyes that read.

The secret wouldst thou know
  To touch the heart or fire the blood at will?
Let thine own eyes o'erflow;
  Let thy lips quiver with the passionate thrill;
Seize the great thought, ere yet its power be past,
And bind, in words, the fleet emotion fast.

Then, should thy verse appear
  Halting and harsh, and all unaptly wrought,
Touch the crude line with fear,
  Save in the moment of impassioned thought;
Then summon back the original glow, and mend
The strain with rapture that with fire was penned.

Yet let no empty gust
  Of passion find an utterance in thy lay,
A blast that whirls the dust
  Along the howling street and dies away;
But feelings of calm power and mighty sweep,
Like currents journeying through the windless deep.

Seek'st thou, in living lays,
  To limn the beauty of the earth and sky?

Before thine inner gaze
  Let all that beauty in clear vision lie;
Look on it with exceeding love, and write
The words inspired by wonder and delight.

Of tempests wouldst thou sing,
  Or tell of battles—make thyself a part
Of the great tumult; cling
  To the tossed wreck with terror in thy heart;
Scale, with the assaulting host, the rampart's height,
And strike and struggle in the thickest fight.

So shalt thou frame a lay
  That haply may endure from age to age,
And they who read shall say:
  "What witchery hangs upon this poet's page!
What art is his the written spells to find
That sway from mood to mood the willing mind!"

The Path

The path we planned beneath October's sky,
   Along the hillside, through the woodland shade,
Is finished; thanks to thee, whose kindly eye
   Has watched me, as I plied the busy spade;
Else had I wearied, ere this path of ours
Had pierced the woodland to its inner bowers.

Yet, 'twas a pleasant toil to trace and beat,
   Among the glowing trees, this winding way,
While the sweet autumn sunshine, doubly sweet,
   Flushed with the ruddy foliage, round us lay,
As if some gorgeous cloud of morning stood,
In glory, mid the arches of the wood.

A path! what beauty does a path bestow
   Even on the dreariest wild! its savage nooks
Seem homelike where accustomed footsteps go,
   And the grim rock puts on familiar looks.
The tangled swamp, through which a pathway strays,
Becomes a garden with strange flowers and sprays.

See from the weedy earth a rivulet break
   And purl along the untrodden wilderness;
There the shy cuckoo comes his thirst to slake,
   There the shrill jay alights his plumes to dress;
And there the stealthy fox, when morn is gray,
Laps the clear stream and lightly moves away.

But let a path approach that fountain's brink,
   And nobler forms of life, behold! are there:
Boys kneeling with protruded lips to drink,
   And slender maids that homeward slowly bear
The brimming pail, and busy dames that lay
Their webs to whiten in the summer ray.

Then know we that for herd and flock are poured
   Those pleasant streams that o'er the pebbles slip;
Those pure sweet waters sparkle on the board;
   Those fresh cool waters wet the sick man's lip;
Those clear bright waters from the font are shed,
In dews of baptism, on the infant's head.

What different steps the rural footway trace!
   The laborer afield at early day;

The schoolboy sauntering with uneven pace;
  The Sunday worshipper in fresh array;
And mourner in the weeds of sorrow drest;
And, smiling to himself, the wedding guest.

There he who cons a speech and he who hums
  His yet unfinished verses, musing walk.
There, with her little brood, the matron comes,
  To break the spring flower from its juicy stalk;
And lovers, loitering, wonder that the moon
Has risen upon their pleasant stroll so soon.

Bewildered in vast woods, the traveller feels
  His heavy heart grow lighter, if he meet
The traces of a path, and straight he kneels,
  And kisses the dear print of human feet,
And thanks his God, and journeys without fear,
For now he knows the abodes of men are near.

Pursue the slenderest path across a lawn:
  Lo! on the broad highway it issues forth,
And, blended with the greater track, goes on,
  Over the surface of the mighty earth,
Climbs hills and crosses vales, and stretches far,
Through silent forests, toward the evening star—

And enters cities murmuring with the feet
  Of multitudes, and wanders forth again,
And joins the climes of frost to climes of heat,
  Binds East to West, and marries main to main,
Nor stays till at the long-resounding shore
Of the great deep, where paths are known no more.

Oh, mighty instinct, that dost thus unite
  Earth's neighborhoods and tribes with friendly bands,
What guilt is theirs who, in their greed or spite,
  Undo thy holy work with violent hands,
And post their squadrons, nursed in war's grim trade,
To bar the ways for mutual succor made!

The Death of Slavery

O thou great Wrong, that, through the slow-paced years,
Didst hold thy millions fettered, and didst wield
The scourge that drove the laborer to the field,
And turn a stony gaze on human tears,
Thy cruel reign is o'er;
Thy bondmen crouch no more
In terror at the menace of thine eye;
For He who marks the bounds of guilty power,
Long-suffering, hath heard the captive's cry,
And touched his shackles at the appointed hour,
And lo! they fall, and he whose limbs they galled
Stands in his native manhood, disenthralled.
A shout of joy from the redeemed is sent;
Ten thousand hamlets swell the hymn of thanks;
Our rivers roll exulting, and their banks
Send up hosannas to the firmament!
Fields where the bondman's toil
No more shall trench the soil,
Seem now to bask in a serener day;
The meadow-birds sing sweeter, and the airs
Of heaven with more caressing softness play,
Welcoming man to liberty like theirs.
A glory clothes the land from sea to sea,
For the great land and all its coasts are free.

Within that land wert thou enthroned of late,
And they by whom the nation's laws were made,
And they who filled its judgment-seats obeyed
Thy mandate, rigid as the will of Fate.
Fierce men at thy right hand,
With gesture of command,
Gave forth the word that none might dare gainsay;
And grave and reverend ones, who loved thee not,
Shrank from thy presence, and in blank dismay
Choked down, unuttered, the rebellious thought;
While meaner cowards, mingling with thy train,
Proved, from the book of God, thy right to reign.

Great as thou wert, and feared from shore to shore,
The wrath of Heaven o'ertook thee in thy pride;
Thou sitt'st a ghastly shadow; by thy side
Thy once strong arms hang nerveless evermore.
And they who quailed but now
Before thy lowering brow,

Devote thy memory to scorn and shame,
And scoff at the pale, powerless thing thou art.
And they who ruled in thine imperial name,
Subdued, and standing sullenly apart,
Scowl at the hands that overthrew thy reign,
And shattered at a blow the prisoner's chain.

Well was thy doom deserved; thou didst not spare
Life's tenderest ties, but cruelly didst part
Husband and wife, and from the mother's heart
Didst wrest her children, deaf to shriek and prayer;
Thy inner lair became
The haunt of guilty shame;
Thy lash dropped blood; the murderer, at thy side,
Showed his red hands, nor feared the vengeance due.
Thou didst sow earth with crimes, and, far and wide,
A harvest of uncounted miseries grew,
Until the measure of thy sins at last
Was full, and then the avenging bolt was cast!

Go now, accursed of God, and take thy place
With hateful memories of the elder time,
With many a wasting plague, and nameless crime,
And bloody war that thinned the human race;
With the Black Death, whose way
Through wailing cities lay,
Worship of Moloch, tyrannies that built
The Pyramids, and cruel creeds that taught
To avenge a fancied guilt by deeper guilt—
Death at the stake to those that held them not.
Lo! the foul phantoms, silent in the gloom
Of the flown ages, part to yield thee room.
I see the better years that hasten by
Carry thee back into that shadowy past,
Where, in the dusty spaces, void and vast,
The graves of those whom thou hast murdered lie.
The slave-pen, through whose door
Thy victims pass no more,
Is there, and there shall the grim block remain
At which the slave was sold; while at thy feet
Scourges and engines of restraint and pain
Moulder and rust by thine eternal seat.
There, mid the symbols that proclaim thy crimes,
Dwell thou, a warning to the coming times.

The Return of the Birds

I hear, from many a little throat,
  A warble interrupted long;
I hear the robin's flute-like note,
  The bluebird's slenderer song.

Brown meadows and the russet hill,
  Not yet the haunt of grazing herds,
And thickets by the glimmering rill,
  Are all alive with birds.

Oh choir of spring, why come so soon?
  On leafless grove and herbless lawn
Warm lie the yellow beams of moon;
  Yet winter is not gone.

For frost shall sheet the pools again;
  Again the blustering East shall blow—
Whirl a white tempest through the glen,
  And load the pines with snow.

Yet, haply, from the region where,
  Waked by an earlier spring than here,
The blossomed wild-plum scents the air,
  Ye come in haste and fear.

For there is heard the bugle-blast,
  The booming gun, the jarring drum,
And on their chargers, spurring fast,
  Armed warriors go and come.

There mighty hosts have pitched the camp
  In valleys that were yours till then,
And Earth has shuddered to the tramp
  Of half a million men!

In groves where once ye used to sing,
  In orchards where ye had your birth,
A thousand glittering axes swing
  To smite the trees to earth.

Ye love the fields by ploughmen trod;
  But there, when sprouts the beechen spray,
The soldier only breaks the sod
  To hide the slain away.

Stay, then, beneath our ruder sky;
Heed not the storm-clouds rising black,
Nor yelling winds that with them fly;
Nor let them fright you back,—

Back to the stifling battle-cloud,
To burning towns that blot the day,
And trains of mounting dust that shroud
The armies on their way.

Stay, for a tint of green shall creep
Soon o'er the orchard's grassy floor,
And from its bed the crocus peep
Beside the housewife's door.

Here build, and dread no harsher sound
To scare you from the sheltering tree,
Than winds that stir the branches round,
And murmur of the bee.

And we will pray that, ere again
The flowers of autumn bloom and die,
Our generals and their strong-armed men
May lay their weapons by.

Then may ye warble, unafraid,
Where hands, that wear the fetter now,
Free as your wings shall ply the spade,
And guide the peaceful plough.

Then, as our conquering hosts return,
What shouts of jubilee shall break
From placid vale and mountain stern,
And shore of mighty lake!

And midland plain and ocean-strand
Shall thunder: "Glory to the brave,
Peace to the torn and bleeding land,
And freedom to the slave!"

May Evening

The breath of Spring-time at this twilight hour
Comes through the gathering glooms,
And bears the stolen sweets of many a flower
Into my silent rooms.

Where hast thou wandered, gentle gale, to find
The perfumes thou dost bring?
By brooks, that through the wakening meadows wind,
Or brink of rushy spring?

Or woodside, where, in little companies,
The early wild-flowers rise,
Or sheltered lawn, where, mid encircling trees,
May's warmest sunshine lies?

Now sleeps the humming-bird, that, in the sun,
Wandered from bloom to bloom;
Now, too, the weary bee, his day's work done,
Rests in his waxen room.

Now every hovering insect to his place
Beneath the leaves hath flown;
And, through the long night hours, the flowery race
Are left to thee alone.

O'er the pale blossoms of the sassafras
And o'er the spice-bush spray,
Among the opening buds, thy breathings pass,
And come embalmed away.

Yet there is sadness in thy soft caress,
Wind of the blooming year!
The gentle presence, that was wont to bless
Thy coming, is not here.

Go, then; and yet I bid thee not repair,
Thy gathered sweets to shed,
Where pine and willow, in the evening air,
Sigh o'er the buried dead.

Pass on to homes where cheerful voices sound,
And cheerful looks are cast,
And where thou wakest, in thine airy round,
No sorrow of the past.

Refresh the languid student pausing o'er
The learnèd page apart,
And he shall turn to con his task once more
With an encouraged heart.

Bear thou a promise, from the fragrant sward,
To him who tills the land,
Of springing harvests that shall yet reward
The labors of his hand.

And whisper, everywhere, that Earth renews
Her beautiful array,
Amid the darkness and the gathering dews,
For the return of day.

October, 1866

'Twas when the earth in summer glory lay,
 We bore thee to thy grave; a sudden cloud
Had shed its shower and passed, and every spray
 And tender herb with pearly moisture bowed.

How laughed the fields, and how, before our door,
 Danced the bright waters!—from his perch on high
The hang-bird sang his ditty o'er and o'er,
 And the song-sparrow from the shrubberies nigh.

Yet was the home where thou wert lying dead
 Mournfully still, save when, at times, was heard,
From room to room, some softly-moving tread,
 Or murmur of some softly-uttered word.

Feared they to break thy slumber? As we threw
 A look on that bright bay and glorious shore,
Our hearts were wrung with anguish, for we knew
 Those sleeping eyes would look on them no more.

Autumn is here; we cull his lingering flowers
 And bring them to the spot where thou art laid;
The late-born offspring of his balmier hours,
 Spared by the frost, upon thy grave to fade.

The sweet calm sunshine of October, now
 Warms the low spot; upon its grassy mould
The purple oak-leaf falls; the birchen bough
 Drops its bright spoil like arrow-heads of gold.

And gorgeous as the morn, a tall array
 Of woodland shelters the smooth fields around;
And guarded by its headlands, far away
 Sail-spotted, blue and lake-like, sleeps the sound.

I gave in sadness; it delights me not
 To look on beauty which thou canst not see;
And, wert thou by my side, the dreariest spot
 Were, oh, how far more beautiful to me!

In what fair region dost thou now abide?
 Hath God, in the transparent deeps of space,
Through which the planets in their journey glide,
 Prepared, for souls like thine, a dwelling-place?

Fields of unwithering bloom, to mortal eye
  Invisible, though mortal eye were near,
Musical groves, and bright streams murmuring by,
  Heard only by the spiritual ear?

Nay, let us deem that thou dost not withdraw
  From the dear places where thy lot was cast,
And where thy heart, in love's most holy law,
  Was schooled by all the memories of the past.

Here on this earth, where once, among mankind,
  Walked God's belovèd Son, thine eyes may see
Beauty to which our dimmer sense is blind
  And glory that may make it heaven to thee.

May we not think that near us thou dost stand
  With loving ministrations, for we know
Thy heart was never happy when thy hand
  Was forced its tasks of mercy to forego!

Mayst thou not prompt, with every coming day,
  The generous aim and act, and gently win
Our restless, wandering thoughts to turn away
  From every treacherous path that ends in sin!

The Order of Nature

[FROM BOETHIUS' DE CONSOLATIONE]

Thou who wouldst read, with an undarkened eye,
The laws by which the Thunderer bears sway,
Look at the stars that keep, in yonder sky,
Unbroken peace from Nature's earliest day.
The great sun, as he guides his fiery car,
Strikes not the cold moon in his rapid sweep;
The Bear, that sees star setting after star
In the blue brine, descends not to the deep.

The star of eve still leads the hour of dews;
Duly the day-star ushers in the light;
With kindly alternations Love renews
The eternal courses bringing day and night.
Love drives away the brawler War, and keeps
The realm and host of stars beyond his reach;
In one long calm the general concord steeps
The elements, and tempers each to each.

The moist gives place benignly to the dry;
Heat ratifies a faithful league with cold;
The nimble flame springs upward to the sky;
Down sinks by its own weight the sluggish mould.
Still sweet with blossoms is the year's fresh prime;
Her harvests still the ripening Summer yields;
Fruit-laden Autumn follows in his time,
And rainy Winter waters still the fields.

The elemental harmony brings forth
And rears all life, and, when life's term is o'er,
It sweeps the breathing myriads from the earth,
And whelms and hides them to be seen no more:
While the Great Founder, he who gave these laws,
Holds the firm reins and sits amid his skies
Monarch and Master, Origin and Cause,
And Arbiter supremely just and wise.

He guides the force he gave; his hand restrains
And curbs it to the circle it must trace:
Else the fair fabric which his power sustains
Would fall to fragments in the void of space.
Love binds the parts together, gladly still
They court the kind restraint nor would be free;
Unless Love held them subject to the Will
That gave them being, they would cease to be.

Tree-Burial

Near our southwestern border, when a child
Dies in the cabin of an Indian wife,
She makes its funeral-couch of delicate furs,
Blankets and bark, and binds it to the bough
Of some broad branching tree with leathern thongs
And sinews of the deer. A mother once
Wrought at this tender task, and murmured thus:
"Child of my love, I do not lay thee down
Among the chilly clods where never comes
The pleasant sunshine. There the greedy wolf
Might break into thy grave and tear thee thence,
And I should sorrow all my life. I make
Thy burial-place here, where the light of day
Shines round thee, and the airs that play among
The boughs shall rock thee. Here the morning sun,
Which woke thee once from sleep to smile on me,
Shall beam upon thy bed, and sweetly here
Shall lie the red light of the evening clouds
Which called thee once to slumber. Here the stars
Shall look upon thee—the bright stars of heaven
Which thou didst wonder at. Here too the birds,
Whose music thou didst love, shall sing to thee,
And near thee build their nests and rear their young
With none to scare them. Here the woodland flowers,
Whose opening in the spring-time thou didst greet
With shouts of joy, and which so well became
Thy pretty hands when thou didst gather them,
Shall spot the ground below thy little bed.
"Yet haply thou hast fairer flowers than these,
Which, in the land of souls, thy spirit plucks
In fields that wither not, amid the throng
Of joyous children, like thyself, who went
Before thee to that brighter world and sport
Eternally beneath its cloudless skies.
Sport with them, dear, dear child, until I come
To dwell with thee, and thou, beholding me,
From far, shalt run and leap into my arms,
And I shall clasp thee as I clasped thee here
While living, oh most beautiful and sweet
Of children, now more passing beautiful,
If that can be, with eyes like summer stars—
A light that death can never quench again.
"And now, oh wind, that here among the leaves
Dost softly rustle, breathe thou ever thus

Gently, and put not forth thy strength to tear
The branches and let fall their precious load,
A prey to foxes. Thou, too, ancient sun,
Beneath whose eye the seasons come and go,
And generations rise and pass away,
While thou dost never change—oh, call not up,
With thy strong heats, the dark, grim thunder-cloud,
To smite this tree with bolts of fire, and rend
Its trunk and strew the earth with splintered boughs.
Ye rains, fall softly on the couch that holds
My darling. There the panther's spotted hide
Shall turn aside the shower; and be it long,
Long after thou and I have met again,
Ere summer wind or winter rain shall waste
This couch and all that now remains of thee,
To me thy mother. Meantime, while I live,
With each returning sunrise I shall seem
To see thy waking smile, and I shall weep;
And when the sun is setting I shall think
How, as I watched thee, o'er thy sleepy eyes
Drooped the smooth lids, and laid on the round cheek
Their lashes, and my tears will flow again;
And often, at those moments, I shall seem
To hear again the sweetly prattled name
Which thou didst call me by, and it will haunt
My home till I depart to be with thee."

The Two Travellers

'Twas evening, and before my eyes
  There lay a landscape gray and dim—
Fields faintly seen and twilight skies,
  And clouds that hid the horizon's brim.

I saw—or was it that I dreamed?
  A waking dream?—I cannot say,
For every shape as real seemed
  As those which meet my eyes to-day.

Through leafless shrubs the cold wind hissed;
  The air was thick with falling snow,
And onward, through the frozen mist,
  I saw a weary traveller go.

Driven o'er the landscape, bare and bleak,
  Before the whirling gusts of air,
The snow-flakes smote his withered cheek,
  And gathered on his silver hair.

Yet on he fared through blinding snows,
  And murmuring to himself he said:
"The night is near; the darkness grows,
  And higher rise the drifts I tread.

"Deep, deep, each autumn flower they hide;
  Each tuft of green they whelm from sight;
And they who journeyed by my side,
  Are lost in the surrounding night.

"I loved them; oh, no words can tell
  The love that to my friends I bore;
They left me with the sad farewell
  Of those who part to meet no more.

"And I, who face this bitter wind
  And o'er these snowy hillocks creep,
Must end my journey soon, and find
  A frosty couch, a frozen sleep."

As thus he spoke, a thrill of pain
  Shot to my heart—I closed my eyes;
But when I opened them again,
  I started with a glad surprise.

[THE TWO TRAVELLERS]

'Twas evening still, and in the west
A flush of glowing crimson lay;
I saw the morrow there, and blest
That promise of a glorious day.

The waters, in their glassy sleep,
Shone with the hues that tinged the sky,
And rugged cliff and barren steep
Gleamed with the brightness from on high.

And one was there whose journey lay
Into the slowly-gathering night;
With steady step he held his way,
O'er shadowy vale and gleaming height.

I marked his firm though weary tread,
The lifted eye and brow serene;
And saw no shade of doubt or dread
Pass o'er that traveller's placid mien.

And others came, their journey o'er,
And bade good-night, with words of cheer:
"To-morrow we shall meet once more;
'Tis but the night that parts us here."

"And I," he said, "shall sleep ere long;
These fading gleams will soon be gone;
Shall sleep to rise refreshed and strong
In the bright day that yet will dawn."

I heard; I watched him as he went,
A lessening form, until the light
Of evening from the firmament
Had passed, and he was lost to sight.

The Land of Dreams

A mighty realm is the Land of Dreams,
  With steeps that hang in the twilight sky,
And weltering oceans and trailing streams,
  That gleam where the dusky valleys lie.
But over its shadowy border flow
  Sweet rays from the world of endless morn,
And the nearer mountains catch the glow,
  And flowers in the nearer fields are born.

The souls of the happy dead repair,
  From their bowers of light, to that bordering land,
And walk in the fainter glory there,
  With the souls of the living hand in hand.
One calm sweet smile, in that shadowy sphere,
  From eyes that open on earth no more—
One warning word from a voice once dear—
  How they rise in the memory o'er and o'er!

Far off from those hills that shine with day,
  And fields that bloom in the heavenly gales,
The Land of Dreams goes stretching away
  To dimmer mountains and darker vales.
There lie the chambers of guilty delight,
  There walk the spectres of guilty fear,
And soft low voices, that float through the night,
  Are whispering sin in the helpless ear.

Dear maid, in thy girlhood's opening flower,
  Scarce weaned from the love of childish play!
The tears on whose cheeks are but the shower
  That freshens the blooms of early May!
Thine eyes are closed, and over thy brow
  Pass thoughtful shadows and joyous gleams,
And I know, by thy moving lips, that now
  Thy spirit strays in the Land of Dreams.

Light-hearted maiden, oh, heed thy feet!
  O keep where that beam of Paradise falls:
And only wander where thou mayst meet
  The blessed ones from its shining walls!
So shalt thou come from the Land of Dreams,
  With love and peace to this world of strife:
And the light which over that border streams
  Shall lie on the path of thy daily life.

The Burial of Love

Two dark-eyed maids, at shut of day,
Sat where a river rolled away,
With calm sad brows and raven hair,
And one was pale and both were fair.
Bring flowers, they sang, bring flowers unblown,
Bring forest-blooms of name unknown;
Bring budding sprays from wood and wild,
To strew the bier of Love, the child.

Close softly, fondly, while ye weep,
His eyes, that death may seem like sleep,
And fold his hands in sign of rest,
His waxen hands, across his breast.
And make his grave where violets hide,
Where star-flowers strew the rivulet's side,
And bluebirds in the misty spring
Of cloudless skies and summer sing.

Place near him, as ye lay him low,
His idle shafts, his loosened bow,
The silken fillet that around
His waggish eyes in sport he wound.
But we shall mourn him long, and miss
His ready smile, his ready kiss,
The patter of his little feet,
Sweet frowns and stammered phrases sweet;

And graver looks, serene and high,
A light of heaven in that young eye,
All these shall haunt us till the heart
Shall ache and ache—and tears will start.
The bow, the band shall fall to dust,
The shining arrows waste with rust,
And all of Love that earth can claim,
Be but a memory and a name.

Not thus his nobler part shall dwell
A prisoner in this narrow cell;
But he whom now we hide from men,
In the dark ground, shall live again:
Shall break these clods, a form of light,
With nobler mien and purer sight,
And in the eternal glory stand,
Highest and nearest God's right hand.

Christmas in 1875

[SUPPOSED TO BE WRITTEN BY A SPANIARD]

No trumpet-blast profaned
The hour in which the Prince of Peace was born;
No bloody streamlet stained
Earth's silver rivers on that sacred morn;
But, o'er the peaceful plain,
The war-horse drew the peasant's loaded wain.

The soldier had laid by
The sword and stripped the corselet from his breast,
And hung his helm on high—
The sparrow's winter home and summer nest;
And, with the same strong hand
That flung the barbèd spear, he tilled the land.

Oh, time for which we yearn;
Oh, sabbath of the nations long foretold!
Season of peace, return,
Like a late summer when the year grows old,
When the sweet sunny days
Steeped mead and mountain-side in golden haze.

For now two rival kings
Flaunt, o'er our bleeding land, their hostile flags,
And every sunrise brings
The hovering vulture from his mountain-crags
To where the battle-plain
Is strewn with dead, the youth and flower of Spain.

Christ is not come, while yet
O'er half the earth the threat of battle lowers,
And our own fields are wet,
Beneath the battle-cloud, with crimson showers—
The life-blood of the slain,
Poured out where thousands die that one may reign.

Soon, over half the earth,
In every temple crowds shall kneel again
To celebrate His birth
Who brought the message of good-will to men,
And bursts of joyous song
Shall shake the roof above the prostrate throng.

[CHRISTMAS IN 1875]

Christ is not come, while there
The men of blood whose crimes affront the skies
Kneel down in act of prayer,
Amid the joyous strains, and when they rise
Go forth, with sword and flame,
To waste the land in His most holy name.

Oh, when the day shall break
O'er realms unlearned in warfare's cruel arts,
And all their millions wake
To peaceful tasks performed with loving hearts,
On such a blessed morn,
Well may the nations say that Christ is born.

The Poems of William Cullen Bryant

IV

HYMNS WRITTEN AT VARIOUS TIMES

The Editor's Commentary

In common with Whittier, Bryant luxuriated in hymns; one might say that the four-square beat, the common measure, was in their blood. Bryant's tunes are the more traditional, just as his spirit was the more orthodox. But the underlying devotion lifts the lines above pattern-making, and the purpose triumphs over the platitude.

Although the note of unfettered inspiration is scarcely heard in these hymns, they are not without religious rapture. The devout singer as well as the seer is manifest in the straightforward quatrains, especially in "A Broken and a Contrite Heart," "How Amiable Are Thy Tabernacles," "The Truth Shall Make You Free," "Thou, God, Seest Me," "The Freeman's Hymn," "The Aged Pastor," "In Memoriam," and the low-pitched but uplifting "Centennial Hymn."

"A Broken and a Contrite Heart, O God, Thou Wilt Not Despise"

O God, whose dread and dazzling brow
Love never yet forsook!
On those who seek thy presence now
In deep compassion look.

Aid our weak steps and eyesight dim
The paths of peace to find,
And lead us all to learn of Him
Who died to save mankind.

For many a frail and erring heart
Is in thy holy sight,
And feet too willing to depart
From the plain way of right.

Yet, pleased the humble prayer to hear,
And kind to all that live,
Thou, when thou seest the contrite tear,
Art ready to forgive.

"The Lord Giveth Wisdom"

Mighty One, before whose face
Wisdom had her glorious seat,
When the orbs that people space
Sprang to birth beneath thy feet!

Source of Truth, whose beams alone
Light the mighty world of mind!
God of Love, who, from thy throne,
Watchest over all mankind!

Shed on those who, in Thy name,
Teach the way of Truth and Right,
Shed that Love's undying flame,
Shed that Wisdom's guiding light.

"The Earth Is Full of Thy Riches"

Almighty! hear thy children raise
The voice of thankfulness and praise,
To Him whose wisdom deigned to plan
This fair and bright abode for man.

For when this orb of sea and land
Was moulded in thy forming hand,
Thy calm, benignant smile impressed
A beam of heaven upon its breast.

Then rose the hills, and broad and green
The vale's deep pathway sank between;
Then stretched the plains to where the sky
Stoops and shuts in the exploring eye.

Beneath that smile earth's blossoms glowed,
Her fountains gushed, her rivers flowed,
And from the shadowy wood was heard
The pleasant sound of breeze and bird.

Thy hand outspread the billowy plains
Of ocean, nurse of genial rains,
Hung high the glorious sun and set
Night's cressets in her arch of jet.

Lord, teach us, while the admiring sight
Dwells on Thy works in deep delight,
To deem the forms of beauty here
But shadows of a brighter sphere.

"How Amiable Are Thy Tabernacles!"

Thou, whose unmeasured temple stands,
  Built over earth and sea,
Accept the walls that human hands
  Have raised, O God! to thee.

And let the Comforter and Friend,
  Thy Holy Spirit, meet
With those who here in worship bend
  Before thy mercy seat.

May they who err be guided here
  To find the better way,
And they who mourn and they who fear
  Be strengthened as they pray.

May faith grow firm, and love grow warm,
  And hallowed wishes rise,
While round these peaceful walls the storm
  Of earth-born passion dies.

"Thou, God, Seest Me"

When this song of praise shall cease,
  Let thy children, Lord, depart
With the blessing of thy peace
  And thy love in every heart.

Oh, where'er our path may lie,
  Father, let us not forget
That we walk beneath thine eye,
  That thy care upholds us yet.

Blind are we, and weak, and frail;
  Be thine aid forever near;
May the fear to sin prevail
  Over every other fear.

"His Tender Mercies Are Over All His Works"

Our Father! to thy love we owe
All that is fair and good below.
Life, and the health that makes life sweet,
Are blessings from thy mercy seat.

Oh Giver of the quickening rain!
Oh Ripener of the golden grain!
From Thee the cheerful day-spring flows,
Thy balmy evening brings repose.

Thy frosts arrest, thy tempests chase
The plagues that waste our helpless race,
Thy softer breath, o'er land and deep,
Wakes Nature from her winter sleep.

Yet, deem we not that thus alone
Thy bounty and thy love are shown,
For we have learned with higher praise
And holier names to speak thy ways.

In woe's dark hour our kindest stay,
Sole trust when life shall pass away,
Teacher of hopes that light the gloom
Of Death, and consecrate the tomb.

Patient with headstrong guilt to bear,
Slow to avenge and kind to spare,
Listening to prayer and reconciled
Full soon to thy repentant child.

"Thy Word Is Truth"

O thou, whose Love can ne'er forget
  Its offspring, Great Eternal Mind!
We thank thee that thy truth is yet
  A sojourner among mankind;

A light before whose brightness fall
  The feet arrayed to tread it down,
A voice whose strong and solemn call
  The cry of nations cannot drown.

Thy servants, at this sacred hour,
  With humble prayer thy throne surround,
That here, in glory and in power,
  That light may shine, that voice may sound;

Till Error's shades shall flee away,
  And Faith, descending from above,
Amid the pure and perfect day,
  Shall bring her fairer sister Love.

"Except the Lord Build the House"

Ancient of Days! except thou deign
  Upon the finished task to smile,
The workman's hand hath toiled in vain,
  To hew the rock and rear the pile.

Oh, let thy peace, the peace that tames
  The wayward heart, inhabit here,
That quenches passion's fiercest flames,
  And thaws the deadly frost of fear.

And send thy love, the love that bears
  Meekly with hate, and scorn, and wrong,
And loads itself with generous cares,
  And toils, and hopes, and watches long.

Here may bold tongues thy truth proclaim,
  Unmingled with the dreams of men,
As from His holy lips it came
  Who died for us and rose again.

In Memoriam

Two hundred times has June renewed
Her roses since the day
When here, amid the lonely wood,
Our fathers met to pray.

Beside this gentle stream that strayed
Through pathless deserts then,
The calm, heroic women prayed,
And grave, undaunted men.

Hymns on the ancient silence broke
From hearts that faltered not,
And undissembling lips that spoke
The free and guileless thought.

They prayed, and thanked the Almighty One
Who made their hearts so strong,
And led them, towards the setting sun,
Beyond the reach of wrong.

He made for them that desert place
A pleasant heritage,
The cradle of a free-born race,
From peaceful age to age.

The plant they set—a little vine—
Has stretched its boughs afar,
To distant hills and streams that shine
Beneath the evening star.

Their fields are ours—these fields that smile
With summer's early flowers;
Oh, let their fearless scorn of guile,
And love of truth, be ours.

"I Will Send Them Prophets and Apostles"

All that in this wide world we see,
Almighty Father! speaks of Thee;
And in the darkness, or the day,
Thy monitors surround our way.

The fearful storms that sweep the sky,
The maladies by which we die,
The pangs that make the guilty groan,
Are angels from thy awful throne.

Each mercy sent when sorrows lower,
Each blessing of the wingèd hour,
All we enjoy, and all we love,
Bring with them lessons from above.

Nor thus content, thy gracious hand,
From midst the children of the land,
Hath raised, to stand before our race,
Thy living messengers of grace.

We thank thee that so clear a ray
Shines on thy straight, thy chosen way,
And pray that passion, sloth, or pride,
May never lure our steps aside.

The Death of Channing

While yet the harvest-fields are white,
   And few the toiling reapers stand,
Called from his task before the night,
   We miss the mightiest of the band.

O thou of strong and gentle mind,
   Thy thrilling voice shall plead no more
For Truth, for Freedom, and Mankind—
   The lesson of thy life is o'er.

But thou in brightness, far above
   The fairest dream of human thought,
Before the seat of Power and Love,
   Art with the Truth that thou hast sought.

"The Truth Shall Make You Free"

Lord, from whose glorious presence came
  The truth that made our fathers free,
And kindled in their hearts the flame
  Of love to man and love to thee.

Bow the great heavens, thy throne of light,
  And fill these walls, as once, of yore,
Thy spirit rested in its might
  Upon the ark that Israel bore.

Here, let thy love be strong to draw
  Our wavering hearts to do thy will,
And hush them with the holy awe
  That makes the rebel passions still.

And while thy children, frail and blind,
  Here bend in humble prayer to thee,
Oh, shed, abroad, on every mind,
  The truth that made our fathers free.

"His Mother Kept All These Sayings in Her Heart"

As o'er the crade of her Son
  The blessèd Mary hung,
And chanted to the Anointed One
  The psalms that David sung,

What joy her bosom must have known,
  As, with a sweet surprise,
She marked the boundless love that shone
  Within his infant eyes.

But deeper was her joy to hear,
  Even in his ripening youth,
And treasure up, from year to year,
  His words of grace and truth.

Oh, may we keep his words like her
  In all their life and power,
And to the law of love refer
  The acts of every hour.

"Other Sheep I Have, Which Are Not of This Fold"

Look from the sphere of endless day,
  Oh, God of mercy and of might!
In pity look on those who stray,
  Benighted, in this land of light.

In peopled vale, in lonely glen,
  In crowded mart by stream or sea,
How many of the sons of men
  Hear not the message sent from thee.

Send forth thy heralds, Lord, to call
  The thoughtless young, the hardened old,
A wandering flock, and bring them all
  To the Good Shepherd's peaceful fold.

Send them thy mighty word to speak
  Till faith shall dawn and doubt depart,—
To awe the bold, to stay the weak,
  And bind and heal the broken heart.

Then all these wastes, a dreary scene,
  On which, with sorrowing eyes, we gaze,
Shall grow with living waters green,
  And lift to heaven the voice of praise.

"Whatsoever He Sayeth Unto You, Do It"

"Whate'er he bids, observe and do";
Such were the words that Mary said,
What time the Holy One and True
Sat where the marriage feast was spread.

Then, at his word, the servants sought
The streams from Cana's fountains poured,
And lo! the crystal water brought
Was ruddy wine upon the board.

Whate'er he bids observe and do;
Such be the law that we obey,
And greater wonders men shall view
Than that of Cana's bridal day.

The flinty heart with love shall beat,
The chains shall fall from passion's slave,
The proud shall sit at Jesus' feet
And learn the truths that bless and save.

"Proclaim Liberty throughout the Land"

Go forth, O Word of Christ! go forth,
O Truth of God supremely strong!
To banish, from the groaning earth,
All forms of tyranny and wrong.

For where the Word of Christ prevails
To touch a nation's mighty heart,
The oppressor's pride before it quails,
The links of bondage fall apart.

When the pure faith by Jesus taught
Its conquering course on earth began,
Where'er the blessèd news was brought
The fettered slave stood up a man.

Still may thy heralds, Lord, proclaim
The gracious message published then,
And teach the world, in Jesus' name,
How love makes free the sons of men.

The Freeman's Hymn

In eastern lands a servile race
May bow to thrones and diadems;
And hide in dust the abject face,
Before the glare of gold and gems.

For us, we kneel to One alone;
And freemen worship only Him
Before the brightness of whose throne
The proudest pomps of earth are dim.

And therefore to his children here
This bright and blooming land He gave,
Where famine never blasts the year,
Nor plagues, nor earthquakes glut the grave;

A land where all the gifts unite
That Heaven bestows to make life sweet;
A land of peace, a land of light,
A land where truth and mercy meet.

"Receive Thy Sight"

When the blind suppliant in the way,
By friendly hands to Jesus led,
Prayed to behold the light of day,
"Receive thy sight," the Saviour said.

At once he saw the pleasant rays
That lit the glorious firmament;
And, with firm step and words of praise,
He followed where the Master went.

Look down in pity, Lord, we pray,
On eyes oppressed by moral night,
And touch the darkened lids and say
The gracious words, "Receive thy sight."

Then, in clear daylight, shall we see
Where walked the sinless Son of God;
And, aided by new strength from Thee,
Press onward in the path He trod.

"This Do in Remembrance of Me"

All praise to Him of Nazareth,
  The Holy One who came,
For love of man, to die a death
  Of agony and shame.

Dark was the grave; but since he lay
  Within its dreary cell,
The beams of heaven's eternal day
  Upon its threshold dwell.

He grasped the iron veil, he drew
  Its gloomy folds aside,
And opened, to his followers' view,
  The glorious world they hide.

In tender memory of his grave
  The mystic bread we take,
And muse upon the life he gave
  So freely for our sake.

A boundless love he bore mankind;
  Oh, may at least a part
Of that strong love descend and find
  A place in every heart.

"Thou Hast Put All Things under His Feet"

O North, with all thy vales of green!
  O South, with all thy palms!
From peopled towns and fields between,
  Uplift the voice of psalms.
Raise, ancient East! the anthem high,
And let the youthful West reply.

Lo! in the clouds of Heaven appears
  God's well-belovèd Son;
He brings a train of brighter years;
  His kingdom is begun;
He comes a guilty world to bless
With mercy, truth, and righteousness.

Oh, Father! haste the promised hour,
  When at His feet shall lie
All rule, authority, and power,
  Beneath the ample sky:
When He shall reign from pole to pole,
The Lord of every human soul.

When all shall heed the words He said,
  Amid their daily cares,
And, by the loving life He led,
  Shall strive to pattern theirs;
And He who conquered Death shall win
The mightier conquest over Sin.

The Aged Pastor

Thy love, O God! from year to year,
Has watched thy faithful pastor here,
Till fifty years of toil have now
Engraved their tokens on his brow.

Fast have the seasons rolled away;
A moment in thy sight were they,
Yet while their rapid course was run,
What mighty works thy hand has done!

What empires rose, and, at thy frown,
In sudden weakness crumbled down!
What barriers, reared by earth and hell,
Against thy truth, gave way and fell!

Meanwhile, beneath thy gracious sight
This flock has dwelt in peace and light,
By living waters gently led,
And in perennial pastures fed.

Oh, when before thy judgment seat
The pastor and his flock shall meet,
May thy benignant voice attest
Their welcome to thine endless rest.

The Star of Bethlehem

As shadows cast by cloud and sun
  Flit o'er the summer grass,
So, in thy sight, Almighty One!
  Earth's generations pass.

And while the years, an endless host,
  Come pressing swiftly on,
The brightest names that earth can boast
  Just glisten, and are gone.

Yet doth the Star of Bethlehem shed
  A lustre pure and sweet;
And still it leads, as once it led,
  To the Messiah's feet.

And deeply, at this later day,
  Our hearts rejoice to see
How children, guided by its ray,
  Come to the Saviour's knee.

O Father, may that holy Star
  Grow every year more bright,
And send its glorious beam afar
  To fill the world with light.

The Captive Loosed

When, doomed to death, the Apostle lay,
  At night, in Herod's dungeon-cell,
A light shone round him like the day,
  And from his limbs the fetters fell.

A messenger from God was there,
  To loose his chain and bid him rise,
And lo, the Saint, as free as air,
  Walked forth beneath the open skies.

Chains yet more strong and cruel bind
  The victims of that deadly thirst
Which drowns the soul, and from the mind
  Blots the bright image stamped at first.

Oh, God of Love and Mercy, deign
  To look on those, with pitying eye,
Who struggle with that fatal chain,
  And send them succor from on high.

Send down, in its resistless might,
  Thy gracious Spirit, we implore,
And lead the captive forth to light,
  A rescued soul, a slave no more.

The Pastor's Return

From ancient realms, from many a seat
Of art and power beyond the sea;
From fields o'er which the blessed feet
Of Jesus walked in Galilee;

From snow-capped peak and glorious vale,
That listen to the cataract's voice,
Led by the hand of God, we hail,
Once more, the pastor of our choice.

The reaper takes his place again,
Where the white harvest skirts the way,
With sinews strengthened to sustain
The heat and burden of the day.

And while our hearts, with one accord,
Welcome him to his cherished home;
As Thou hast blessed his wanderings, Lord,
Oh, bless his labors yet to come!

The Centennial Hymn

Through calm and storm the years have led
Our nation on, from stage to stage—
A century's space—until we tread
The threshold of another age.

We see where o'er our pathway swept
A torrent-stream of blood and fire,
And thank the Guardian Power who kept
Our sacred League of States entire.

Oh, chequered train of years, farewell!
With all thy strifes and hopes and fears!
Yet with us let thy memories dwell,
To warn and teach the coming years.

And thou, the new-beginning age,
Warned by the past, and not in vain,
Write on a fairer, whiter page,
The record of thy happier reign.

The Poems of William Cullen Bryant

V

APPENDIX:

EARLY AND UNCOLLECTED POEMS

The Editor's Commentary

When "Thanatopsis" was first printed, it appeared with four stanzas prefixed to the poem on the subject of death but, otherwise, had no connection with it; they were, it now seems, never intended for publication. Nevertheless this Appendix begins with the first printed version of "Thanatopsis," not only as a literary curiosity, but as an example of a poet's critical acumen.

In a paper published in PMLA (*Publications of the Modern Language Association of America*) for June, 1937, Professor Tremaine McDowell carefully examines Bryant's practice in composition and revision. His research discloses that instead of allowing the unconscious to dictate the work and leaving the impromptu results as they came, Bryant was an assiduous reviser. Readers may be not only surprised but rewarded by comparing the curious version that appeared in the *North American Review* in 1817 (reprinted in this Appendix) with the poem as it was revised by Bryant (see page 10), and shaped into the poem we know.

The uncollected poems vary in appeal and value. Most of them are merely youthful imitations. Perhaps the most interesting if not the most ingratiating are "The Bee in the Tar-Barrel" and "The Rats and Mice." Both poems are full of allusions to contemporary political problems—the ever-vexing tariff, the spoils system, the plight of the Cherokee Indians, the politicians' contempt for the fundamental tenets of democracy—but the humor is as broad as the satire is deep.

Thanatopsis

[EARLY VERSION]

Not that from life, and all its woes
    The hand of death shall set me free;
Not that this head, shall then repose
    In the low vale most peacefully.

Ah, when I touch time's farthest brink,
    A kinder solace must attend;
It chills my very soul, to think
    Of that dread hour when life must end.

In vain the flatt'ring verse may breathe,
    Of ease from pain, and rest from strife,
There is a sacred dread of death
    Inwoven with the strings of life.

This bitter cup at first was given
    When angry Justice frowned severe;
And 'tis the eternal doom of heaven
    That man must view the grave with fear.

—Yet a few days, and thee
The all-beholding sun shall see no more
In all his course; nor yet in the cold ground,
Where thy pale form was laid, with many tears,
Nor in the embrace of ocean, shall exist
Thy image. Earth, that nourished thee, shall claim
Thy growth, to be resolv'd to earth again;
And, lost each human trace, surrend'ring up
Thine individual being, shalt thou go
To mix forever with the elements,
To be a brother to th' insensible rock
And to the sluggish clod, which the rude swain
Turns with his share, and treads upon. The oak
Shall send its roots abroad, and pierce thy mould.

Yet not to thy eternal resting-place
Shalt thou retire alone—nor couldst thou wish
Couch more magnificent. Thou shalt lie down
With patriarchs of the infant world—with kings,
The powerful of the earth, the wise, the good,
Fair forms, and hoary seers of ages past,
All in one mighty sepulchre.—The hills
Rock-ribb'd and ancient as the sun, the vales

Stretching in pensive quietness between,
The venerable woods, the floods that move
In majesty, and the complaining brooks
That wind among the meads and make them green,
Are but the solemn decorations all
Of the great tomb of man.—The golden sun,
The planets, all the infinite host of heaven,
Are glowing on the sad abodes of death
Through the still lapse of ages. All that tread
The globe are but a handful to the tribes
That slumber in its bosom.—Take the wings
Of morning, and the Borean desert pierce—
Or lose thyself in the continuous woods
That veil the Oregon, where he hears no sound
Save his own dashings—yet the dead are there,
And millions in those solitudes, since first
The flight of years began, have laid them down
In their last sleep. The dead reign there alone.—
So shalt thou rest; and what if thou shalt fall
Unnoticed by the living, and no friend
Take note of thy departure? Thousands more
Will share thy destiny.—The tittering world
Dance to the grave. The busy brood of care
Plod on, and each one chases as before
His favorite phantom. Yet all these shall leave
Their mirth and their employments, and shall come,
And make their bed with thee!—

The Embargo [WRITTEN IN 1808]

"When private faith and public trust are sold,
And traitors barter liberty for gold;
When fell corruption, dark, and deep, like fate,
Saps the foundation of a sinking state;
Then warmer numbers glow through satire's page,
And all her smiles are darken'd into rage;
Then keener indignation fires her eye,
Then flash her lightnings, and her thunders fly!"

ESSAY ON SATIRE

Look where we will, and in whatever land,
Europe's rich soil, or Afric's barren sand,
Where the wild savage hunts his wilder prey,
Or art and science pour their brightest day,
The monster *Vice* appears before our eyes,
In naked impudence, or gay disguise.

But quit the meaner game indignant muse,
And to thy country turn thy nobler views;
Ill-fated clime! condemn'd to feel th' extremes,
Of a weak ruler's philosophic dreams;
Driven headlong on, to ruin's fateful brink,
When will thy country feel, when will she think!

Satiric muse, shall injured Commerce weep
Her ravish'd rights, and will thy thunders sleep;
Dart thy keen glances, knit thy threat'ning brows,
Call fire from heaven to blast thy country's foes.
Oh let a youth thine inspiration learn—
Oh give him "words that breathe and thoughts that burn"!

Curse of our nation, source of countless woes,
From whose dark womb unreckon'd misery flows,
Th' Embargo rages, like a sweeping wind,
Fear lowers before, and famine stalks behind.
What words, O Muse! can paint the mournful scene,
The saddening street, the desolated green;
How hungry labourers leave their toil and sigh,
And sorrow droops in each desponding eye!

See the bold Sailor from the Ocean torn,
His element, sink friendless and forlorn!
His suffering spouse the tear of anguish shed,
His starving children cry in vain for bread!

On the rough billows of misfortune tost,
Resources fail, and all his hopes are lost;
To foreign climes, for that relief he flies,
His native land ungratefully denies.

In vain Mechanics ply their curious art,
And bootless mourn the interdicted mart;
While our sage *Ruler's* diplomatic skill,
Subjects our councils to his sovereign will;
His grand "*restrictive energies*" employs,
And wisely regulating trade—destroys.

The Farmer, since supporting trade is fled,
Leaves the rude joke, and cheerless hangs his head;
Misfortunes fall, an unremitting shower,
Debts follow debts, on taxes, taxes pour,—
See in his stores his hoarded produce rot,
Or Sheriff sales his profits bring to naught;
Disheartening cares in thronging myriads flow,
Till down he sinks to poverty and woe!
Ye, who rely on Jeffersonian skill;
And say that fancy paints ideal ill;
Go, on the wings of observation fly,
Cast o'er the land a scrutinizing eye;
States, counties, towns, remark with keen review,
Let *facts* convince and own the picture true!

Oh, ye bright pair! the blessing of mankind,
Whom time has sanction'd, and whom fate has join'd,
COMMERCE, that bears the trident of the main,
And AGRICULTURE, empress of the plain;
Who hand in hand, and heav'n-directed, go
Diffusing gladness through the world below;
Whoe'er the wretch, would hurl the flaming brand
Of dire disunion, palsied be his hand!
Like "Cromwell damn'd to everlasting fame,"
Let unborn ages execrate his name!

How foul a blot Columbia's glory stains!
How dark the scene! infatuation reigns!
For French intrigue which wheedles to devour,
Threatens to fix us in Napoleon's power;
Anon within th' insatiate vortex whirl'd,
Whose wide periphery involves the world.

[THE EMBARGO]

Oh, heaven defend, as future seasons roll,
These western climes from Bonaparte's control;
Preserve our freedom, and our rights secure,
While truth subsists, and virtue shall endure!
Lo Austria crouches to the tyrant's stroke,
And bends proud Rome beneath his galling yoke;
Infuriate, reeking with the spoils of war,
O'er prostrate kingdoms rolls his blood-stain'd car;
Embattled hosts in vain his fury meet,
Sceptres and crowns he treads beneath his feet.

Aspiring Belgia, once the patriot's pride,
When barbarous Alva, her brave sons defied;
The nurse of arts, th' advent'rous merchant's boast,
Whose wide-spread commerce whiten'd every coast.
Humbled, degraded, by the vilest arts,
Beneath his iron scourge, succumbing smarts;
The crowded city, the canal's green shore,
Fair haunts of free-born opulence, no more!

Ah, hapless land! where freedom lov'd to dwell,
Helvetia's fall, what weeping bard shall tell!
Warn'd too by Lusitania's fate, beware!—
Columbians wake! evade the deep laid snare!
Insensate! shall we ruin court, and fall,
Slaves to the proud autocrator of Gaul?
Our laws laid prostrate by his ruthless hand,
And independence banish'd from our land!

We who seven years erst brav'd Britannia's power,
By Heaven supported in the gloomiest hour;
For whom our Sages plann'd, our Heroes bled,
Whom WASHINGTON, our pride, and glory led;
Till heaven propitious did our efforts crown
With freedom, commerce, plenty, and renown.

When shall this land, some courteous angel say,
Throw off a weak, and erring ruler's sway?
Rise, injured people, vindicate your cause!
And prove your love of liberty and laws;
Oh wrest, sole refuge of a sinking land,
The sceptre from the slave's imbecile hand!
Oh ne'er consent, obsequious, to advance,
The *willing vassal* of imperious France!

Correct that suffrage you misus'd before,
And lift your voice above a congress roar.

And thou, the scorn of every patriot name,
Thy country's ruin, and her council's shame!
Poor servile thing! derision of the brave!
Who erst from Tarleton fled to Carter's cave;
Thou, who, when menac'd by perfidious Gaul,
Didst prostrate to her whisker'd minion fall;
And when our cash her empty bags supply'd,
Didst meanly strive the foul disgrace to hide;
Go, wretch, resign the presidential chair,
Disclose thy secret measures, foul or fair.
Go, search with curious eye, for hornèd frogs,
Mid the wild wastes of Louisianian bogs;
Or, where Ohio rolls his turbid stream,
Dig for huge bones, thy glory and thy theme.
Go, scan, Philosophist, thy ****** charms
And sink supinely in her sable arms;
But quit to abler hands the helm of state,
Nor image ruin on thy country's fate!

Ah hapless State! with wayward councils curst,
Blind to thy weal, and to thy laws unjust;—
For, where their blasting "*energies*" extend,
Foes undermine and dire divisions rend;—
Who shall sustain thy gradual sinking form,
And guide thee safely through the gathering storm?
What guardian Angel shall conduct thee o'er
Misfortune's ocean to a peaceful shore?—
Remove the source whence all thy troubles rose,
And shield from foreign and domestic foes!

Oh for a WASHINGTON, whose boundless mind,
Infolds his friends, his country, and mankind;
He might restore our happy state again,
And roll our Navy o'er the billowy main;
From all our shores bid lawless pirates fly,
And lift our wond'ring Eagle to the sky!

But vain are reason, eloquence, and art,
And vain the warm effusions of the heart.
E'en while I sing, see Faction urge her claim,
Mislead with falsehood, and with zeal inflame;

Lift her black banner, spread her empire wide,
And stalk triumphant with a fury's stride.
She blows her brazen trump, and at the sound,
A motley throng, obedient, flock around;
A mist of changing hue, o'er all she flings,
And darkness perches on her dragon wings!

As Johnson deep, as Addison refin'd,
And skill'd to pour conviction o'er the mind,
Oh, might some patriot rise! the gloom dispel,
Chase error's mist, and break her magic spell!

But vain the wish, for hark! the murmuring meed
Of hoarse applause from yonder shed proceed;
Enter, and view the thronging concourse there,
Intent, with gaping mouth, and stupid stare;
While in the midst their supple leader stands,
Harangues aloud, and flourishes his hands;
To adulation tunes his servile throat,
And sues successful for each blockhead's vote.

"The advocate of *liberty* I stand,—
Oh were I made a ruler in the land!
Your interests none more cherishes than I,
In your sweet service, may I live and die!
For the dear *people*, how my bowels yearn!—
That *such* may govern be your chief concern;
Then *federalism*, and all its lordling train,
Shall fall disgrac'd before our *equal* reign;
Dismay'd, diminish'd, our fair presence shun,
As shadows shorten to the rising sun;
Spontaneous banquets shall succeed to want,
No tax shall vex you, and no sheriff haunt."

The powerful influence of the knave's address,
In capers droll, the foolish dupes express;
With *horrid* shouts th' affrighted sky is rent,
And high in air their tatter'd hats are sent.

But should truth shine distinguishingly bright,
And lay his meanness naked to the sight;
He tries new arts to blind their willing eyes,
Feeds with new flatt'ries, hammers out new lies;
Exerts his influence, urges all his weight,

To blast the laurels of the good and great;
Till reconfirm'd, the fools uphold him still,
Their creed his *dictum*, and their law his will.

Now morning rises borne on golden wings,
And fresh to toil the waking post-boy springs;
Lo, trudging on his raw bon'd steed he hies,
Dispersing Suns, and Chronicles, and Spys.
Men uninform'd, in rage for something new,
Howe'er unprincipled, howe'er untrue,
Suck in with greedy throat the gilded pill,
Whose fatal sweetness pleases but to kill.
Wide, and more wide the dire contagion flies,
Till half the town is overwhelm'd with lies.
Hence that delusion, hence that furious zeal,
Which wrong-heads cherish, and which hot-heads feel.

Oh, snatch me heaven! to some sequester'd spot,
Where Jefferson, and faction, are forgot;
Where never *Suns* nor *Chronicles* molest,
Duane and Colvin unregarded rest.
Sick of the tumult, where the noisy throng,
In wild disorder, roar of right and wrong;
Where lying pamphlets round the town are sped,
And knowing politicians talk you dead!

In vain *Italia* boasts her genial clime,
Her Rome's proud towers, and palaces sublime;
In vain the hardy Swiss, inur'd to toil,
Draw scant subsistence from a stubborn soil;
Both doom'd alike, to feel, in evil hour,
The giant grasp of huge despotic power!
Touch not their shores, fair freedom dwells not there,
But far remote, she breathes Columbian air;
Yet here, her temple totters to its fall,
Shook from its centre by gigantic Gaul!
Oh, let not prating *History* proclaim,
The foul disgrace, the scandal of our name!
Write not the deed my hand! Oh may it lie,
Plung'd deep, and mantled in obscurity!
Forbid it heaven! that while true honour reigns,
And ancient valour glows within our veins,
(Our standard justice, and our shield our God,)
We e'er should tremble at a despot's nod!

Oh, may the laurels of unrival'd fame,
For ever flourish round your honour'd name!
Ye, who unthrall'd by prejudice, or power,
Determin'd stood in that eventful hour;
Tore the dire secret from the womb of night,
And brought your country's infamy to light!
Go boldly on the deep-laid plot unfold,
Though much is known, yet much remains untold.
But chief to thee our gratitude belongs,
Oh Pickering! who hast scan'd thy country's wrongs,
Whose ardent mind, and keen discerning eye,
Trac'd out the true Embargo policy;
Shew'd that our Chief, unable to control,
The alien yearnings of his dastard soul;
And curst with feelings hostile to our trade,
At beck of France, the dire restriction laid!

Hail first of Statesmen! Massachusetts' pride!
Fam'd in her wars, and in her councils try'd;
Long to thy friends by private worth endear'd,
"In pure majestic poverty rever'd";
At thy rebuke, (though late so monstrous grown,)
Corruption trembles on her venal throne!
Oh, may the people, with attentive eyes,
Peruse thy well-tim'd warnings and be wise!

Mournful reverse! the muse with grief would trace,
The painful scene of thy colleague's disgrace.
Unhappy he, by glare of *office* lur'd,
Renounc'd the truth, and federal faith abjur'd!
With fine spun sophisms, and inflated style,
Strove to mislead, bewilder, and beguile;
O'er presidential error gently spread
The flimsy veil, perverted reason made.
Virtue abash'd beheld th' apostate's zeal,
And freedom trembled for the public weal;
Till Coleman rose, by honest anger led,
And at his touch the gay delusion fled;
The veil disparts, the painted bubbles burst,
The splendid fabric crumbles into dust!

Go on, ye pimps of France! intriguers fell!
Wind your dark ways, and aid the work of hell!
Go, rouse dire *faction* from her gloomy den,

Wake the worst passions in the breasts of men;
O'er a once free, once heaven-protected land,
Impel the tempest with infuriate hand;
Go, lure the simple, with unfaithful views,
To paths where error her wild way pursues;
But soon from heaven, shall justice wing her way,
Arrest your course, and immolate her prey!

So prays the muse;—while bursting on the sight,
Hope's torch diffuses an enlivening light;
And scenes, prophetic of Columbia's rise
To former glory, greet the gladden'd eyes.
Rous'd by the murmurs of the coming storm,
Lo, freedom's genius lifts her radiant form!
Rolls her keen eye, and hovering o'er the land,
Calls in loud thunders to her slumbering band.
Far o'er the realm, electric, unconfin'd,
Flies the quick flame, and runs from mind to mind.
Wak'd from her stupid lethargy, at length
Old Massachusetts, feels returning strength;
Her sons, reflecting, break the baneful league,
With factious zeal, and popular intrigue;
No more they hug delusion's magic chain,
Nor grasp at objects, fleeting, and inane;
But break the charm, false, flatt'ring error binds,
The pleasing mania, that enchain'd their minds.

And now as *Truth* with growing lustre shines,
Before her beams Democracy declines;
Vain are all arts her baffled leaders try,
And vain alike, to flatter or to lie.
From their long sleep alarm'd the people rise,
And spite of sophisms, learn to trust their eyes.

Rise then, Columbians! heed not France's wiles,
Her bullying mandates, her seductive smiles;
Send home Napoleon's slave, and bid him say
No arts can lure us, and no threats dismay;
Determin'd yet to war with whom we will,
Choose our allies, or dare be "neutral" still.

Ye merchants arm! the tyrant Gaul repel,
Your prowess shall the naval triumph swell;

Send the marauders shatter'd whence they came,
And Gallia's cheek suffuse with crimson shame.
But first select, our councils to direct,
One whose true worth entitles to respect:
In whom concentrates all that men admire,
The Sage's prudence, and the Soldier's fire;
Who scorns ambition, and the venal tribe,
And neither offers, nor receives a bribe;
Who firmly guards his country's every right,
And shines alike, in council, or in fight.

Then on safe seas, the merchant's barque shall fly,
Our waving flag, shall kiss the polar sky;
On canvass wings our thunders shall be borne,
Far to the west, or tow'rd the rising morn;
Then may we dare a haughty tyrant's rage,
And gain the blessings of an unborn age.

'Tis done, behold, the cheerful prospects rise!
And splendid scenes the startled eye surprize;
Lo! busy Commerce courts the prosperous main,
And peace and plenty glad our shores again!
Th' industrious swain sees nature smile around,
His fields with fruit, with flocks, his pastures crown'd.

Thus, in a fallen tree, from sprouting roots,
With sudden growth, a tender sapling shoots,
Improves from day to day, delights the eyes,
With strength, and beauty, stateliness, and size,
Puts forth robuster arms, and broader leaves,
And high in air its branching head upheaves.

Turn now our views to Europe's ravag'd plains,
Where murderous war, with grim oppression reigns;
There long, and loud, the storm of battle roars,
With direful portent to our distant shores;
The regal robber, rages uncontrol'd,
No law restrains him, and no faith can hold;
Before his steps, lo! cowering terror flies,
And pil'd behind him, heaps of carnage rise!
With fraud, or force, he spreads his iron sway,
And blood, and rapine, mark his frightful way!

Thus some huge rock of ice, on Greenland's shore,
When bound in frost, the surges cease to roar,
Breaks loosen'd from its base, with mighty sweep,
And thunders horrid o'er the frozen deep.

While thus, all Europe rings with his alarms,
Say, shall we rush, unthinking, to his arms?
No; let us dauntless all his fury brave,
Our fluttering flag, in freedom's gale shall wave,
Our guardian Sachem's errless shafts shall fly,
And terrors lighten from our eagle's eye!

Hear then I cease, rewarded, if my song,
Shall prompt one honest mind, though guided wrong,
To pause from party, view his country's state,
And lend his aid to stem approaching fate.

To Death [WRITTEN IN 1815]

Oh, thou whom the world dreadeth! Art thou nigh,
To thy pale kingdom, Death, to summon me?
While life's scarce-tasted cup yet charms my eye,
And yet my youthful blood is dancing free
And fair in prospect smiles futurity.
Go, to the crazed with care thy quiet bring;
Go to the galley-slave who pines for thee;
Go to the wretch whom throes of torture wring,
And they will bless thy hand, that plucks the fiery sting.

I from thine icy touch with horror shrink,
That leads me to the place where all must lie;
And bitter is my misery to think
That in the springtime of my being, I
Must leave this pleasant land, and this fair sky;
All this hath charmed me from my feeble birth;
The friends I love, and every gentle tie;
All that disposed to thought, or waked to mirth;
And lay me darkly down, and mix with the dull earth.

The Farewell [WRITTEN IN 1809]

"O thou, whose cherished image seems
 A portion of my heart,
Whose eyes of light make glad my dreams,
 Farewell, for now we part.
The sail is swelling in the bay
That bears me on my distant way,
For years to rove the dreary sea—
For years—and think of only thee.

"Yet will that beauteous image make
 The dreary sea less drear,
And thy remembered smile will wake
 The hope that tramples fear,
When I shall face the tempest's wrath,
Or struggle through the dangerous path
Where the blue icebergs, vast and steep,
Drifting and dashing, crowd the deep.

"Then, too, when heaven with clouds is dark
 And wild winds sweep the vale,
Wilt thou not think of him whose bark
 Strives with the polar gale?
Wilt thou not think, and softly pray
For the sea-wanderer far away,
That, all his toils and perils o'er,
His hand may clasp thy hand once more?

"But shouldst thou hear no more of me,
 Or hear that I have died
And sleep within that icy sea,
 Or on its desert side,
Will not a pang thy bosom press,
Even in thy pride of loveliness—
A tear in thy sweet eyelids shine
For him whose latest thought was thine?"

Ode

TO CONNECTICUT RIVER• [WRITTEN IN 1808]

Why should I blush to sing the rural lay,
Where fair CONNECTA winds its gentle way?
While smiling Spring, on southern breezes borne,
With snowy pinions scents the breath of morn;
And throws her dewy wreaths, with laughing glee,
O'er the green mead and germinating tree!

Could I thy charms, celebrious stream, rehearse,
In glowing numbers and exalted verse;
Me, did the Muse of poesy inspire,
With Maro's strains, or Pope's celestial fire;
Like the rough Tiber, or the gentler Thame,
Should classic honours flourish round thy name.

On thy green banks, let flowers perennial bloom,
And forests shade thee with a grateful gloom;
Bright towns ascending, flourish on thy shore,
And cultur'd gardens spread their balmy store!

When all is hush'd, and buoyant breezes sleep,
I view the mirror of thy level deep;
The sun reflected from thy bosom shine,
With piercing beams, and splendours all divine;
There glittering clouds, and glowing skies are seen,
The towering forest, and the humble green.

[ODE]

Oft, when soft breezes agitate thy tide,
I mark thy waves in quick succession ride;
While the small fry, disporting rise to sight,
Their nimble fins with crimson edges bright;
And from her perch the frighted heron springs,
Soaring aloft with azure tinted wings!

Here, foaming o'er the rugged rocks, he roars,
Through dreary chasms, along unfertile shores;
There, where yon gay parterre adorns his side,
He rolls a gentle and majestic tide!

Spread widely round, what beauties crowd the scene,
High waving woods, and meadows broad and green;
Tall spire-crown'd churches glitter to the day,
And clust'ring domes their humbler heads display;
In blue perspective, distant mountains rise,
And Tempe's charms renew'd, attract th' admiring eyes!

Long may thy sons in useful arts renown'd,
With waving cornfields hide the furrow'd ground;
Hung thick with fruitage bid the orchard bend,
And from the vine the clustering grape depend;
Plant the young wood, the flowery garden spread,
And give the dome to lift its ample head.

Long may thy Merchants borne on canvass wing,
From various climates, wealth, and wisdom bring;
Exotic wealth, that earth or ocean yields,
The icy north, or India's purple fields!

Oh, ne'er may war, with gloomy front appear,
Nor hostile armies prowl for plunder here!
May heaven-born peace, amid the sylvan dell,
Erect her throne, and long delight to dwell;
Led by her hand, may smiling plenty pour,
The copious bounties of her flower-crown'd store!

The Genius of Columbia [WRITTEN IN 1810]

Far in the regions of the west,
  On throne of adamant upraised,
Bright on whose polished sides impressed,
  The sun's meridian splendours blazed,
Columbia's Genius sat and eyed
  The eastern despot's dire career;
And thus with independent pride,
  She spoke and bade the nations hear.

"Go, favoured son of glory, go!
  Thy dark, aspiring aims pursue!
The blast of domination blow,
  Earth's wide extended regions through!
"Though Austria, twice subjected, own
  The thunders of thy conquering hand,
And tyranny erect her throne
  In hapless Sweden's fallen land!

"Yet know, a nation lives, whose soul
  Regards thee with disdainful eye;
Undaunted scorns thy proud control,
  And dares thy swarming hordes defy;
"Unshaken as their native rocks
  Its hardy sons heroic rise;
Prepared to meet thy fiercest shocks,
  Protected by the favouring skies.

"Their fertile plains and woody hills
  Are fanned by freedom's purest gales!
And her celestial presence fills
  The deepening glens and spacious vales."
She speaks; through all her listening bands
  A loud applauding murmur flies;
Fresh valour nerves their willing hands,
  And lights with joy their glowing eyes!

Then should Napoleon's haughty pride
  Wake on our shores the fierce affray;
Grim terror lowering at his side,
  Attendant on his furious way!
With quick repulse, his baffled band
  Would seek the friendly shore in vain,
Bright justice lift her red right hand,
  And crush them on the fatal plain.

For the Fourth of July [WRITTEN IN 1812]

Should justice call to battle,
  The applauding shout we'd raise;
A million swords would leave their sheath,
  A million bayonets blaze.
The stern resolve, the courage high,
  The mind untam'd by ill,
The fires that warmed our leader's breast
  His followers bosoms fill.
Our fathers bore the shock of war;
  Their sons can bear it still!

The same ennobling spirit
  That kindles valor's flame,
That nerves us to a war of right,
  Forbids a war of *shame;*
For not in Conquest's impious train
  Shall Freedom's children stand;
Nor shall in guilty fray be raised
  The high-souled warrior's hand.
Nor shall the patriot draw the sword
  At Gallia's proud command.

No! by our fathers' ashes,
  And by their sacred cause,
The Gaul shall never call us slaves,
  Shall never give us laws;
Even let *him* from a swarming fleet
  Debark his veteran host,
A living wall of patriot hearts
  Shall fence the frowning coast,—
A bolder race than generous *Spain,*
  A better cause we boast.

The Bee in the Tar-Barrel [WRITTEN IN 1831]

I heard a bee, on a summer day,
  Brisk and busy, and ripe for quarrel—
Bustling, and buzzing, and bouncing away,
  In the fragrant depth of an old tar-barrel.

Do you ask what his buzzing was all about?
  Oh, he was wondrous shrewd and critical:
'Twas sport to hear him scold and flout,
  And the topics he chose were all political.

And first and foremost he buzzed of tar,
  And called the heads of the government asses,
To let it be carried off so far,
  And changed, at Trinidad, for molasses.

For we got the West India trade too soon
  From the British folks—he had not a doubt of it;
For himself, he'd have scorned the thing "as a boon,"
  But kept at work till he cheated them out of it.

Then plaintive and piteous his humming grew,
  And I thought him complaining of indigestion;
But I listened again, and at length I knew
  He had got upon the Indian question.

The world, he declared, would all look glum,
  To see us coax the Cherokee nation
From their fathers' graves, from the whites and rum,
  Their pockets lined with a compensation.

Next, tones of fury and wrath were heard—
  And I started back with sudden wonder;
For the staves were shaken, the hoops were jarred,
  And it seemed the barrel was filled with thunder.

" 'Twas a crime to fill the land with groans,
  'Twas a deed," he said, "most foul and ugly,
To turn our poor unfortunate drones
  From the public hive, where they lodged so snugly."

And next—but I started at the sound
  Of noses blown and people walking;
And I saw some thirty Nationals round,
  And found I had dozed while Ketchum was talking.

The Rats and Mice [WRITTEN IN 1839]

Once on a time, as saith our story,
  Within a single edifice,
A nation flourished in its glory,
  Whose citizens were rats and mice.
The politics they prospered under
Passed far and widely for a wonder,
So based were they on reason's laws,
  And equal rights of vermin;—
So planned, the general good to cause,
  And cleanly keep Justitia's ermine.

The mice were populous by legions,
But mostly in the upper regions,
Where cracks and crevices so small were,
That none but mice could go at all there.
But there they got a name and grew,
  Established trade and ports of entry,
And made improvements not a few,
  In cupboards, case and pantry.

The rats rejoiced in cellar spacious,
  Where finding ample fare,
  With little thought or care,
They grew remarkably audacious,—
  Great statesmen they, and rhetoricians,
  And eke by nature politicians.
  On every great occasion,
  The counsel of the nation
  Assembled duly in
  An empty barrel bin
  Yclept Ratopolis,
  Where dog and cat police
  And foul monopolies,
  And all affairs of state,
  Gave rise to much debate.

Long lived this great mouse-ratic union,
  While enemies were hurt to see
  The wondrous peace and courtesy
With which the parties held communion.
At length some busy story-teller
  Began to noise it through the house,
That everything down in the cellar
  Worked badly for the mouse.

Instead of persons fat and sleek,
They seemed but shadows, thin and weak,
Those cellar mice,—poor starveling wretches,
Like what we're told are seen in churches!
For food,—while rats were proud to waste it,—
These famished mice dared hardly taste it.

And worse,—'twas rumored that
Full many a tyrant rat
Had sold his neighbors to the cat!
Resolved to have investigation
In general council of the nation,
Some garret-mice there brought the charge
Against the race of rats at large.

Up jumped a hundred rats or more,
In furious haste to get the floor;
The one that did, in speech er-rat-ic,
Cried, "Mr. Speaker, I should like to know
What, with our cellar-mice, they have to do
Who live up in the attic!

"Our institutions are our own,
We swear they must be left alone;
Our mice (for they indeed belong to us,)
Are better off than those who make the fuss;
A subject that we deign not to discuss,
But let the canting saints,
Who make these sad complaints,
Their whiskers show the cellar side
And we the question will decide,
By means far briefer than haranguing,
That is to say, by *hanging!*"

A grey old mouse, that caught the Speaker's eye,
In nick of time, thus made reply:—
"I hold that mice of sense
Will vote to save expense
Of further inquisition,—
And take with full reliance,
This chivalrous defiance,
As equal to confession.
None but the guilty deprecate
The lightning flash of free debate."